Through the year with Frederick Coutts

Through the Year
with
Frederick Coutts

Daily readings
edited and arranged by

Peter M. Cooke

Foreword by
General Erik Wickberg (R)

International Headquarters of The Salvation Army
101 Queen Victoria Street, London EC4P 4EP

PETER M. COOKE

is a soldier at Upper Norwood Corps, British Territory,
having spent his formative years in Nottingham. After
serving for a number of years in the public sector, he is
currently employed in the Literary Department, International Headquarters. He is a noted salvationist poet and
songwriter.

Cover by Jim Moss Graphics

Printed in Great Britain by
The Campfield Press, St Albans

Foreword

It gives me much pleasure to write this foreword to these choice selections drawn from the writings of General Frederick Coutts.

My first contact with the young officer who was to become our eighth General dates back to the early thirties, when he wrote his 'musings' in *The Officer* under the modest pen-name of 'Ensign'. Those contributions delighted his contemporaries and before long brought him from the British field to the Literary Department of International Headquarters. At that time I was stationed in the Overseas Department and we met from time to time.

There and then began a literary output which in quantity and quality must be said to be remarkable. Very few Army leaders have been able to combine top leadership with such literary work. Of course, Frederick Coutts loved to write. He had read so much and digested and pondered what he had read, that it was for him a necessity to share with others the riches not only of his sources but of his own thinking and his own conclusions.

Early on he introduced into Army literature a new quality which to some, at the time, was slightly disturbing but which met a real need and to many of us came as a refreshing breeze. His theology was thoroughly 'Army', but he had the gift of presenting the old truths in a new way. From his wide reading he brought insights and illustrations that made him a respected and accepted teacher.

For six years I worked closely with him as his Chief of the Staff and during those years I had occasion to admire his diligence and exactitude in all he did. We often shared literary discoveries that had a bearing on our common Army ideals.

When the General retired I asked him to take on volume six of our official Army history. This was a delicate task, as the period covered a sensitive era. I venture to think, however, that nobody could have done a better work than did General Coutts with that volume. He was able also, as a very last task, to complete volume seven. Also in retirement he wrote such important books as *No Continuing City* (the autobiography) and *Bread for my Neighbour.*

As a source of meditation his book on holiness, *The Call to Holiness*, and his selected sermons, *In Good Company*, as well as the New Testament commentaries which he edited from *The Soldier's Armoury*, will richly repay readers of all categories.

I heartily welcome and recommend the publication of this volume.

Erik Wickberg,
General (R).

1 January

Most of us are good at beginnings. The new diary . . .
fondly bought for father by his younger daughter is
regularly filled in—for the first week or so. Her brother's
new exercise book is neat and spotless—for the first two
pages. . . . Almost every new project is a thing of
delight—until the novelty has worn off. The reason is that
many of us lack what the theology of a past age used to
call 'final perseverance' or, more colloquially, the power
to stick it. . . .

In the spiritual realm John Bunyan symbolised this half-
heartedness in the person of Mr Pliable. At first he was all
for the Celestial City. Christian was too slow for him.
'Come on, let us mend our pace' was his continual cry.
But a single obstacle—the Slough of Despond—was
enough to send him home with his hair muddied, his
clothes dirtied and his ardour dampened. 'Is this the
happiness you told me of? If I get out of here, you can
possess the brave country alone!'

There are two main reactions to the sloughs and
stumbling-blocks which lie across the human pathway.
Pliable's is one of them and the most common. It is to
abandon what first appeared an entrancing task and to
write oneself off as a dead failure. There is comfort—
though a false comfort—even in that. If I can't make the
grade, why waste time and effort trying? It's just not in
me. How foolish to demand of myself that of which
plainly I am not capable! Better resign myself to
remaining what I am. So rationalising failure, I accept
what is easier to regard as inevitable.

On the other hand, failure can be a spur. . . .

The Officer, January, February 1949

2 January

muddied

. . . Failure can be a spur. Christian was just as ~~mirely~~

1

as Pliable, but he struggled to the side nearest the wicket gate. The Slough compelled him to exert his strength to get out. A handicap can force a man to greater effort. It is the handicap in a race which determines the speed of the winner. If the race be in his pocket, he will not exert himself unduly. But if he be heavily handicapped, he will go flat out. In other words, as is his handicap, so is his strength.

. . . Doctor Toynbee has gathered a mass of evidence from all parts of the world and from all periods of history to prove that when conditions have been easy nations have degenerated and finally disappeared. On the other hand, enduring civilisations have been built under conditions which made easy living impossible. As their day, so has the strength of nations been. *The S— Army*

This is as true of movements; ~~our own movement~~ is a notable example. The Army's great age of expansion was when personal and social righteousness was such a passion with us that to bullying rioter and prejudiced magistrate alike we cried: 'Out of our way! This is the King's business!' Opposition was the breath of life to us. As our handicap, so was our strength.

Now if a parallel movement is to take place in the realm of the spirit, I must give God a chance to verify his promise in my life. Any remedy for an ailment deserves fair trial and, if my weakness is to be made strong, I must take the cure. . . .

The Officer, January, February 1949

3 January

Astronomers have described how tiny a fraction of the sun's rays falls upon the surface of the globe. Of all the heat and light which the sun pours out, our world takes no more than 'a swallow might sip skimming across the surface of a lake'. So our greatest demands upon Infinite Power are, by comparison, infinitesimal. At the same time, the grace of God is no magician's wand. There is no heavenly abracadabra which can transform a weakling into a moral giant overnight. Growth in character is not exempt from the laws of progress which govern other skills. As Dom Bernard Clements used to say: 'If we wish to reach the upper storeys of a building, we do not expect to jump up and in from the pavement; we climb up, as all the saints have done, one step at a time.' The strengthening power of grace is like the strengthening power of a rich friendship. The yield may be small at first, but it rises in geometrical progression.

The communist will argue that history is behind his aims; that the one-class society of his dreams is the predestined goal to which the world is moving. If a man believes that this is so, then for him it is so. Faith can feed on a fallacy and yet supply immense drive. But what matters for the believer is the truth that the stars in their courses are fighting for righteousness. That is, when I seek to do God's will, I have all his mighty power behind me. 'Who can be our adversary if God is on our side?' The promise of Scripture comes alive in experience. Thus a man discovers for himself—and no discoveries are more worthwhile than those which we make for ourselves—that as his day, so can be his strength.

This is not of works, lest any man should boast. The will, and the power, to victory is his, shared by us.

The Officer, January, February 1949

4 January

. . . Prayer, like every other means of grace, is something regularly to be practised if its worth is to be proved.

Far too many people still think of prayer as an aid to which they can turn in an emergency. So cried the sailors at the opening of Shakespeare's *The Tempest*. 'All lost! All lost! To prayers! To prayers!'

This is an ancient failing. The Old Testament refers to such people, of whom it says: 'They . . . are at their wits' end. Then they cry unto the Lord.' Prayer is looked upon as an emergency cord to be pulled when danger threatens. It is regarded as an airman does his parachute— handy in case of an accident; all the same, he devoutly hopes the moment may never come when he has to use it. In other words, prayer is considered the straw at which a drowning man will clutch.

Now it would be quite wrong if I gave anyone the impression that God will not answer the sharp, swift prayer of sudden need. He does hear and he does answer. Being 'Our Father' he can do no other, just as any parent worthy of the name will at once go to the help of his boy in danger, no matter how wilfully perverse the lad may previously have been. The 'God help me' of the man who feels himself going down for the last time is never ignored.

But prayer is more than an occasional cry for help. It is a means of grace which, when regularly used, can bring to us each the daily strength of which we stand in daily need. After all, it is a poor business if a man turns to God only when he is in a hole. . . .

The Officer

5 January

Prayer is not a subtle way of getting what we want; rather is it the means of learning what God wants. Prayer is more than asking; prayer implies fellowship with God, and true fellowship rises far above either giving or taking. So that no one may misunderstand me, let me repeat that God will answer the repentant cry of the man who does not usually pray, but such a cry is no more the last word in prayer than a child's shrill demand for food is the last word in conversation.

. . . During the last war we had our national days of prayer. . . . Moved by the wish of the king, or the need of the hour, or the peril of some loved one, many who did not regularly attend any place of worship flocked to church for prayer. But, of that number, I can well imagine that not a few went home again without having gained that emotional uplift or sudden accession of moral strength which they had counted on receiving.

That was not to be wondered at. The kind of man I now am does not depend on what I had for breakfast this

4

morning. It depends on the kind of life I have been living, and the kind of food I have been in the habit of eating since boyhood. If I have been consistently starved, one good meal will not put me on my feet again. On the contrary, it would probably make me feel desperately ill.

So with prayer. . . .

The Officer

6 January

A solitary cry for help is good in its way, but it isn't enough. The true worth of prayer becomes best known to the man who makes a habit of prayer. In this, as with the rest of life, it is practice that makes perfect. When [a famous cricketer] was asked the source of his skill on the cricket field, he replied: 'It's being ah't i' t'middle iv'ry day as does it.' So with the means of grace; their value increases in direct proportion to their regular use. We had no better example of this than King George V. Public worship on Sunday morning was a habit with him. If, for example, he was in India and travelling by train on a Sunday, about 11 in the morning the train would be halted, the chaplain summoned and divine worship held. The result of this habit was reflected in the king's character.

Will you now begin to make regular use of this means of grace called prayer? I sometimes think that the effort required to do so is like the effort needed to learn to swim. The nervous beginner has to accept the instructor's word that the water will not suck him down but hold him up. Once he commits himself to the water he finds this to be true. All that his swimming master has said becomes part of his own personal experience. Experience verifies what previously was but theory.

So with prayer. Make trial, and you will discover for yourself that though 'prayer is not an easy way of getting what we want, it is the only way of becoming what God would have us be'.

The Officer

Communion with God in Christ should form a large part of the Christian life. The term covers all kinds of prayer from the simple prayer of petition to that of silent waiting upon God. Where it becomes habitual it exercises—often unconsciously—a transforming influence. 'Moses wist not that . . . his face shone.'

There is no short cut to genuine fellowship with God. If we are careless in our daily work, allow ourselves to say spiteful things about another, or give way to inconsiderate moods, our prayer life is bound to suffer. Further, if we indulge ourselves, allow some recreation to be too absorbing, be taken up exclusively with light or trashy reading, are irregular in our use of the means of grace, then we cannot expect to enjoy any deep fellowship with God. . . .

C. F. Andrews, devoted missionary to India, once said: 'When I was young . . . I was very active and used to spend the day in ceaseless activities. Indeed, I would almost grudge the time spent in quiet and meditation. . . . With this thought in mind I worked . . . with hardly any pause or time for rest. . . . I did not realise my grievous blunder. But when I came to India . . . I had to learn a new lesson. . . . If we do not give our time and our earnest longing to find Christ in the silence of our inner lives, then we shall lose our true life altogether. We may gain other things, but we shall have lost the best thing of all. . . . We must find Christ in solitude, in the inner chamber of our hearts, when we are praying and are all alone. And if we find him thus, both in action and in rest, we shall indeed win the victory.'

International Company Orders 1944

8 January

Nothing enriches the soul and widens the mind more than praise of God as God. When, for example, Paul does so, he breaks out with: 'All comes from him, all lives by him, all ends in him. Glory to him for ever, Amen!' (Romans 11:36, *Moffatt*).

Sometimes we find little to adore because our conception of God is little. We must have made him in our own image. Not inward, but upward and outward must we look to glimpse his greatness. In Jesus we see his character. In nature we sense his power. In history we can mark the sweep of his judgments. . . .

'What art thou then, my God?' exclaimed Augustine. 'What, I ask, save the Lord God. . . . Highest, best, most mighty, most merciful, most just. . . . What can I say, my God, my life, my holy joy? Or what can anyone say when he speaks of thee?'

'If you want to take some pleasure in prayer,' said a French writer, 'you must never think of God save as the most enchanting ideal of courtesy and kindness, so loving, compassionate and pitiful that the very thought of him makes you weep for joy.' That is well said, it is true—but it is not the whole truth. We must not lose sight of the righteous God who looks for righteousness in his worshippers. No emphasis on one particular attribute of God must cause us to forget the rest. . . .

'Count your blessings' is trite advice, but always timely.

International Company Orders 1944

9 January

There are two opposed ideas of prayer—one which thinks of prayer as a means of persuading God to do what we want; the other in which we seek to be ready to do as God wishes, and pray that all for whom we intercede may be equally obedient to his voice. Prayer 'in Christ's name' never says 'Thy will be changed', but always and with all earnestness 'Thy will be done'—done, that is to say, in the active sense—carried out, put into practice.

Frequently we speak of prayer that 'changes things' and prayer which 'moves the mighty arm of God'. The truth in these and kindred phrases should not blind us to their possible misuse. . . . Not to get an answer may be the answer.

God hears all prayers. How he answers is his affair. Of one thing we may be sure—he answers according to infinite love and wisdom. One basic fact with him is that as all men are different, no two prayers can of necessity be answered alike. Each is judged—so to speak—on its merits. That is not a cause for complaint, but for gratitude.

International Company Orders 1944

10 January

Petition is one of the earliest forms of prayer. The child asks God for a fine day for the outing, for some special birthday present, for God to 'bless daddy and mummy, and all kind friends'. When we were children, we thought like children and prayed like children. Now we have become men and women we have put away childish things, but that certainly must not include taking everything to God in prayer. . . .

We ought to pray. We have the authority of Jesus for that (Luke 18:1). If God is our Father and we his children, it cannot be wrong to bring every need to him. Spiritual needs will come first, of course; material ones will then find their proper place. We are first of all to seek God's righteousness; what is needful for our temporal welfare will then be given.

Nevertheless, God likes us to tell him of all our needs, whatever these may be, just as a good earthly father is pleased when his children think so much of him that they will speak to him without reserve of all their wants. But this truth should be balanced with the fact that we ought always to pray in his name. Jesus said 'Whatsoever ye ask in my name'. The last three words are all-important; they mean 'in harmony with my character and my spirit'. We are intended to make our wants known to God as did Jesus—that is, in active faith, leaving the answer in God's hands, knowing that no prayer goes unanswered.

International Company Orders 1944

11 January

No Jew was ever fond of the sea. The Bible always refers to the sea in its most forbidding guises (eg Isaiah 57:20,

James 1:6). Fourteen days in a gale, without food, the crew wearied and partly undisciplined, all hope abandoned by many, yet Paul was able to give thanks. Never did the apostle show up better than on this voyage. With him was no repining, no complaint against God or man. He felt sure that the God who through Christ had called him to do the work of an evangelist would continue to care for him. . . .

Hannington of Uganda, when dragged out by the natives and about to be martyred, 'laughed at the very agony of the situation and then sang: "Safe in the arms of Jesus"'. Jesus himself, on the eve of his own death, 'took bread . . . and the cup'—both symbols of his own self-offering—and 'gave thanks'.

. . . In 1909 four men were coming back from the South Polar regions. Their diet consisted of horseflesh and a few biscuits. One of the company, Frank Wild, was so ill that he couldn't eat his horseflesh. Shackleton slipped his own ration—one biscuit—into his companion's hand. It was all so quietly done that the others didn't notice the action. Wrote Wild afterward in his diary: 'The bread I ate with you was more than bread.' That solitary biscuit meant more to him than a luxurious dinner.

Paul's calm example worked wonders. The ship's company followed suit. What about our example in saying grace? Do we do so in restaurants and in works' canteens as well as at home?

International Company Orders 1944

12 January

All the Master's years of preparation did not make him feel that therefore he could, during the brief and pressing 36 months of the ministry, dispense with prayer. He never seems to have thought that because his meat was 'to do the will of him who sent me', that therefore he was excused turning back to the source of grace and replacing patiently and carefully the virtue he spent so gladly. Because time was short and evil urgent, defiant, advancing, that—to him—did not mean that he must not take a moment off

9

from helping the stricken and opposing the devil. . . . We may judge by the ration of his life, the balance of his time, the way in which he allotted his days . . . that he considered any disregard of, any restriction on, the life of prayer to be a criminal mistake deserving the ruin of the whole enterprise.

The value of a prayer does not depend upon its length. The recorded prayers of Jesus were short, though we know he spent many hours in prayer. The only known exception to this is his high priestly prayer in John 17. Nor do we pray to supply God with information. We cannot tell him anything he does not know. The 'thou knowest, O Lord . . .' type of prayer is often addressed, not to God, but to another person. Prayer is not just asking. It is better understood as a man's whole attitude toward God. . . . Those who pray become the friends of God. In the prayers of Jesus, praise, adoration and intercession as well as petition all found a place.

In the prayer life of Jesus precept and practice were one. At every point they met and mingled. Christ's teaching about prayer was the fruit of his own secret life of prayer: his life of prayer was simply his teaching in action.

International Company Orders 1944

13 January

The sight of him so often in communication with his Father moved one of his disciples to say: 'Lord, teach us to pray.'

Jesus answered with what we call the Lord's prayer. In the language he spoke (Aramaic) this prayer was like a piece of poetry—having both rhythm and rhyme. . . . Though 'Our Father' is not a poem in our language, its sentences are very dear to us through much use. We must watch that we don't reduce it to the level of a recitation, and should always think of what we are saying when we repeat it.

In this model prayer, God comes first, then the needs of all . . . (our neighbours and ourselves together), last of all ourselves alone.

After we have called him 'Our Father' . . . the first three phrases . . . are concerned with God's nature and purpose. This teaches us—among others things—that our first thoughts in prayer should not be for ourselves, but for God. We hallow God's name not merely by coming to his house to worship him, or even by behaving reverently in his presence. Those are both good things and should not be neglected. But we truly hallow God's name when we live worthily of him and when our lives reflect his Spirit, which is the Spirit of Jesus.

Plainly we cannot get to know his Spirit unless we spend some time in his presence. . . . The more we pray to God, the better shall we know him, and thus shall better understand what showing forth his Spirit means.

International Company Orders 1944

14 January

The second petition helps us to tell God what we desire. We long that he shall reign. For God's Kingdom to come means that his will shall be done by all men. The reason why there is so much misery and distress in the world is that men's selfish ways of living hinder the working of God's love. Here and there, however, we can see signs of his Kingdom coming, for whenever a man turns to him in sorrow for his sin and with a desire to do better for the future, then God's Kingdom is set up in yet another life. The third petition is not very different from the second. God has a purpose for the world, and helping to carry it out—that is, doing his will—is not a grim, unpleasant task we would prefer to evade, but a happy adventure in which we can find great joy.

The important words to remember in 'Give us this day our daily bread' are 'us' and 'our'. We are not asking God to supply only our own wants, but those of his children everywhere—for all men are his children. This means we cannot use the Lord's prayer selfishly, as if we were the only people in the world who matter to God. . . .

Last of all we come to three petitions for ourselves. . . . We need to pray all three, and certainly can never afford

11

to neglect the first. When we are sorry for our sin and ask his forgiveness, God will pardon us at once. . . . But we must also do to others what we wish God to do to us. . . . If we still cherish grudges, then that is a sin in his sight, and so we are not fully forgiven. . . .

All around us are . . . 'the sights that dazzle and the tempting sounds'. We so easily yield to the lure of these things. . . . To debate within ourselves, 'Shall I . . . ?' 'Shall I not . . . ?' is going more than halfway towards yielding. . . . Last of all, if we should by mischance or by our own folly fall into evil ways, we pray that God in his mercy will deliver us from their power and forgive us our sin. . . .

International Company Orders 1944

15 January

Those of us who have wrestled with the writings of the apostle Paul . . . will know how this converted rabbi set out his thoughts on the divine purpose in history in the Epistle to the Romans. Some scholars think that chapters 9 and 11 inclusive are the notes of an address which he was in the habit of delivering on this particular subject. . . . In his appearances in Jewish synagogue and Gentile lecture hall the apostle may frequently have felt himself called upon to justify the ways of God to man, and these chapters probably formed the substance of his argument.

Those ways, he concluded, were 'past finding out'. As the context makes clear, that was a cry of adoration. A believer was bowing before the loving wisdom of a redeeming God. On the lips of those who continually seek a sign however, the same phrase could be a wail of despair. God is a God who hides himself, so that the man whose only sources of information are secular must inevitably be driven to suppose that God, if there be a God, is doing precious little. He is either unconcerned or impotent. . . .

'O God, do you exist?' cried Chopin after the capture of Warsaw by the Russians in 1831. '. . . You do, and yet you do not take vengeance.'

Were we to rely on the news agencies for information we might almost judge that God had despaired of the world and, as in the days of Noah, had abandoned the ungodly to their fate. Yet we would be wrong, for the real news is seldom in the newspapers. Significant events are rarely front page news, if only because men do not perceive their significance until after a lapse of time which may run to centuries. There can be a great and mighty headline and the Lord be not in the headline—nor in what follows below. . . .

The Officer, July, August 1951

16 January

The truth is that God's events are rarely headlines. Some of the most important happenings in the divine economy have a way of not appearing in human history books at all. . . .

We who serve God's Kingdom should never allow ourselves either to be unduly exalted or greatly cast down by the news of the hour. Those who mark such events with banner headlines and a double column spread are themselves aware of the transitory nature of what they are publicising. They are the first to push yesterday's political sensation off the page in order to feature today's society scandal, which in turn will give place to tomorrow's international crisis. Little abides more than 24 hours. The resignation of a Minister of State or the dismissal of a general is but a seven days' wonder. A casual shake of the kaleidoscope and the pattern is changed. Another shake— and the coloured pieces assume yet another variation of colour and form. . . .

Be assured that God is not idle. 'My Father worketh,' said Jesus. Nor is he indifferent. . . . Divine goodness is not weak, though sometimes it looks weak compared with the weapons of this world.

But while evil cannot but be destructive for that is its nature, it is heartening beyond words to be given the privilege of serving in a redemptive economy in which a seeming triviality like a cup of cold water is not wasted. Therefore be steadfast, unmovable. No labour is vain in the Lord.

The Officer, July, August 1951

17 January

. . . I was in Bandung, a city in Indonesia with over a million people and, at a weeknight meeting in a public hall, was welcomed by the Moslem representative of the Provincial Governor, himself a Moslem. The speaker referred to the Pantjasila, or five principles, upon which community life in Indonesia is based, the first of which is belief in God. To my surprise—though a welcome surprise—the congregation began to applaud. Half-a-dozen nuns seated in the second row applauded. Two young Dutch priests at the opposite end of the row joined in. Salvationists began to clap. Moslems shared in the sound. Soon the whole meeting was applauding. 'When I go home,' I said in response, 'I shall tell my western friends that, for the first time in my life, I have heard a public meeting applaud a declaration of belief in God.'

I know that the word 'God' did not mean the same to everyone in the hall that night but, from the initial agreement that he is, we can go on to the Christian assertion that he is the God and Father of our Lord Jesus Christ. In short, he is our Father. And if our Father, then he is the one to whom I can commit my life in trustful obedience, knowing that the creator of all things visible and invisible is also the Father who cares for each of his children. And this faith, far from being childish or infantile, an attitude to life unworthy of a grown man, is an expression of spiritual and intellectual maturity.

Essentials of Christian Experience, pp 1, 2

18 January

It has been well said that next to the foolishness of denying the existence of God is that of trying to prove his existence. The Bible does neither—but is content to affirm that he is and to declare what he has done.

We begin with 'the Father'.

All serious thinking about life begins with the fact that God is. The 'death of God' school is itself dying. It remains true—as Francis Bacon said—that 'a little philosophy bringeth men's minds about to religion'. It is far too readily and gratuitously assumed that believers in God constitute a dwindling minority, principally drawn from the less intelligent sections of the community. There are those who would like it that way. The fact is, however, that there are millions of men and women—Roman Catholics, Jews, Moslems, Orthodox, Protestant—whose first article of faith is 'I believe in God'. Not all have the same understanding of God, but all believe according to the measure of their understanding. . . .

. . . To deny God is not an act of liberation, a glorious freedom nobly gained. It is to deliver oneself over to the grosser forms of credulity, with the clear possibility of descending to the level of the bushman clutching his ju-ju.

The believer affirms that this is God's world. At the heart of things is not a dark, empty hole, but a Father to whose love we may at all times commit ourselves.

Essentials of Christian Experience, pp 1, 3

19 January

God everlastingly remains greater than we can know. His ways are always higher than our ways and his thoughts than our thoughts. As Teersteegen observed, 'a God comprehended is no God'. No man, whatever his ecclesiastical authority, knows all the answers about God and about life. Our best judgments are subject to the limitations both of our factual knowledge and of our spiritual discernment. Over every assessment we are compelled to write 'E & O E' (errors and omissions excepted). The most inspired of God's servants can know only in part and can prophesy only in part. In our moments of greatest certainty, when we are most sure that our own actions are right and that our judgment of the actions of other people is doubly right, we have to remind ourselves, with Paul, that we see through a glass, darkly.

The rabbis had a legend that Moses saw God through a window of horn, and there are commentators who see an allusion to this in the Apostle's phrase. Be this correct or not, the truth remains that though revelation be granted, mystery abides. Revelation and mystery, like light and darkness, day and night, keep company together. They depend upon each other for their existence and significance. This being so, we can hardly quarrel with life as God made it. Like Carlyle's lady who agreed to accept the universe, we can but do the same. We know—but we know only in part. We see through a glass darkly—but still we see.

Essentials of Christian Experience, pp 47, 48

20 January

Belief in the existence of God—this central fact of all our thinking—was the great contribution made by the Hebrew people to the world. They did not arrive at this conviction in a day. They were slow—slower than they ought to have been, we may think, as we read and reread their religious history—to welcome and to understand God's continuous and progressive disclosure of himself to them. But we can say with certainty that the greatest of their prophets confidently believed that the universe had been created and was sustained by one God whose ways and thoughts were infinitely higher than those of man. Yet his might was subordinate to his love, for while he was 'strong in power', yet he showed himself tender toward the children of men, feeding his flock like a shepherd and gathering the lambs in his arm. In this ancient thought of God, which culminated and took final shape in what Jesus had to say about his Father, we may note how men understood him to be ruler over nature, and ruler over human nature, and ruler over time.

. . . Whatever additional information we may now possess about the origin of the universe—and that will always remain much of a mystery—but increases our sense of 'wonder, love and praise' at the creative power of God.

God's sovereign power was seen by men in the way in which he sustained the world order which he himself had called into being. . . . As soldiers move to the left or right at the bidding of their officer, so God orders the stars in their courses. As a man can hold a tiny pool of water in his palm, so God holds the oceans in the hollow of his hand. As a shopkeeper tosses his goods on and off the scale, weighing them with a rapidity born of much practice, so God is master of mountains.

But he is ruler over human nature and over time. . . .

International Company Orders 1941

21 January

God not only 'by wisdom made the heavens and stretched out the earth above the waters', but he also 'smote Egypt in their firstborn and brought out Israel from among them with a strong hand'. Even the obstinate will of the Pharaoh had to bow before the might of God. No man could prevail against that. To try to do so was indeed 'to kick against the pricks'.

. . . A tradesman may clean the scale of his weighing machine by blowing on it. Pouf!—and the dust flies to the four corners of the shop. So—in God's sight—the nations of the world are 'a mere drop in the bucket, no more to him than dust upon the balance' *(Moffatt)*. Elsewhere the prophet saw that even Assyria was under God's control. In his blindness the heathen conqueror thought only of the might of his own arm and of the plunder that awaited him. Nonetheless, he was an instrument in the hands of God, used by divine power to further the divine purpose. The same fact held good with regard to Cyrus. Though the Persian emperor might be unaware of the significance of what he was doing, yet God was using him none the less to further Israel's restoration.

Pilate had to hear the same truth from the lips of Jesus. When the Master would make no reply, the governor broke out with: 'You will not speak to me? Do you not know it is in my power to release you or crucify you?' To which Jesus made answer: 'You could have no power over me, unless it had been granted you from above.' . . . The trial and crucifixion of Jesus were not events outside the scope of God's control. He was ruler even of Pilate. . . .

We must cling to this faith today. However much certain men may appear to hold the destiny of the human race—for good or ill—in their hands, yet God is master of their plans.

International Company Orders 1941

22 January

'His mercy endureth *for ever*!' This is true of all God's attributes. Men are the victims of time. In vain they try to seize it by the forelock. The hours slip past too quickly, and even the greatest and busiest are left lamenting—as did Cecil Rhodes: 'So little done; so much to do.' But God is at no such disadvantage. He is 'from everlasting to everlasting'. He has eternity for the achievement of his purposes, and we can be certain that they will not fail.

Let this be our comfort when our own plans crumble because of lack of success, or have to be left unfinished because time has stolen up on us unawares. God and his will are not subject to any such limitations. Faith in his sovereign power puts iron into men's convictions. Such a creed sustained the Hebrew nation through its tragic exile in Babylon, and upheld the persecuted covenanters in Scotland. Jesus accepted this faith and lived in the strength thereof. He refused to be panicked when a storm broke out on the Sea of Galilee. Had his disciples no faith? And in Gethsemane he accepted anew the death that awaited him as part of the will of a sovereign God. 'The cup which my Father hath given me, shall I not drink it?' Let us stay our anxious minds on the truth that he who rules is also *our* Father.

International Company Orders 1941

23 January

Even before Jesus came, God's ancient people had come to know him as One with whom there was forgiveness . . . (Psalms 103:8-12 and 130:1-8; Isaiah 55:6, 7). But because these passages are so full of grand comfort, we must not imagine that the last word had been said on the subject. We have to remember that God's dealings were presumed to be limited to his chosen people. At any rate, his mercy was thought so to be. And even within Israel, while sins of frailty and thoughtlessness could be forgiven, sins done presumptuously (Psalm 19:13) . . . deliberately and with knowledge aforethought, were held to put the sinner beyond the pale. We can best appreciate this by noting how the religious leaders of Christ's own day regarded his teaching about sin and its forgiveness as far too free and easy, striking at the very foundations of their age-old law.

This, of course, was not so. The life and death of Jesus evoked in men a deeper sense of the essential shamefulness of sin. His work and teaching made the gulf between a holy God and sinful men seem more impassable than ever. And yet men found that, in spite of his knowledge of their darkened hearts and stained imaginations, he was willing to keep them company and to allow his friendship to be the bridge that would carry them over into new ways of clean and honest living. That had seemed an impossibility. So it was, and is, and always will be—from the human point of view. It was God who provided the way of redemption. He 'was in Christ reconciling the world to himself'.

Now this shuts out the thought—still mistakenly held by a few—that somehow Jesus, by his sacrifice, saved men from an angry God who would not otherwise have been willing to forgive. Far from that being true, our faith is that in Jesus God's love is most fully and perfectly revealed. The cross stands in time for what God is throughout eternity. That fact is the reason for our penitence and the motive which prompts both our adoring worship and our loving service.

International Company Orders 1941

24 January

The dictionary describes a thing of beauty as one which arouses our admiration, and to which there is an inward response of delight. For example—a swallow, a rose, a racehorse, are all beautiful. The spire of Salisbury Cathedral is beautiful, as is the Golden Gate, San Francisco, and the view of Landale Valley, from the eastern shore of Windermere. Opinions sometimes differ as to what constitutes beauty. There are those who cannot distinguish between paste and pearl, and mistakenly prefer the cheap and flashy to the genuinely lovely. Such varying judgments only prove that 'it is not the eye, but the soul, that sees'. Beauty is always marked by *simplicity* and *proportion*. This is as true of a building as an animal, a ship, a painting, or a sentence. . . .

Beauty is a sign of love. No other explanation is possible. Ruskin, who continually emphasised the connection between beauty and love in his *Seven Lamps of Architecture,* tells of his surprise at the ugliness of certain huge statues on the front of a church in Rome. One day he climbed on to the roof to make a closer inspection, and discovered that the sculptor had not carved an inch wherever his work would normally be out of sight. He did his best with the fronts, but, argued Ruskin, he might as well have saved his labour, for the man who cared so little for his craft that he could skimp it in such a sorry fashion was not capable of producing anything of genuine beauty. . . .

Everywhere in nature is this hallmark of love. Beauty is not a rare thing, reserved for the peacock or the costly orchid. It is as present (said Sir J. A. Thompson) 'in the minute chiselling of the moth's egg shell as in the graceful lines of a crane, the hidden down feathers of the eagle, or the cedars of Lebanon'. Nature is so crammed with beauty because its creator is Love. God might possibly have constructed a world on stark factory lines, capable of supporting life—but purely utilitarian. Instead, he has given us a home where he 'hath made everything beautiful in its time'.

International Company Orders 1942

25 January

The Hebrew Hymn of Creation reaches back to the dawn

20

of time—'in the beginning'. When that was—no one knows. Various calculations have been made as to the age of the universe, but most of them consist of so many noughts that the mind is simply bewildered. . . .

Science does not contradict the story of God's creative power, but fills in the details of the outline supplied by Scripture. In both instances, the emphasis is on *God's* activity. Indeed . . . 'the story of creation is told with perfect accuracy in the words: "And God said, Let there be light."' Good people have nothing to fear from scientific research into the origin of the universe in which we live. Much of that work is necessarily speculative, but no new facts brought to light can ever eliminate God. 'All things were made by him, and without him was not anything made that was made.' However far science peers backward into the dark, it cannot think of any age or state that was not the product of pre-existing conditions. Before the dawn of creation must have been Mind. That Mind we believe to be God, and in the wonder of earth's story we see how he prepared a home where his children might live.

With this conclusion men so opposite in outlook as Lord Kelvin and Charles Darwin agree. Wrote the former: 'I do not say, with regard to the origins of life, that science neither affirms nor denies creative power. Science positively *asserts* creative power.' Darwin but echoed those words when, referring to the drama of creation, he said: 'This grand sequence of events the mind refuses to accept as the result of blind chance. The understanding revolts from such a conclusion.'

. . . The universe was created by an *Almighty* God.

International Company Orders 1941

26 January

In his poem *The Torchbearers* Alfred Noyes has described how Kepler, the early 17th-century German astronomer, was disputing with those who thought that the universe was the product of chance, and how at last he quoted the way in which his wife had disposed of so illogical a position:

21

One night
When I was tired and all my mind adust
With pondering over atoms, I was called
To supper, and she placed before me there
The most delicious salad. It would appear—
I thought aloud—that if these pewter dishes,
Green hearts of lettuce, tarragon, slips of thyme,
Slices of hard-boiled egg and grains of salt,
With drops of vinegar, water and oil,
Had in a bottomless gulf been flying about
From all eternity, one sure certain day
The sweet invisible hand of happy chance
Would serve them as a salad.
   'Likely enough,'
My wife replied, 'but not so good as mine,
Nor so well dressed. Come, John, say grace.'
The universe was created by an *Almighty* God. . . .

International Company Orders 1941

27 January

The universe was created by an *Almighty* God. God said,
'Let there be'—and there was. 'As easy as talking' is the
way in which we sometimes describe a not very difficult
task. That is the suggestion here. The writer to the
Hebrews expressed the same idea in the phrase (11:3) 'We
understand that the worlds were formed by the word of
God.' He only needed to speak—and it was so.

The greatness of this inspired Hebrew account is seen
more clearly when contrasted with other pagan stories of
creation. Tablets discovered on the site of Nineveh have
told us how the Babylonians thought that Marduk, the
god of light, fought the dragon Tiamat, who personified
chaos. Not until he had slain this upholder of disorder
and its relations, could he use its skin to make the dome of
the sky and proceed with the work of creation.

Putting the two accounts side by side, which is superior?
The Hebrew story has a dignity and reasonableness while
the other takes refuge in grotesque invention. . . . Each
nation had its own god. When there was war on the earth
there was confusion in the heavens. As against that idea of

a multitude of warring deities, the Hebrews believed in *one* Almighty God, who was in supreme control. Life was not at the mercy of whatever tribal idol was thought to be strongest. Such ideas reduced religion to a worship of chance. Who knew which god would deliver a man, just as who could foresee when a storm of hail would spoil a peasant's crops, or a stroke of lightning bring a tree crashing down upon his simple dwelling?

No! said the inspired teachers of the Hebrew race. God is in command. He has set the stars in their courses. The winds are his messengers. 'Fire and hail, snow and vapours . . . , fulfil his word.' Nature is yet another expression of himself. That is the language of Psalm 148 in which the universe is called upon to praise the Creator. In that chorus we can join.

International Company Orders 1941

28 January

Continuing our study of God's creative work, it may not be out of place to remind ourselves of its immense scope. We live on the surface of a spinning ball that sails through space like a ship on a vast ocean. Yet our world is but one of the thousands of millions of stars revealed by a modern telescope. . . . Yet while the colossal scale and design of the infinitely great is awe-inspiring, the infinitely little evokes no less wonder. The writer of Proverbs (30:25, 26) marvelled at the wisdom of the ants and conies. Though so tiny, they fulfilled a useful purpose and men could learn from their industry. Here again was design, and that, together with the beauty which Jesus noted in a wild flower, are two of God's hallmarks stamped on all his handiwork. . . .

Nature has been planned for a purpose, and—what is more—for a good purpose. When the heavens and the earth were finished, 'God saw'—so runs the Hymn of Creation—'that it was very good'. Order and design are apparent in the infinitely large as well as the infinitely small.

'Our universe,' wrote Ernst Haekel, 'knows only one

sole God, and this Almighty God rules the whole of nature without exception. We see him at work everywhere. To him the whole world is subject. . . . If a body falls to the ground at the rate of 15 feet per second, if three atoms of oxygen to one of sulphur always produce sulphuric acid . . . then these phenomena are the immediate operations of God, equally with the blossoms of plants, the movements of animals, the thoughts of mankind. We all exist by God's grace—the stone as well as the water, the insect no less than the pine tree.'

International Company Orders 1941

29 January

Evidence of design can be seen in so frail a creature of a summer's day as a butterfly.

The 17,000 tubes in the compound lens of a butterfly's eye are formed and developed in each insect by a co-operative process so complicated that it defies description. It includes all the preliminary arrangements in the egg, caterpillar and chrysalis stage, and the contributory processes whereby food—taken in and digested—is conveyed to build up the intricate structure of the lens. . . . These include the remarkable power of reproducing, not only itself, but all the latest 'accidental improvements' in its indescribably complicated instruments; for, unless these improvements are transmitted as they are acquired, they disappear. They certainly are acquired. They certainly are transmitted. The argument weighs heavily against . . . any easy acceptance of happy accidents as an explanation of a vast and harmonious system of law.

A similar illustration of amazingly complicated design can be seen in the human nervous system, with—to take only one example—250,000 fibres in the optic nerve, each of which is capable of 'innumerable degrees of sensation'. To argue that such an intricate design is born of chance is to make unbelief harder to accept than belief!

International Company Orders 1941

30 January

Again and again students of nature have been amazed by the way in which animals and insects know just how to act. An engineer may work out elaborate mathematical formulae in order to build a suspension bridge, linking cliff to cliff, but spiders have been joining branch to branch with their finespun webs for ages. . . . We might also compare the retractable carriage of an aeroplane which lessens air resistance with the way in which seagulls in flight 'retract' their feet; the ant hills of the termites which—according to size—are proportionately taller than man's concrete skyscrapers. . . .

The beauty of God's handiwork was a favourite theme with Jesus. When he spoke of the loveliness of the lily we must not think of our rare English flower. . . . The bluebell in the wood—untended by man—is clothed by God with beauty. We can rightly take this as a further sign of the Creator's affection for his creatures—for beauty is the product of love. Ruskin once climbed an Italian cathedral to inspect some of the statuary, and, finding that at the back—out of sight—they were only half-finished, broke out in condemnation of the sculptor as an hireling, a fellow who could not possibly have been in love with his work.

Contrast that with the work of craftsmen who take a delight in each separate article they make. The beauty which they evoke from grained wood or wrought metal is a sign of their pleasure in their craft. And of God it was truly said that 'He hath made everything beautiful in its time' (Ecclesiastes 3:11, *RV*). For this further gift we can but thank him, with an added prayer that his beauty—which is the beauty of holiness—may be seen in our lives as well.

International Company Orders 1941

31 January

In 1908 when Bryan and Taft were rivals for the presidency of the USA, an American, who was a keen

25

astronomer, received a visit from a friend who was an ardent politician. The visitor spent some time gazing through the powerful telescope belonging to his host, and then said: 'So you tell me that most of those planets are bigger than our earth?' 'Undoubtedly so!' 'And is this globe only a speck among innumerable millions of stars, some of which are whirling masses of fire like the sun?' 'Almost certainly so!' The questioner was silent. Then, as he rose to go, he remarked: 'Well, I guess it doesn't much matter whether Bryan or Taft gets in.' . . .

From the dawn of time and thought men have been both startled and bewildered by the contrasts existing within themselves and also between themselves and their surroundings.

Compared with the animals, man is inferior in strength and speed to many—and yet he has dominion over all. Compared with 'thy heavens . . . the moon and the stars . . . what is man?' Today—more than ever—we feel the force of that remark. The astronomer—groping his way through the problems presented by the sky above— reckons that the unit of time in star-life may well be a million years. And ours is three-score years and ten! Yet Tennyson's question has still to be answered:

> Tho' world on world in myriad myriads roll
> Round us, each with different powers,
> And other forms of life than ours,
> What know we greater than the soul? . . .

International Company Orders 1941

1 February

The difference between man and the universe in which he lives does help him to cultivate a sense of proportion. At the same time, this contrast must not oppress him. Thomas Hardy, speaking through the mouth of one of his characters—Lady Constantine—thought that astronomy was a bad subject for a man to study because it made him so conscious of human insignificance and the worthless-ness of human life. Wrote he: 'At night, when human discords and harmonies are hushed, there is nothing to moderate the blow with which the infinitely great, the stellar universe, strikes down upon the infinitely little, the mind of the beholder.'

But those words just beg the question. Is the mind of man 'infinitely little'? The quip about 'the trouble of ants in the glare of a million million suns' is nothing more than the worship of size. To argue that man is therefore of small account in God's sight is like arguing that, in a case of fire, a mother should grab the mangle instead of the baby because it weighs more. We must not confuse bigness with greatness. If we pile up the material universe in one scale, and then place in the other the mind that has triumphed over matter and penetrated the secrets of the most distant stars, which is of most value?

'Man is but a reed, weakest in nature,' said Pascal, 'but a reed which thinks. Were the universe to crush him, man would still be more noble than that which has slain him.' And why? Because man rejoices in the divine blessings of mind and soul. The fruits of these—love, thought, joy, worship—are the really noble and enduring qualities of life. They stamp man as the crown of creation. They were given him when God said, 'Let us make man in our image.' By comparison with the universe, man may be a 'frail creature of dust', yet he is also 'little less than divine'. . . .

International Company Orders 1941

2 February

Seeing that he is made in the likeness of God, what then follows?

He has intelligence and a capacity greater than that of any other creature for using his intelligence. It is true that a household pet can behave intelligently. . . . But the tiniest child has greater possibilities than the wisest and friendliest old dog. The animal is at a dead end. The child may become a Lincoln or a Herod, a Wilberforce or a Nero. He has endless possibilities either way. The gift of intelligence can have either a savour of life unto life or of death unto death.

He possesses a conscience—a moral sense which enables him to *distinguish* between right and wrong. Added to this is the power of free will which enables him to *choose* between right and wrong. The faculty of conscience may be faulty and in need of correction. Even in Scripture we come across practices which, though followed by godly men in the past, are now considered wrong. . . . But we have been given a perfect moral standard—the mind of the Master—as the rule of Christian faith and practice. When that is set before us, conscience swings round to it like the compass needle to the pole. As we stand before Christ we recognise that he is *the* standard, and that we sadly fall short.

Free will is the power of choice, and carries with it the responsibility for choice. When every allowance has been made for the handicap of a bad environment, and for the fact that life may have given man a raw deal, he is still responsible for doing his best with the cards he has. It is better to have made a good thing of a poor hand than a poor thing of a good hand. . . .

International Company Orders 1941

3 February

Man is a spiritual being. This is the choicest of blessings. Man can commune with God, and God with man—a fellowship not limited to time but capable of endless perfecting throughout eternity. Only by the daily exercise of this privilege can man grow to his full stature. Just as rain and fresh air and sunlight are good for a thriving plant, so there is nothing which develops our human powers more fruitfully than the worship of God.

J. H. Fabre, the naturalist, was once demonstrating before a class in a science laboratory. He placed two small birds in a bell jar from which the oxygen had been exhausted. As might be expected, the birds panted, struggled, gasped and died. 'Whatever is in the jar?' asked the boys. 'Nitrogen' replied Fabre. 'Then what a terrible poison nitrogen must be!' they said in chorus. 'Not at all' answered their teacher. 'Nitrogen is in the air all around us. We are breathing it now. It was the absence of oxygen that killed the birds.'

In like manner, it is only in God that we can live and move and have our being. If he be withdrawn or, more correctly, if we shut him out, the soul withers up. If a man refuses to make use of this highest of all his capacities— the capacity for fellowship with God—then he limps through life like a cripple, as mis-shapen as any twisted invalid. Man realises his chief end only when his life glorifies his Creator. 'And we best glorify him,' said a 17th-century teacher, 'when we grow most like him.'

International Company Orders 1941

4 February

On church notice boards we often read 'Divine worship —11 am and 6.30 pm'. The announcement may be true enough, but it is by no means the whole truth. The Christian worship of God has never been an affair of 'services' only, but is part of the whole business of Christian living. If worship be a matter of offering something worthwhile to God, then growth in character by his grace is the 'living sacrifice' which, in the new dispensation, we offer him in place of the blood of beasts in the old. Worship may first of all be an attitude of the soul, but it must also include the outward expression of that inner attitude in the market-place and in the home.

Were worship only a method of going through a particular routine in a building set apart for such a purpose, then we might carry through such a ritual on the appointed day and, for the rest of the week, yield to business or pleasure the supreme devotion of our lives. But worship reaches out beyond one short hour on one day in seven. Perverted and debased, it can sink to a superstitious fear which reveals itself, for example, in the use of mascots or a silly dread of the number 13. Rightly directed, it is the supreme adoration which we give to Almighty God, of whose demand for such a surrender we have become livingly aware and to which we joyfully accede. In such an act we acknowledge that we are entirely dependent upon him and that he is the source of all we can need.

Here then is a 'totalitarian' claim. God will brook no rival. Man cannot serve God and Mammon. The Christian in the Roman Empire could not offer to Caesar the pinch of incense which would acknowledge him as 'lord and god'. . . . Early-day salvationists could not cease from standing in the highways and byways to make known the gospel just because a government tried to forbid them. . . . Nor can we in the 20th century give to any pleasure or pursuit or secular demand that complete surrender of the will which belongs to God alone.

International Company Orders 1947

5 February

With the poor in the East what to eat, to drink and to wear occupied of necessity the greater part of their time and attention. We must not think that the Master was blind to those physical needs. Far from it; not for nothing was he the eldest son of a widow with a large family. But he certainly taught that people could get too pre-occupied with their material wants. To him, God was a heavenly Father who would no more allow one of his children to fall by the way than an earthly father could the child of his care. . . . The song of the birds and the beauty of the flowers appealed to him as proof of the Father's care. God was the Creator of the natural world and, looking upon it, Jesus, like his Father on the seventh day, saw that 'it was very good'. To him, nature was not 'red in tooth and claw' but 'all which he beheld was full of blessings'.

If God be admitted as the Creator and sustainer of life, then worry becomes needless. More than that, it is useless. About events under our control we should rightly be concerned. But concerning those which we, with all the goodwill in the world, have no power to alter, we can but trust. Our chief duty is to seek God's Kingdom; useless anxiety which distracts us from that first purpose is a positive sin. . . . What Jesus taught, he himself practised. His whole life was one of trust, and in this the best of his followers have ever sought to copy him. 'In nothing be anxious,' wrote Paul to the Philippians (4:6, *RV*). That advice was not the platitude of a man who had led a sheltered life, but came from a missionary who had breasted every storm that could blow. . . .

As children of God we are called upon to trust him without demanding precise explanations at every end and turn. This may sound a hard saying, but we can be given 'faith in the night as well as the day'.

International Company Orders 1947

6 February

It is hard for us to realise what it meant to the Master to be despised and rejected of men. He had come to save his people from their sin, but one result of his coming was to make their condemnation the more certain. . . . The more you love people, the harder it is to see them going wrong. Now remember how passionately the Master's great heart longed to see his people fulfil their God-given mission. Jesus was the fulfilment of all that the law and the prophets had foretold, and for his nation to reject him was to turn their backs upon their true destiny, and to bring upon themselves the disasters which Jesus so clearly foresaw (Luke 19:41-44). . . .

Dark and unwelcome though the appointed pathway seemed, Jesus acknowledged it to be God's way for him. What this obedience cost him, we cannot tell. Hebrews 5:8 gives us a hint, for the second half of the verse probably means: 'He learned what obedience cost through suffering.' Part of that price—more spiritual and mental than physical—lay in the fact that his prayer was not answered. He who had rebuked anyone for saying 'If' to him (Mark 9:23), now said 'If' himself. His request that the cup should pass was not allowed. Here he comes very close to us, for our prayers are not always answered. . . . A further part of the price lay in the fact that even his three closest friends were found wanting in the emergency. . . . He had to tread the winepress alone.

There was but one resource left to Jesus. He did not lose his sense of God's nearness, and in the strength of him whose presence had always been the most real of all the facts of human experience the Master said: 'Not what I will, but what thou wilt.'

International Company Orders 1947

7 February

One of the first principles of happiness and usefulness in life is that a man should accept himself for what he is. Few among us may be front bench orators, but that does not mean we cannot give a word of testimony in the open-air meeting. Not all bandsmen are soloists, but that does not mean that secondary parts are to be despised. Are not accompaniments every whit as important as solos?

No one is free from certain limitations. With one man it may be his age. The spirit is willing, but the flesh is weak. With another it may be his health. . . . With another, his lack of opportunity. Not all men get the same chance. 'Full many a flower is born to blush unseen.' But none of these facts is any reason for neglecting whatever gift you may possess. As the squirrel said to the mountain:

> If I cannot carry forests on my back,
> Neither can you crack a nut. . . .

Sins of omission were serious offences in the eyes of Jesus. Simon the Pharisee was rebuked because he gave no water and proffered no kiss. The priest and the Levite showed up badly because they did nothing to help the injured traveller. The foolish virgins were guilty of no sin of commission; they just forgot to do something—to bring a reserve of oil for their lamps. . . . To fail to do something because we cannot do everything is to stand condemned. . . .

We cannot truly worship God unless we work for him with such powers as we may possess. Each of us has some talent to be used for his glory. What are you doing with yours?

International Company Orders 1947

8 February

Is there any difference *in principle* between making one

loaf (or five) into sufficient to feed a crowd in a few moments, and making one grain of wheat into a hundred between spring and harvest? We cannot explain how the first was done—but neither can we the second. It is true that growers everywhere make use of the mysterious processes of reproduction, but any explanation of the miracle of life—whether in plant, animal or child—is beyond us. We have gratefully to accept it as given.

There is no doubt that our globe—as part of God's universe—could provide enough to feed the peoples of the world. That many go without is not his fault. Human ignorance, inefficiency and selfishness are responsible for much of the want that prevails. Obviously these notes cannot discuss the intricate problems of distribution involved in the world's food supply, but it does seem plain that any man-made barriers which interfere with the feeding of human beings stand condemned in God's sight. They make a mock of his providential care and nullify his will that none should perish. . . .

Nature is not a system of forces working independently of God and interposed between us and him. The source of all nature's activity is a good and gracious Creator. . . .

We live by the labours of others. Let us remember the duty we owe our fellow-men in return.

International Company Orders 1942

9 February

We are not asked to deny the bitter facts of sorrow and loss. They stare us in the face; we cannot shut our eyes to them. But even the unwanted birth of a child is an opportunity for yet another human soul to know the joy of fellowship with the Father, and for the Father to show that the sins of the parents need not be visited upon the child.

Even an undesired baby is unique, an unrepeatable individual, like none other. The majesty of the infinitely great should not blind us to the worth of the seemingly insignificant. No two roses are cut to the same pattern.

33

The crest of each wave differs from the next. No man's fingerprints are exactly the same as his neighbour's. Each living person is one on his own and God so regards him.

Our Father in Heaven is not like a top executive in a huge combine who may give direction in matters of principle but leaves the details to his subordinates. He may do this because he cannot cope with all the details or because he does not want to be bothered with them. But are we to say that God cannot cope or does not care?

Jesus and our Need, pp 39, 40

10 February

The existence of evil in a universe over which a good God rules has been a standing problem since the dawn of conscious thought, and may appear to contradict what Jesus said about the Father's care.

. . . All suffering is not wholly evil. For example, some forms of pain serve as warnings. That is its function in the animal world. The pet house-dog learns to avoid the hard stone wall, and pussy the bramble bushes, because the memory of previous pains suffered acts as a danger signal. This is also true to a most helpful degree so far as our bodies are concerned. The aching tooth bids me visit a dentist. A stab of pain in the lungs tells me that I ought to consult a doctor. Without such warnings the body might well decay and a man be unaware of its sorry condition.

Some forms of suffering lead to new and deepened sympathies, so that good comes out of evil. One illustration of this is to be found in the way in which some of the world's leading generals have come to be opposed to their own profession. Experience has taught them to feel for the victims of the evil for which they themselves have been in a measure responsible. . . . There is a suffering born of the struggle to learn. A parent might do his child's homework for him, thus saving the boy the effort of finding the right answer. But would that be wise, let alone truly helpful? Would it profit the lad in the long run? No!

He must wrestle with his own school problems and master them.

There is also the evil which arises out of 'man's inhumanity to man'. . . .

International Company Orders 1941

11 February

When people want to know why God does not intervene to prevent, say, a war, they are assuming that the sins and follies of rulers of nations call for different treatment from those committed by lesser people. But a lie is a lie whoever tells it—errand boy or minister of state. Both will be judged according to the light each possessed. Admittedly a man of influence may—by his choice of evil—bring suffering upon a far greater number. But it must not therefore be assumed that God is indifferent to the resultant havoc.

While it cannot be denied that distressing calamities—such as an earthquake in India or a flood in China—seem to challenge religious faith, yet we believe that none of these things can 'separate us from the love of God, which is in Christ Jesus our Lord'. In passing final judgment upon the matter, we must remember that while we may have to share in suffering which is the result of another man's sin, we also share in blessings which we ourselves may have done little to deserve and certainly less to produce. . . .

Finally . . . stands the assurance—given by Jesus—that we are precious in the sight of the Father. Of course, the man who wants to argue that Jesus was mistaken can do so. But nothing less than a downright refusal to accept what he said as true can dispose of his words that we 'are of more value than many sparrows'. Flowers and birds achieve a perfection of beauty in God's world. How much more then his children? And indeed, as we ourselves grow in years and in grace, we find this truth confirmed by personal experience.

International Company Orders 1941

12 February

To some it may have seemed as if their task in explaining the nature and work of the Third Person in the Trinity was made additionally difficult for want of a human being with whom they could identify the Holy Spirit as the eternal Son is identified with the Christ of Galilee.

Yet there is one human figure in whom we can see the Holy Spirit fully and freely at work; him we acknowledge as the incarnate God—Jesus of Nazareth. For the Father gave not 'the Spirit by measure unto him'. 'The heaven was opened and the Holy Ghost descended . . . upon him' at the Jordan. 'Full of the Holy Ghost' he 'was led . . . into the wilderness'. 'In the power of the Spirit' he came to Nazareth where his testimony was: 'the Spirit of the Lord is upon me'.

When, therefore, we desire to see the Holy Spirit at work in his most revealing manner, we look to Jesus, whose words and deeds manifest the character and power of the Spirit equally as they reveal the nature of the Father. He is the 'incarnation' of the Spirit. There is no higher holiness than his. No richer degree of spirituality is possible than he made manifest. We cannot improve on him! . . . A life filled with the Spirit is in all things like to Jesus. As the puritan, John Owen, wrote: 'There is no grace that is not to be found in Christ: and every grace is in him in its highest degree.'

This truth may provoke two reactions. . . .

The Officer, May, June 1950

13 February

This truth may provoke two reactions. On the one hand we are awed by the beauty of holiness displayed by Jesus. The fruit of the Spirit is seen in him as in no one and nowhere else. The best of men have the defects of their qualities, but opposite virtues found their unity in him. The rhythm of his life was perfect; the circle of graces complete; the balance true; the blend faultless. Who can rise to this perfection?

Yet we may be encouraged by the sanity of his example. The holiness of Jesus did not despise eating and drinking, dining with publicans and Pharisees alike, playing with small children, soothing harassed mothers, enjoying the quiet of Bethany as well as the cut and thrust of public argument—all experiences which fall to our lot. The Holy Spirit was in him and with him as much amid the crowd in Capernaum who jostled him . . . as when 'rising up a great while before day, he went out, and departed into a solitary place, and there prayed'. All he did was 'in the power of the Spirit'.

Now the temptation which besets many well-intentioned people is to associate the Spirit's power with the extraordinary, the unusual, even the bizarre—as if the strangeness of an experience was an authentic sign of the Spirit's presence. Yet the example of Jesus should not lead us to think so. He never spoke with 'tongues'. There is no record that he was ever caught up to any third heaven. The gospels mention no spiritual ecstasies which he enjoyed. And while it is not for anyone to cast so much as the faintest shadow of disparagement upon any blessing enjoyed by any of the Lord's people, yet Jesus remains the pattern. The servant must not suppose himself greater than his Lord—either in raptures or in tribulations.

The Officer, May, June 1950

14 February

In his reminiscences, *Sometime, Never,* Wilfred Pickles has described how, as a lad in the Halifax Public Library, he suddenly came across the *Oxford Book of English Poetry.* Time stood still as he succumbed to the magic spell of words. Halifax was forgotten until, moved by a sudden impulse, he hid the book (which he later replaced) beneath his coat and hurriedly left the library.

Then, as a builder's labourer, connecting a drain pipe to a main sewer, he astonished his mate by standing in the trench and reciting from 'A Shropshire Lad'.

> In summer time on Bredon
> The bells they sound so clear; . . .   •

Thereafter to the youthful Wilfred poetry was never a string of meaningless words, the fad of the highbrow, the cult of the aesthete. No more could he escape her magic.

... We do not need to have been very bad in order, by God's grace, to be made good—though at the crisis point we may doubtless feel bad enough. ... Our dungeon may be that of our own fears and misgivings. Self, rather than sinning, may hold us prisoner. But from any and all of these outward signs of inward failure we may be delivered by committing ourselves without reserve to Jesus as Saviour and Lord.

So the new birth may well be that moment when, in an act of penitent self-surrender to Christ, the Lord becomes a living reality and his daily presence our all-sufficiency.

Essentials of Christian Experience, pp 18-20

15 February

The experience called conversion can express itself in different ways for different people. No two human encounters with the grace of God are ever exactly the same. To some conversion is such a drastic change that it can be described only as in Oliver Cooke's chorus: 'I know a place where night is turned to day'. And that not in a slow dawn where light imperceptibly brightens the sky, but with the suddenness of a lightning flash which illuminates what has hitherto been pitch black.

But to others among us conversion may be more truthfully likened to slow dynamite. We have always believed in such general truths that God is love, that in his mercy sin can be forgiven, and that by his grace temptation can be overcome. ... But there comes a moment when these truths to which we have long given passive assent suddenly become compellingly alive. They seize us by the throat. They demand that we live by them. The slow burning fuse, first set alight maybe in the Sunday afternoon company meeting, now reaches the powder barrel and our adolescent sophistications are blown sky high. Saving truth confronts us and demands that we accept as a matter of personal conviction the gospel which we have heard from the days of our childhood.

Outwardly there may be little change in the externals of our living. . . . But inwardly that moment of illumination and dedication is never to be forgotten.

Essentials of Christian Experience, pp 17, 18

16 February

. . . As General Orsborn wrote: 'God wills for his people an uttermost salvation.'

That has always been God's will for his people. The meaning of the word 'holy' was deepened by the prophets and altogether transformed by the coming of Jesus, yet the New Testament can freely quote the Old Testament command, 'Be ye holy; for I am holy', because that has always been the purpose of God. The word itself comes from a root meaning separated, and with Israel it was the divine will that they should be separate from their neighbours in faith and practice. With the new Israel it is still his will that we should be separate from the world in habits because we are separate at heart. We are to be a peculiar people, his very own, possessing and possessed by the faith that works by love. . . .

Often 'to will is present with me, but how to perform . . . I find not'. But with God it is axiomatic that what he wills he can perform. So my sanctification, like my salvation, lies in yielding myself to him with whom all things are possible.

Here then is ground which believers may feel firm beneath their feet. Here personal desire and scriptural teaching meet to provide the open door by which grace may fully enter. The experience of holiness is not merely one for which I long nor to which I am counselled by my teachers. This is that which God wills and which, with man's active consent, can be fulfilled in every life.

The Call to Holiness, pp 5, 6

17 February

This is where we must give the life of holiness as exemplified in Jesus a fair chance. Some of us do not do that. We do not take the trouble to look long enough at him. We pay more attention to a human interest picture in the daily paper. We gaze more intently at the TV screen. . . .

Ought we not to give this spiritual ideal at least equal time and attention? Sometimes we say of a person who may not have impressed us favourably at first blush: 'He improves with knowing.' Reverently we may say the same of the life of holiness as exemplified in Jesus. . . .

Finally, look with eyes for none but him, for only he can stir us out of our lazy content with the lower levels of spiritual living. . . . Our human nature, left to itself, always clings to the lower levels. Despite Longfellow's 'Excelsior', few of us seize the banner with the strange device, 'Holiness unto the Lord', and are lost to sight making for the summit of the holy hill of God.

Only Jesus can rouse us into making such an attempt. Then look to him that he may quicken you with holy desire which, by the presence and power of the Holy Spirit, may find its fullest expression in holy—that is to say, Christ-like—living.

The Call to Holiness, pp 20, 21

18 February

. . . Life compels men to acknowledge the existence of those inner self-contradictions which, apart from the grace of God, can be their ruin. Because of those character flaws, it is man's nature to be dissatisfied with his nature, but how to shape it nearer to his heart's desire is beyond him.

Now the Christian faith did not invent this dilemma. . . . For example, the rabbis of our Lord's day taught that in man there were two natures, so that he was in the unhappy position of being drawn in opposite directions at one and the same time. He was—in the most literal sense—

distracted; that is to say, he was drawn apart. And, though employing different terms, the Greeks said much the same. There has come down to our own times the familiar imagery of the soul as the charioteer whose unenviable task it was to drive in double harness two horses, one of noble breed, the other the exact opposite. The noble horse was reason; the untamed horse was passion—whose brute strength dragged the chariot earthwards.

To what the Greeks said the Romans added their own melancholy amen. When the apostle Paul was in his early teens there died a Roman philosopher many of whose sayings can still be found in any standard dictionary of quotations. One such reads: 'I see and approve the better; I follow the worse,' and the apostle, who was a child of both worlds—Jewish and Gentile—summed up man's continuing plight in the well-worn phrase: 'The good that I would I do not: but the evil which I would not, that I do. . . . O wretched man that I am! . . .'

What is the remedy offered?

Essentials of Christian Experience, pp 63-65

19 February

What is the remedy offered? The Christian faith . . . first of all . . . recognises that these are the facts of life. In the second place it offers a remedy. That is to say, when the Christian faith speaks of men as sinners, it is not so much sitting in judgment on them as realistically accepting them for what they are. What is called the doctrine of original sin is this recognition of man's imperfections. Which is another way of saying that no social or material progress can—of its own outworking—eliminate that innate selfishness, which is the root of all sinful actions, from man's nature. Like his own shadow, man cannot be rid of this plague. Here is a literal old man of the sea whom he cannot shake off his shoulders. The Christian faith accepts these facts, and accepts them without despairing of their victims, because it can offer a remedy. . . .

What is the remedy offered? Three possibilities await man. The first is that there is no hope for him. As he is he will remain. The second is that man can mend his own ways. He can take himself in hand, lifting himself up, as it were, by his own hair. The third—which is the Christian possibility—is that man cannot change himself but that he can be changed or converted.

Essentials of Christian Experience, p 65

20 February

The first possibility is that there is no hope for man. You can't change human nature. But who says this? The apologist for current injustices, for one. Especially where the wrongs done to others work out, either directly or indirectly, to his own profit. It is in his interest so to let matters run. So he damps down all hopeful endeavour with his own self-interested fatalism.

The drop-out echoes this attitude—because he himself doesn't want to be changed. He prefers to remain as he is. . . . Our Lord had to put a question of this kind to the cripple who had been lying at the pool of Bethesda for 38 years. 'Do you want to get better again?' For where there is no desire there can be little hope.

And the pessimist agrees that there is no hope for man, especially if he is a disillusioned intellectual. 'Man, who began in a cave behind a windbreak', wrote H. G. Wells, 'will end in the disease-soaked ruins of a slum.' This should be seen for what it is—a counsel of despair.

Essentials of Christian Experience, pp 65, 66

21 February

The second possibility is that man can mend his own ways. He can lift himself up by his own bootstraps. Of course, it is open for anyone who desires to think this possible to do so. But on this the deserved comment is that there is not much evidence available to encourage such optimism, either for individuals or for society.

The truth is that if it be thought a vain dream to change human lives by means of the Christian faith, it is a vainer dream still to try to help men without it. It is always Jekyll who proves the undoing of Hyde. It is never our own unsupported desires for goodness which triumph over the evil which does so easily beset us. 'Who on earth can set me free from the clutches of my own sinful nature?' There is but one answer: 'God alone, through Jesus Christ our Lord.'

This leaves the third possibility, the Christian one, that though man cannot change himself he can be changed.

Christian character is not and never can be self-induced. No sleight of hand can produce Christlikeness from that doubtful mixture which we know unregenerate human nature to be. As well might the most skilful cook despair of producing a wholesome meal out of sour milk, rancid butter and stale flour. But despair of ourselves is not a bad thing if it leads us to cast ourselves without reserve upon the saving power of God. The old proverb which declares that God helps those who help themselves is by no means the whole truth. The witness of the Christian gospel is that God waits to help the man who cannot help himself.

Hence the truth that 'the Lord's hand is not shortened, that it cannot save; neither his ear heavy, that it cannot hear.'

Essentials of Christian Experience, pp 66, 67

22 February

Further, if this word stands for a religious experience, it also stands for a desirable experience. Holy belongs to the same family of words as hale—in hale and hearty—which is related to health and healthy.

Nothing is more desirable than health and never is health more desirable than when we have lost it. We move heaven and earth to regain it. We don't regard invalidism as desirable—much less ideal. We're sorry for the man who is battling with indifferent health. Hard lines for poor old so-and-so to be under the weather again. We try to advise him. Why not call in Dr Finlay? Or consult Dr Kildare? But never in the name of sanity do we regard physical ill health as either praiseworthy or desirable.

By the same token neither is any state of moral or spiritual ill health. In our own rough-and-ready way we say so ourselves. Of some acquaintance the verdict is: you just can't depend on him. Take care; he'll let you down. In our bones we sense some flaw in his nature which means that, under pressure, he can't be counted on. . . .

Now against this state of spiritual ill health—the condition of far too many of us—can be set the state of spiritual health which is called holiness. This is plainly desirable—if only by contrast with what is so plainly undesirable. And the experience becomes more desirable still when we see it exemplified at its best in the life of our Lord and Saviour Jesus Christ.

Address—27 June 1965

23 February

In common with the creed our Salvation Army articles of faith describe [our Lord and Saviour Jesus Christ] as 'truly and properly man'. This does not mean he was not divine. On the contrary, his divinity is truly seen in the fact that here was man at his best. In all the rest of us who go by the name of man none is at his best, for in all of us the image of God has been disfigured by sin. Only in Jesus do we see man as he ought to be. Though tempted in all points like we are, his life never cracked under the strain. And to his example as ideal, men of all ages and in all places have turned—whether a Bonhoeffer in the Flossenburg prison or a Gandhi in his Indian ashram. 'The hymn "Jesus, the very thought of thee",' wrote Livingstone in his journal, 'rings in my ears as I cross the wilderness of Africa and makes me wish I was more like him.' And don't we all?

This is the second element in the meaning of the word holiness. If it stands for nearness to God, it also means likeness to Jesus—and there could be nothing more desirable than that.

Finally, this is a possible experience. . . . But this experience of moral and spiritual health is gained not as we depend upon our own strength—which is so often in question—but as we depend upon Another, even our Lord and Saviour.

Address—27 June 1965

24 February

One reason why some of us lose heart in the Christian warfare is that we under-rate what has been called 'the magnificent might' of him who said: 'All power is given unto me in Heaven and in earth', and mistakenly suppose that there are situations from which his help is excluded. This is more of a practical than a theoretical atheism. We do not so much disbelieve his existence as deny his presence. We think that he cannot be with us when we need him most or, even if he is with us, deny him as powerless to help.

In the days of his flesh there were those who supposed there were human problems beyond his wit and wisdom.

For example, there was the distracted father who brought his epileptic boy to Jesus. The Master had been away on the Mount of Transfiguration. By themselves the disciples had been powerless to help and critical onlookers had enjoyed their discomfiture; so that all the father could say when Jesus returned was: 'If thou canst do anything, have compassion on us and help us!'

But Jesus could not accept this advance-questioning of his ability to help. So he picked up the phrase 'If thou canst', put it in quotes as it were, and passed it back to the father. What was lacking was not power on the part of Jesus but faith on the part of the parent. Those who want the Saviour's help must not begin by questioning his power to help. . . .

IHQ Archives

25 February

. . . So insidious are the infiltrations of the principle of worldliness that no outward sign or symbol by itself can provide adequate protection. The worldling is not just the corner-boy who wastes his substance in an amusement arcade, nor the film-fan who fills his leisure with casual pleasures of an inferior quality. For the most part they are indifferent to Christ. Nor is the term 'worldliness' to be applied only to commercialised amusements. Wardour Street couldn't care less about true religion. But the world—using the term in its New Testament sense—is definitely hostile to Christ and can reveal its presence and power in the lives of those who declaim most loudly against it. Worldliness is the temptation which so easily besets the religious and respectable—as the gospel story bears witness.

Two leading examples will serve to illustrate the point.

The raising of Lazarus so alarmed the Jewish priest-hood that, taking counsel together under Caiaphas, they agreed that Jesus threatened their 'place and nation' and should therefore be put to death.

Mark the order. Their 'place' came first. The high priest and his colleagues felt that their time-honoured privileges were in danger. (Remember that a worldling is one who takes action only when his own interests are threatened.) Though versed in the piety of the Psalms, at home in their ancient Scriptures, the guardians of the accredited sacrifices and the leaders of what was—until Jesus came—God's best thing, these men were a worldly-minded set who moved into action only when they deemed their own security to be imperilled.

So with Pilate. . . .

The Officer, September, October 1950

26 February

We revise our notion of meekness most searchingly when we consider him who was 'meek and lowly in heart'. Meekness and lowliness were the Master's favourite graces. He said so himself, and his actions witnessed to the truth of his personal testimony. But the Jesus of history was no pale Galilean. There was what has been called 'a stormy north side' to him. Whittier wrote some lines about the Quaker Joseph Sturge:

> Tender as a woman, manliness and meekness
> In him were so allied
> That they who judged him by his strength or weakness
> Saw but a single side.

So Jesus cannot be written off merely as 'gentle Jesus'. Meekness is controlled strength, and of that there are abundant examples in the gospels. Here is the Master in the Jewish synagogue on the Sabbath. A man with a deformed hand is present in the congregation—planted there by the Pharisees who wish to charge Jesus with Sabbath breaking. Mark describes how the callous faces about him move the Master to anger, but controlled by love he says to the sufferer: 'Stretch forth thine hand.'

Such an incident floods this grace with life and light.

The Call to Holiness, pp 99, 100

27 February

. . . Jesus said to the woman in the house of Simon the Pharisee: 'Thy faith hath saved thee.'

What then is this 'faith' which can effect so revolutionary a change in human life? More than 80 years ago the Army Mother . . . delivered her mind and soul on this very matter in an address entitled 'A true and a false faith'.

I follow in her steps by saying that the faith which saves is not merely a description of the Christian religion as, for example, 'the faith . . . once delivered unto the saints', where the word stands for a body of doctrine. Articles of faith can be learned by heart, and repeated in public worship Sunday by Sunday, without ever becoming the power of God unto salvation.

Nor is the faith that saves to be equated with the small boy's definition of faith as believing what you know ain't true. Nor with the more sophisticated suggestion that faith is believing what you cannot prove.

For faith does not stand by itself. Its purpose and power lie in the object or person in whom that faith reposes.

47

Faith misdirected—that is to say, faith in some nostrum or superstition—can do more harm than good. . . . But the faith which saves can be defined as that trust in God which leads to obedience to God.

Essentials of Christian Experience, pp 41, 42

28 February

You can trust the God who has revealed himself in Jesus to meet your deepest need. Most probably that need is for forgiveness and cleansing from the guilt and power of sin. These may sound old-fashioned phrases but they speak to present need. You can commit yourself without reserve to the God whose word in Christ is: 'Him that cometh unto me I will in no wise cast out.'

There is no need for anyone to doubt this word—as some of our sophisticates do. 'I wish it were true', said Theodore Dreiser, 'that there was someone to whom a man in his misery might turn . . . someone of whom the declaration "Come unto me . . . and I will give you rest" were true.' To which the answer is that no man need rely upon another man's testimony. Every man can find out for himself whether God is as good as his word.

Then those who have accepted Jesus as Saviour should remember the Army Mother's words that faith will lead not merely to that single act of obedience which brought about your salvation but 'to live in obedience to him'.

. . . Is ours continued obedient faith? For we do imperil our salvation if we fail to respond to any further word of command which may reach us from the Lord who is our Saviour.

Essentials of Christian Experience, p 44

29 February

When Jesus was on earth some of his critics took him to task because he was too radiant. He shocked them by comparing his service to a wedding feast. When two young folk in Palestine were married, they did not go away for a honeymoon but kept open house for a week. They wore their best clothes. Their friends waited on them. They had all they wanted. Never again would they have another week like that in all their lives, and their friends—'children of the bridechamber' they are called—shared in the glowing happiness of the newly-weds.

Jesus gave that title to his disciples. The suggestion is that he and they were happy as the day is long. 'Children of joy' was a description of the first believers. 'Praising we plough, singing we sail' said Clement of Alexandria of those who loved the Master. 'Death lay in wait for the Christian at every turn,' wrote T. R. Glover of those early followers of Jesus, 'yet they were the happiest people of the day.'

'Your joy', said Jesus to his disciples, and it was his gift to them, 'no man taketh away from you'. From Perpetua, facing the arena in Carthage with the cry, 'This is my coronation', and Hugh McKail condemned to execution in four days announcing to the silent crowd, 'Good news! I am within four days' journey of seeing Jesus', to the nameless believer chalking upon the Gestapo van taking her to death, 'Jesus Christ is risen!', there has ever been an undefeatable joy about those who know Jesus as Saviour and are dedicated to his business. Compared to this the regimented laughter of a studio audience is but the crackling of thorns under a pot. . . .

Jesus and our Need, pp 47-49

1 March

From entrance into the Kingdom turn now to the principles which govern the conduct of those who are members of the Kingdom. Perhaps 'principles' is a better word than 'laws', for law suggests obedience to some external restraint, whereas a principle is a truth which rules us from within.

These principles, then, are only two in number, but, to help us to understand how they work, Jesus gave a number of illustrations of them in action, and these we know as the Sermon on the Mount. For the moment, it is enough for us to note that those who have entered the Kingdom are called upon to love God and their neighbour 'with all the heart, and with all the understanding, and with all the soul'. That is to say, these two principles of love to God and man unite feeling, thought and will in Christian action. . . .

It is not wrong to suppose that Jesus can hardly have *liked* all the people he met. Would he care for the ways of the crafty Caiaphas, or did he like the means by which Judas secured his arrest? What we can say with conviction is that he certainly *loved* them all—Caiaphas and Judas as well. That is, he continuously and consistently sought their highest welfare. For that is what the New Testament means by love—not an affair merely of the emotions, though emotion may play its due part. Nor only a matter of the mind, though enlightened intelligence may tell us that we ought to seek our neighbour's good as our own. But love as exemplified by Jesus was an activity in which feeling, thought and will were equally conjoined. In other words, the life of love in the Kingdom is not a preference for heart over head, but a union of both in the service of others.

The Kingdom of God, pp 12, 13

2 March

The life and teaching of Jesus was God's establishment of the Kingdom, and he who set it up will see to its final triumph. We know it to be the Father's good pleasure to bring the Kingdom to its final power and glory. Our task . . . is to serve the Kingdom here and now in the spirit of Jesus. The rest we can leave with God who knows his business much better than we do. Keep this in mind, and you will be neither disturbed nor disheartened by the changes and chances of life. . . .

The Kingdom is not Utopia, nor the welfare state, nor is it allied to any particular regime, east or west. The Kingdom is not of this world, though its servants will seek to redeem the world in which they live after the pattern set by their Master. They will try to be the salt—and prevent the world turning hopelessly sour; the leaven—and save it from going flat.

. . . They will seek first the Kingdom which is 'of God'. If Jesus would not serve Rome, neither would he work for the Jewish dream of the kingdom of 'our father David'. His love and loyalty were wholly and unalterably pledged to 'the Kingdom of my Father'. There our heart and treasure should lie as well. As General Bramwell Booth wrote: 'One sinner saved by grace will outlast the British Empire.' That goes for all other empires also. Only the Kingdom abides.

The Kingdom of God, pp 44, 45

3 March

Look in the gospels where you will, you will find little account of what Jesus said to publicans and sinners. We know that he went into their homes and was glad to be in their company for he had come to seek and to save those who were lost, but we have no record of what he said to them at their meal tables. The sins he denounced were mostly those of religious people such as the Pharisees; the rules of life he gave were for his disciples. It almost seems as if he never laid down any laws when eating and drinking with those who were classed as sinners, for he knew that his laws could not be kept without his Father's grace. So it was to his disciples that 'he opened his mouth'. . . .

Take one beatitude only to serve as an illustration for all. The third reads: 'Blessed are the meek: for they shall inherit the earth.'

. . . Some of us may . . . have been put off by 'the devil's darling sin—the pride that apes humility', which is pride drawing attention to itself by sporting humility as a conspicuous cloak. But, as Archbishop Temple used to say, humility is not thinking little about oneself; it is not thinking about oneself at all—a happy state of mind and soul which comes about when all our attention is given to Jesus.

. . . The Master said that those who thus thought nothing of themselves would be greatest in the Kingdom. Now why this emphasis on humility? We shall be able to answer that question better when we recall the harm done by pride, its opposite number. . . .

The Kingdom of God, pp 26-28

4 March

When we love men we care for them as God cares, which is caring till it hurts.

A Bible translator working among the Bantu of the Congo basin was searching for the native equivalent of the love of God when he heard a mother crooning over her child. When asked to explain the meaning of the word she was using she replied: 'White man, that word means that when I think of what will befall my baby girl when she grows up, it hurts me.' The translator had his word. That is how God loves, and the extent of his hurt is to be seen on the cross.

When we love men we see them as God sees them. It was said of Dick Sheppard that he had a 'God-sight' of his fellows. That was why he laboured to exhaustion for their salvation. So to love men means that we stop at nothing to help them. C. T. Studd spoke of his desire to run 'a rescue shop within a yard of Hell'. The expression may or may not be to our taste, but that was his way of saying—and practising—a love that would not let men go, not even on the lip of eternal loss. That is love's calculated risk.

William Temple used to say that the only true progress was progress in love. Progress in technology is no true progress at all unless it is the work of men who care, in whose lives caring directs the exercise of their gifts. In the 20th century we are being made to learn afresh this necessary truth. A man may understand all mysteries and all knowledge, and be able scientifically to remove islands from their beds in the Pacific, yet without love it profits him and his fellows nothing. Is this not a text to be inscribed on the lintels of every research station? . . .

The Call to Holiness, pp 60, 61

5 March

. . . What is perfection anyway? Is it not the pot of gold always in the next field but one? In the arts are not the best of players always seeking a perfection of accomplishment beyond that which they now possess? Else why should a Schweitzer climb into the organ loft at St Paul's and spend the long hours of daylight in rehearsal before a night recital and, when told that most organists were content with a couple of hours, reply with serious humour: 'Then I must be a worse organist than most.'

With the image of Jesus before him, who can count himself to have attained? Yet with that same image before him and all the compulsive power of that Example to stimulate him, who cannot but long to attain? God's will is expressed for us in Jesus. It is that we should stand 'holy and without blame before him' as did his dearly beloved Son. Let every believer embrace that will as his own.

The Call to Holiness, pp 50, 51

6 March

Wrote John Wesley to one of his itinerant preachers: 'You never learned, either from my conversation or preachings or writings, that "holiness consisted in a flow of joy". I constantly told you quite the contrary. I told you it was love . . . the image of God stamped on the heart; the life of God in the soul of man; the mind that was in Christ, enabling us to walk as Christ also walked.'

. . . And first of all we look to Jesus for pattern.

Scholars point out that 'looking unto' is a very strong phrase, and is a translation of a single Greek word used nowhere else in the New Testament. One of its meanings is to look fixedly at, to look at a person or object to the exclusion of all else. A modern translation reads: 'with no eyes for anyone else but Jesus'.

Look to him only or exclusively, for about us there are all manner of caricatures of the holy life. . . . How can holiness be accepted as life abundant, which it is, if it is thought to be repression run riot. How urgent the need to keep a right pattern before us so that our heart's longings be not mocked nor our spiritual desires misdirected.

But more than pattern is needed—and more than pattern can be found when we look to Jesus. This ideal, when accepted, has a compulsive power enabling us to grow like him.

The Call to Holiness, pp 17-19

7 March

Let the body be strengthened in goodness by regular habits of eating and sleeping and if you are a games fan, let it be to play and not to watch. . . . The mind can be strengthened in goodness as well. No modern psychologist has made any advance on Philippians 4:8. Here is how J. B. Phillips has translated the verse. 'If you believe in goodness and if you value the approval of God, fix your minds on the things which are holy and right and pure and beautiful and good.' A man's reading can be as wide as he pleases so long as it is clean. . . . It is as right and proper to love as to eat, but even a Billy Bunter does not read Mrs Beeton all day.

And, for the strengthening of the soul, let your whole being be turned toward Jesus. Set yourself that way like a flower sets itself toward the sun. . . . Just allow the regular use of the means of grace so to keep your whole life open to Jesus that, in any unexpected moment of temptation, you can say with confidence, 'He will keep me from falling'. . . . Say it over and over again if necessary until the dark cloud of evil has passed. Here lies victory. . . .

The reason why we lay such emphasis on looking to Jesus is that he knew what it was to be tempted. We think of him wrongly if we say he was not able to sin. The glorious truth is that he was able not to sin—and it is to this that we must cling. For what he could do, in his strength we can do. That is the answer to all our temptations.

Jesus and our Need, pp 83, 84

54

8 March

. . . The holiness of Jesus was not only the negative grace of sinlessness. Holiness is not a conscious rectitude, a continual watching of my step lest the wrong foot be put forward first. Separation, by itself, is not enough. Holiness is not just not doing things and not going places. I am not made good solely by what I do not do.

Think of Scrooge. He never went to the theatre or haunted low dives, yet no one would call him a holy man. And why? Because there was absent from his life the one particular element which constitutes the very essence of Christian holiness.

. . . With Jesus there was the quality of love which is the first of the fruits of the Holy Spirit's presence. The cease-less activity of love as expressed in the life of Jesus is the distinctive element in the Christian experience of holiness. Therefore Christlikeness is holiness. Where Christ is enthroned, there is holiness. Yet holiness is never an 'imitation' of Christ, if by that is meant a self-conscious external patterning. Christian holiness will spring from the inward possession of that same Holy Spirit who was in Jesus and by whose power he wrought and taught.

So the blessing of holiness is never an 'it'. No one should say: 'I've got it!', for the experience is personal and the source of the experience is personal. . . . The work of the Spirit was perfectly exemplified in Jesus and he can make us like him, not through any outward conformity but by the workings of inward grace.

Essentials of Christian Experience, pp 13, 14

9 March

There is nothing so saddening as sin.

This is true both for the doer and the onlooker. For all its bright promises and glamorous appearance, sin leaves a man the sadder though not always the wiser. It takes many people a long time to learn the true nature of sin—and some never learn at all.

Perhaps we ourselves are not wholly convinced on this

point until we have eaten of the tree of the knowledge of good and evil. We begin by taking life at its face value. Innocent ourselves, we do not dream that others are not so simple-hearted as we are. We assume that everything which glitters is gold. Like a child reading the advertisements on a hoarding or in a newspaper, our nature is to believe what we read, whether the offer be to teach the piano, to cure stammering, to end blushing or to produce the looks of a Helen of Troy—'send 12 penny stamps for our illustrated prospectus'! Only later does it dawn on us that the world is full of deceits, and some of us take that lesson so hardly that we swing to the equally wrong conclusion that there is nothing in the world but deceit.

That is not true, though it is true that there is no deceiver like sin. It promises liberty and ends with slavery. It offers a widening experience of life and finishes by robbing a man of that one pearl of great price—his own integrity. If its most modest bait is that of a good time to be had by all, there is usually a good hangover to follow. And the worst hangovers do not merely make the head feel fit to burst; it is the heart which is more like breaking. . . .

Jesus and our Need, pp 27, 28

10 March

Whatever sin may promise it is the ruin of a man's fellowship with his neighbour. . . . In the Bible story Samson brought the house down on his foes, but when we sin we are often the death of our friends. That is sad enough but sadder still is the fact that sin is the end of man's fellowship with God.

Now how can we be armed against this thing that flatters only to deceive and woos only to ruin?

In the days of his flesh Jesus met many men and women who were so bewitched. Some cried to him in their desperate need and others cursed him because their need was so desperate. To watch Jesus helping those who were at their wits' end is matter for a lifetime of study, but those who wish can quickly look up two instances only. The Scripture references are: John 5:8 and John 8:11.

These stories tell us that Jesus could not condone sin. That is one way the world has of dealing with this trouble. . . .

Of course, that attitude is no remedy. It is the outlook of the man who, because he himself is going down for the last time, does not want anyone else to be saved.

Nor did Jesus only condemn sin. . . . To condone is wrong; to condemn is not enough; the word that redeems is 'sin no more'. And the man who hears that word of mercy also receives divine grace whereby it may be obeyed. . . .

Is not this the best way to deal with that universal sickness known as sin? I know of no other.

Jesus and our Need, pp 28-31

11 March

We all know ourselves to be open to temptation.

None of us can escape this assault . . . upon the will. The New Testament speaks of our three great foes as the world, the flesh and the devil—and each is a source of temptation.

'The world' can be the world of low standards. Not a few of our acquaintances think that the great folly lies not in doing wrong but in being found out. So, if they can put a fast one over and get away with it, they are quite content. And they think we are being unnecessarily righteous when we do not take their line. Our refusal is a rebuke to them . . . so they laugh at our scruples and the laugh increases the force of the temptation.

Other temptations arise from 'the flesh', though we must not read this as if any of our bodily instincts were in themselves sinful and therefore must be suppressed. . . . Temptation arises when one appetite would seek satisfaction at the expense of the rest, or when a particular instinct imperiously demands fulfilment without regard for any considerations of right or wrong.

Then there is the devil who must be reckoned with. For evil is far stronger than lowered social standards or even the misdirection of our physical appetites. In the days of

Jesus men and women felt themselves to be bound by Satan (Luke 13:16), and One stronger than Satan was required to set them free.

How then shall we meet this threefold challenge?

Jesus and our Need, pp 11, 12

12 March

How then shall we meet this threefold challenge? The answer depends in part upon what kind of a person we really are. . . . Satan is not going to waste his time putting before me ideas which have no appeal.

As a rule we are tempted where we are weakest. To recognise this is to be prepared beforehand. And in order to be prepared in advance, let your mind be filled with the strongest possible counter-suggestion. . . .

The strongest possible counter-suggestion to the approach of evil is the presence of Jesus. Let him fill the mind. When a room is quite full no more people can gain admittance. If Jesus by his Spirit has full possession of our lives, then the tempter cannot find so much as a toehold.

'I can point out times and places', wrote Mark Rutherford, 'where I should have fallen if I had been able to rely on nothing better than a commandment or a deduction. But the pure, calm, heroic image of Jesus confronted me and I succeeded. I had no doubt what he would have done, and through him I did not doubt what I had to do.'

We may say that temptations crowd about us as do people in the rush hour. Maybe; but if you are out with some special friend even the rush hour crowds mean less than nothing. There is only one person whose company you value.

Now if your companion is Jesus. . . .

Jesus and our Need, pp 12, 13

13 March

Now if your companion is Jesus. . . .

You may well make him your companion for he knew

what it was to be tempted. He was not born with some kind of magic armour against which the fiery darts of the tempter were helpless. He was tempted in all points like as we are—and not less tempted but more. After all, it is he who never yielded to Satan's power who knows to what lengths the tempter can go. Satan has no need to bring his full power to bear on us. . . . A man who cannot stand much pain but who faints at the least twinge never knows what pain can really mean. And the man who yields at the first approach of temptation cannot know the full malignancy of its powers. Jesus never yielded. He endured the worst that Satan could do—and triumphed. Thus he knows what temptation means and 'is able to succour them that are tempted'. . . .

Be honest. . . . Be busy. . . . Be strong in Christ. . . . When our minds are filled with things lovely, honest, pure, true and of good report, then Satan can find no landing ground and the citadel of the heart is kept inviolate.

Jesus and our Need, pp 13, 14

14 March

'Temptations here upon me press.' That was true for Jesus himself. . . .

As small children we may have seen pictures of Satan in traditional form appearing to the Master during the forty days in the wilderness. Fork, tail, cloven hoof make the evil one plainly recognisable. But surely if ever he appeared as an angel of light it was during that period. Scripture was on his lips. He breathed concern as to the happiest way in which Jesus might fulfil his divine mission. His suggestions wore a most plausible air. Any one of them might have been accepted for a dozen good reasons. If ever Ithuriel's spear was needed to reveal the tempter in his true colours it was then. It may be urged that these were the temptations, not of a mortal man, but of a Saviour. Agreed, and that made them not less searching but more. On no count can it be urged that Jesus was less tempted than we are. Only the soul who has resisted all the wiles of Satan knows their full strength. Many of us know little of Satan's real power because we yield so easily. He has no need to exert himself unduly. We fall so quickly for so little. Only he who resists steadfast in the faith knows how powerful can be the tempter's pull. And spotless Lamb of God though he was, Jesus knew the savage power of that pull.

The experience of holiness does not confer immunity from temptation.

The Call to Holiness, pp 32, 33

15 March

It may . . . strengthen us to remember that he knew the power of temptation not less, but more than, we do. For the richer a man's personality, the more there is of him to be tempted. We need not be surprised—as occasionally we are—at the collapse of some outstanding figure. The wonder is that such occurrences are as rare as they are. The lone climber on the exposed mountain ridge feels the fury of the gale of which the pedestrian, content to plod placidly along in the valley below, is ignorant. . . .

Because Jesus is Captain of our salvation, he was tested by temptation to a degree we have never known—if only for the reason that the tempter has rarely to exert himself to the full to bring us down. The proverbial mess of pottage is enough. The very warfare which our Lord waged with the powers of darkness is an assurance that he knows what superhuman strength is required to fight the good fight of faith, and this he will provide. . . .

So far as our earthly struggles are concerned Jesus has been here. He has passed this way before. He knew—and still knows—the way we take. And our great High Priest also knows how best to help us hold fast our profession. 'In that he himself hath suffered being tempted, he is able to succour them that are tempted' (Hebrews 2:18).

In Good Company, pp 29, 30

16 March

. . . In the wilderness Satan showed Jesus 'all the kingdoms of the world and the glory of them'—that is, what the tempter understood by glory, for what he offered was glory in its most vulgar and transient form. Small wonder that Jesus rejected the offer. It would have been staggering if he, of all people, had been taken in. If, in his mind's eye, he saw across the Mediterranean the glory that was Rome, surely at the same time he saw the vanished glory that had been Macedon's, Assyria's, Babylon's, Egypt's—and we know what he thought of Solomon's. . . .

What the kings of the Gentiles called glory the Master rejected, and warned his disciples against as well. 'So shall it not be among you.' That glory was a poisoned cup. Its tainted delights were cursed with a savour of death unto death—yet they are still so intoxicating that the same man who once tastes the cup can rarely put it down till he has drained it to his own downfall. . . .

Be not deceived, the world has innumerable prizes and rewards with a show of generosity for those who run in its races. Paste is made up to look like pearl and shoddy as wool, so that even the elect are sometimes deceived. And, to further this trickery, catch-penny toys are marked with high prices while durable goods are ticketed so cheaply that we swear to ourselves that they really can't be worth buying. Now and again there lives a man who, by his conduct, exposes the whole ramp—a Francis of Assisi . . ., a Vincent de Paul . . ., a Schweitzer. . . . These, and such as have lived like them, have learned of Jesus who knew that to be crucified was, in reality, to be glorified. The cross, foolishness to the Greek and a stumbling-block to the Jew, is in truth 'glory'.

The Officer, March 1948

17 March

Now God's Kingdom means God's rule. When we say: 'Thy kingdom come', we pray that the rule of God may everywhere be established. Plainly at the moment it is not so established. It is not his will that men should be in want and children go hungry. There are large areas of life where his writ does not run. His rule is either ignored or defied, and the consequent disorder and misery is both a reproach and a challenge to his good government.

One frequent reaction to this is: well, why does not God himself do something about it? If he is almighty, why doesn't he take the worst culprits in hand and either mend or end them? Then, if his rule or kingdom is the beneficent thing believers make it out to be, all men everywhere might stand a chance of enjoying it.

That sounds logical enough, but there is a flaw in the argument—and that at the very beginning.

Who said that God is almighty in the sense that he can do anything? Not I, nor—if you will believe me—any responsible Christian teacher. God will do anything which is *in harmony with his nature*—and those last five words are the all-important qualification. His nature we know to be that of a Father, and he will do nothing inconsistent with that. . . .

Our Father, pp 12, 13

18 March

. . . For example, he is not almighty in the sense that he would make a lie truth. He will not make badness good. He will not make deceit honest. As the Scripture says: 'He cannot deny himself.' He must remain true to his nature.

Now one of the rules which God has laid down, and by which he consistently abides, is that he will not interfere with the freedom of choice he has given to man. He will not coerce. Compulsion is not one of his attributes. Cyril Joad once defined liberty as the right of a man to go to the devil in any way he pleased. I don't like the language of the definition, but I recognise it to be correct in substance and agreeing with the words which Charles Wesley put into the mouth of the impenitent sinner:

Stubborn and rebellious still,
From thine arms of love I fly;
Yes, I will be lost; I will,
In spite of mercy, die.

It is this freedom which makes man a responsible being who can be held accountable for his actions.

You and I, free agents, have chosen to use our God-given freedom to defy God's rule and it is to this defiance of God's rule that the term 'sin' can properly be applied. It is my sin, that which I freely choose and for which I am personally responsible, which is part of the barrier in the way of the coming of God's Kingdom. I, not God, am responsible for that sin. The breaker of the law, not the maker, is held responsible for crime. . . . We must cease blaming God for what he is not responsible, and start to clean our own doorstep, for which we are.

Our Father, pp 13,14

19 March

For, unwelcome though this doctrine may be, it is our refusal to obey God's rule which is the prime cause of our troubles. Man's chief ailment is not his ignorance, so that if he knew more he would do better. When have we known more than in our own age and time? A secondary school-boy 'knows' more than a Paul or a Socrates. Why, we are told that our recent researches into the basic character of nature—I refer to atomic energy—mark a stage in human civilisation comparable only to primitive man's discovery of fire. Yet, so far from this knowledge enabling us to benefit ourselves, we have been warned that if we squander much more of the world's scanty resources of uranium on atomic bombs, we shall have none left for industrial development—that is to say, if after using atomic weapons in self-destruction, there is any industry left to develop! . . .

Finally, if man's ignorance is not the chief barrier to the coming of God's Kingdom, neither is his environment. . . .

. . . As the lamb accompanied Mary wherever she went, so man has his own self, his ego, which clings to him like his shadow. And it is that unregenerate self of mine which is the principal hindrance to the triumph of God's Kingdom in my own life.

If I am sincerely to pray 'Thy Kingdom come', I must welcome God's rule in my own heart and being, and then we shall be one step nearer that rule prevailing in the world at large. And you won't mind my saying, that what goes for me goes for you as well.

Our Father, pp 14-16

20 March

. . . Nowhere in the gospels do we find any word from Jesus as to how and when he became aware of his divine mission, and it is only with extreme diffidence and the utmost reverence that we attempt to read his mind.

Happily the language used to describe his baptism carries clear hints as to the meaning of the event. 'The heaven was opened' declares that here God was at work. The descent of the Spirit indicates that divine strength would be given for his divine task. The voice from Heaven witnessed to the oneness of purpose uniting Father and Son. Thus filled with the Spirit Jesus left the Jordan and, having rejected the plausible but misleading suggestions of the tempter as to how his mission might be accomplished, entered the Nazareth synagogue on the Sabbath day in the power of the Spirit. Whether the quotation from the opening sentences of Isaiah 61 was part of the appointed lectionary for the day, or whether chosen by Jesus himself, it was true that the prophet's words were actually being fulfilled. There was 'no measuring of the Spirit given to *him*! (John 3:34, *J. B. Phillips*). All he said and did was in the power of the Spirit.

In Good Company, p 33

21 March

. . . There was [a] disciple called Nathanael who, at a first meeting, Jesus summed up quickly as 'an Israelite indeed, in whom is no guile.'

Now this phrase 'no guile' must not be understood to mean one who can be gulled. We are too ready to assume that the really good man can easily be taken in. This is one more instance of the wish being father to the thought. How happy all the wide boys would be if they could be sure that no one ever saw through their trickery. It is a frequent assumption that, in a duel of wits, the honest man is bound to come off the worst, and that to meet the world on its own ground one must have more than a touch of the world's low cunning.

But the words 'no guile' should be read along with 'Israelite'. Israel was the name given to the man who, having met God face to face, was so changed by the encounter that thereafter he finished with all forms of knavery and faced life like an honest man. That Jacob was in our Lord's mind is clear from his reference to 'the angels . . . ascending and descending'. But the lesson at Bethel was the first, not the last, by which Jacob was taught to mistrust his wits. This twin, who had deceived his father, outwitted his brother and worsted his uncle, had to learn that there is one who is never taken in—not even by the cleverest schemer.

Was Nathanael early in life the kind of character which Jacob became only later? And what was he thinking as he sat beneath the fig tree? . . .

Jesus and our Need, pp 67, 68

22 March

. . . What was [Nathanael] thinking as he sat beneath the fig tree? The thoughts of youth are traditionally long, long thoughts, and a young idealist would have much to occupy his mind.

An alien army ruled his land. A proud people with centuries of history behind them were not their own masters. The story of their last bid for independence was as near to them as the Battle of Waterloo or the victory of Trafalgar to an English lad today. And the lower the fortunes of Israel sank politically, the more was desired the coming of the Messiah who, in most popular thought, would lead them to victory again.

What part should a young man play in that struggle? Galilee, where Cana was situated, was the home of the resistance movement. Nathanael lived among the highlanders of Jewry. Where should he find the leader who could satisfy his desires and to whom he could yield himself body, mind and soul?

That leader was nearer than Nathanael dreamed. Jesus is never far away from anyone who is honestly trying to think things out . . . if, when we see that he is the One for whom we have been looking we cry as did Nathanael: 'thou art the Son of God'. . . .

This first interview of Jesus with Nathanael concluded by the Master saying that greater things were in store for him in God's service. The heavens would open and reveal their further secrets about redemption's plan. That goes for all the Master's true servants. . . .

Jesus and our Need, pp 68-70

23 March

'Forgive us . . . as we forgive' put into everyday speech . . . means that our attitude to God is determined by our attitude to our fellows. The truth is as simple as that—and yet as difficult as that, for somehow the native impulse is to give tit for tat.

Let a speck of dirt fly into my eye, and instantly the eyelid snaps down in a protective movement. I don't have to will that action; it is an involuntary one, born of a reflex motion in the nervous system. So you lunge at me and, involuntarily, I sidestep the threatened blow and my first reaction is to reply in kind.

So with the emotions. Speak to me in anger, and my reaction is to answer with anger.

So with the mind. Score a joke at my expense, and like

lightning I bethink myself (if I can) of a repartee, a Roland for your Oliver. That is how we seem to be made—to give as good as we get in feelings, words or blows. . . .

It is this seemingly natural urge to get our own back, and this inward sense of justice satisfied when we have done so, which makes the Christian teaching about the forgiveness of injuries seem so idealistic and impracticable, and he who advocates it an impossible dreamer who lives with his head in the clouds.

Idealistic I agree. But I do not regard that word as a reproach in this connection. . . .

IHQ Archives

24 March

. . . Profession without practice [is] worse than useless.

Men who are far from Christ agree with him on this point. It is our critics who are among the loudest in their demand that in our lives deed and word should agree. They are the first with their condemnation if, in their opinion, some believer falls below this standard. That is why the misdeed of some solitary salvationist, overtaken in a fault, hits the headlines. It may be hard to take when those who make no profession at all sit as self-constituted judges upon someone whose practice falls short of his high profession. But in his own twisted way the worldling is unwittingly agreeing with the Christian standard that 'by their fruits ye shall know them'.

After Lenin died his widow was asked how best his life and work could be remembered. 'Do not let your sorrow find expression in any outward veneration of his personality,' she answered. 'Do not raise monuments to him or a palace to his name. Do not organise pompous ceremonies to his memory. In life he took little account of that kind of thing. If you want to honour his name, realise his teachings in your life.' This is what Jesus said about his teaching.

. . . The value of what we profess rises or falls by the life of the anonymous soldier who lives in SW19, the salvationist serviceman at Kneller Hall, the bandsman-student at a redbrick university, the member of our nurses' fellowship in a city hospital, the converted shop steward on the factory floor, the wife and mother on the housing estate. One godly life counts for more than a string of poster hoardings. . . .

Essentials of Christian Experience, pp 7-9

25 March

Here we are truly dealing with the teaching of Jesus in one of its highest flights. What he had to say about the forgiveness of injuries was something new in the world. Nowhere is there so plain a difference between Old and New Testaments. The traditional code was an eye for an eye, a tooth for a tooth. That was, of course, a limitation of the law of revenge. It was a curb on such savage behaviour as that of Lamech who would kill the man who had only wounded him. No, said the Mosaic law, for an eye only an eye. It was an early attempt to make the punishment fit the crime.

But this rule of tit for tat Jesus set aside. Injuries were not to be avenged, but forgiven. I know of nothing he taught so distinctly. Dismiss the idea, if you like, as hopeless in a competitive world. Argue, if you wish, that it gives licence to the injurer to profit at the expense of the injured. Ridicule it as an impossible code for men who prefer to be men, but never say that Jesus did not teach the forgiveness of injuries. By direct statement—what we now call dogma; by parable—what we now call illustration or analogy; and by personal example, he taught that he who would be forgiven must also forgive. . . .

So far as direct teaching is concerned, there are at least a dozen statements on record from Jesus himself. . . . Last of all, Jesus taught the forgiveness of injuries by personal example. . . . 'Father, forgive them.'

All too high-minded . . . for human nature? . . . But it is just the whole point of the Christian faith . . . that that which is impossible to man left to his own devices is possible when he seeks the help of God.

Our Father, pp 23-25

26 March

Jesus was the holy one and to look to him is to have answered many of our questions about the nature of holiness. For questions do arise. It is no use pretending that wayfaring men in general find the highway of holiness easy going. Salvation we understand after our fashion. The simple scriptural imagery of, for example, *The Pilgrim's Progress* supplies us with ways and means by which we can interpret our own experience. As with Christian, the City of Destruction behind us and a sense of personal need within drove us along the path fenced on either side by a wall called salvation. Though, like him, we could not make great haste because we were so laden, at length we reached the place 'somewhat ascending' where, at the sight of the Cross, the burden was loosed from our shoulders and we 'said with a merry heart, "He hath given me rest by his sorrow, and life by his death"'. . . .

But to pass from salvation to sanctification is for some like passing from clear sunshine into a damp, clinging sea mist which hides every landmark and blankets all sense of direction. There are seekers who confess themselves lost in a theological wood where such names as 'the fullness of the Spirit', 'entire sanctification', 'the Canaan rest', 'the second blessing' rise high above their heads and hide the sun from sight. How can this experience be made visible, intelligible and desirable?

The answer is in Jesus and by Jesus, for he who is the Author of our salvation is also the pattern of all holy living.

The Call to Holiness, pp 7-9

27 March

In the first place, Jesus makes holiness visible. . . . The word holiness becomes flesh and dwells among us.

No man was ever holier than Jesus though, in the days of his flesh, the word was never on his lips for the very good reason that he could allow his life to speak for itself. The fourth gospel records Jesus as saying that the Holy

Spirit would 'receive of mine and . . . shew it unto you'. That is to say, the Holy Spirit interprets to us the mind of Jesus, and all that the Spirit bids us do will be in harmony with the example of Jesus. But it is equally true to say that the historic Jesus shows us what the Holy Spirit can do with a human life whom he fully possesses.

And the Holy Spirit fully possessed the Master. The Holy Spirit came upon him at the Jordan. He was led of the Spirit into the wilderness. Temptation ended for a season, he 'returned in the power of the Spirit into Galilee'. God gave not 'the Spirit by measure unto him'. We may reverently believe that, as man, Jesus suffered the limitations of the humanity he embraced. He grew up as we grew up. He learnt by the things he suffered. He increased in wisdom and stature. The only grace of which he did not empty himself was love. The Holy Spirit whose nature, like that of the Father, is love, was his without measure. In him we have an example of what human life can be when filled with the Spirit.

The Call to Holiness, p 9

28 March

And his is also holiness made intelligible—in its naturalness. There was nothing forced or artificial about the goodness of Jesus. We cannot so much as imagine him putting on an act, or behaving in a religious manner because someone was watching him, or assuming a pious tone when speaking of God or to God. His holiness was too much part of the texture of his daily living for that. His goodness expressed itself in his craftsmanship, in yokes that were 'easy', in carpentry which was its own recommendation. . . .

To him the creation of his Father was holy. The flower in the crannied wall spoke of divine care. The lilies of the field—in our tongue, a carpet of bluebells in an English wood—were to be preferred to the glory of Solomon. The Master's followers themselves seized on this truth for, on the walls of the catacombs where they sheltered, brightly coloured birds and fish and palms spoke of their happy delight in all that the Father had made. As Augustine said: 'I find the sky good, the sun good, the moon good, the stars good, the things which are brought forth from the earth and rooted there, all good.'

So can we. We do not honour God the more by plucking the thorn and throwing away the rose. Holiness is not 20th-century asceticism. We are not called upon to deny any human affection in order to be holy in the Father's sight. . . . Holiness is an experience of grace for normal people living normal lives . . . finding their highest happiness in the sanctification of their common joys.

The Call to Holiness, pp 10-12

29 March

. . . The experience of holiness made visible and intelligible in Jesus, appears in him to be most desirable. The repulsion which men sometimes feel over the word is often due to one of three reasons.

Occasionally a believer will discredit his cause by his own inconsistency. But the surprising fact is, remembering how exacting are the standards of Christian living, how rarely such a failure occurs. . . . Mention is frequently made of a single failing, but a lifetime of consistency will go, if not unhonoured, at least often unsung.

Again, few works of modern fiction, like few paragraphs in the press, seem willing to do justice to goodness. It is sin that is news, and sin gives not a few of our writers elbow room in which to earn their bread and butter. . . .

But finally . . . such a life goes against the grain of the natural man. For all of us, apart from grace, are greatly disinclined to gird up our loins and become what God can make us. . . . For all the beauty of the good life made visible in Jesus, it will never become popular with the unregenerate heart. But at least let us see what it is we are rejecting. . . . An impossible ideal? But at least is it not desirable? . . . George Fox used to say: 'Look not at thy temptations but at the Christ, and thou wilt receive power.' To those who thus look all things are possible.

The Call to Holiness, pp 12-14

30 March

If the nature of the Father was fully and finally revealed by the incarnation, the same divine event made clear the nature of the Holy Spirit. For by the incarnation we mean not only the birth of a baby in a manger, but the whole disclosure of God in Christ until 'a cloud received him out of their sight'. If God the Father has always been as Jesus showed him to be, God the Holy Spirit always strives with man with the compassionate strength of Christ. . . .

Jesus as Saviour is already known to us. We recognise him by the 'five bleeding wounds he bears'. Our need of salvation is met in the flesh and blood figure of Jesus of Nazareth. But it would be wrong to limit his work to that primary need. We may not dissociate him from the satisfaction of any of the needs of the human heart. The saying, 'And I, if I be lifted up . . . will draw all men unto me', is not only for the sinner's salvation but for the perfecting of the saints in grace. He who has made salvation real to us will also make holiness real, for holiness is growth in Christlikeness. . . . To learn to walk as he walked is the essence of holiness.

The Call to Holiness, pp 15-17

31 March

The Master early made known the truth for which he was prepared to live and die (Luke 4:16-31). At Nazareth he took part in a synagogue service and, at the request of the leader, read from the roll of the prophet Isaiah. . . .

He reminded his hearers that it was a Gentile widow to whom Elijah was sent, and it was a Gentile soldier whom Elisha healed. At no point had God's mercy and power been limited to the Jews. In the same vein, Jesus later announced that he recognised as mother and brethren, not only those who were bound to him by ties of blood, but all who shared his desire to do the will of the Father (Mark 3:31-35).

This truth about the universal sweep of the Kingdom was stated and restated by Jesus in various parables, of which one more example (Mark 4:30-32) can suffice. . . .

'A grain of mustard seed' was a proverbial Jewish expression for a very small thing, but so tiny a beginning was destined to grow to be a bush or tree so large that 'the fowls of the air'—a common Rabbinical expression for the Gentile nations—would lodge in the branches thereof.

The phrase would also recall to Jewish hearers the imagery of Daniel 4:10-12, where the kingdom of Nebuchadnezzar was likened to a giant tree in whose branches 'the fowls of the heaven dwelt'. Daniel understood this to signify the greatness of Nebuchadnezzar's dominion. So the Master's parable meant that the reign of God, as yet but a living seed, would in time overspread the world. . . .

The Kingdom of God, pp 22, 23

1 April

On one occasion 5,000 men demanded that Jesus become their King (John 6:15). They were ready at his command to march anywhere against anyone. Had the Master agreed there is no knowing what manner of revolt might have swept the country.

But Jesus had not come to set up a kingdom of the Jews, with himself as its national head—and here we come close to one of the principal reasons why his countrymen fell out with him. He did not fit in with the hopes of the nationalists whose ideas about the coming kingdom were Jewish, exclusive and based on force. Nor, on the other hand, did he gain the support of the leaders of organised religion in his day, whose ideas of the Kingdom were just as Jewish and exclusive, but based on certain comprehensive rules of conduct hallowed by centuries of usage. . . .

This Kingdom has been described as God's secret society. No human being can make you join it, but if you are a faithful subject, no human being can expel you from

73

it. There are church rolls and Army rolls and junior rolls—but there is no man-kept roll of the Kingdom. 'The Lord knoweth them that are his.' Some who wear the badges of the Christian faith are not—unfortunately—members of the Kingdom. . . . Jesus released his disciples from the political associations of Israel. Grace, nor race, would bring a man into this Kingdom, and he who does the will of the King belongs to the Kingdom.

No test could be more searching and yet no gate stands open more widely to all.

The Kingdom of God, pp 5-7

2 April

The Kingdom which had come with power in his person, declared Jesus, was inward, spiritual and comprehensive, knowing no limits, no frontiers, no boundaries. In it no sword was to be drawn, no war waged, no power—save that of unwearying love—employed. It was not to be one kingdom among many, struggling for place among the kingdoms of this world by deceits and stratagems. It was to be *The* Kingdom—the only one of its kind and, though without visible organisation, would grow from the smallest of beginnings to be so all-embracing that men would wonder how it had come to include so great 'a multitude . . . of all nations, and kindreds . . . and tongues'.

. . . No gate stands open more widely to all. If the gate . . . stands so widely open, how is it so few enter in thereat? The familiar conversation between Jesus and Nicodemus may give us an answer.

The visitor, a member of the highest governing body in Jewry, was plainly anxious to come to some under-standing with Jesus. He sought the Master out, and began with deferential compliments which were probably sin-cere. But these Jesus straightway brushed aside with the declaration that any one who wished to enter the Kingdom must be 'born again'. . . .

The Kingdom of God, pp 6, 7

3 April

A child is one who is freshly starting out on life. His is a new beginning. So every would-be entrant into the Kingdom—Jew or Gentile—had to begin life anew—ie, be 'born again', and the only power which could accomplish this change was that of 'the Spirit'. . . . The night wind singing in the olive trees provided the Master with an apt answer for the disapproving Nicodemus, for the Hebrew word for 'wind' and 'Spirit' was the same.

The wind blows as God wills; its motions, though mysterious, are ordered. The wind itself cannot be seen, but the signs of its presence can be plain enough. So being 'born again' might be thought by some to be a mystery, but the results of such a new start would be plain for all to see.

Nicodemus had no need to wait till he knew everything about the wind before he spread his sails before it. So he who began life anew by trusting in the power of God to effect the needed change would soon be conscious in himself of the results of that act of committal. All that was asked of any man was this willingness to break with the past, and a desire to do the will of the Father as revealed by Jesus.

No one needed to think he was being asked to bite off more than he could chew. Strength to do the Father's will would come as a man purposed in his heart to do it. He would learn by practice, as he who would learn to swim must begin by taking the plunge. . . . Then will come from above the strength to live as befits a member of the Kingdom.

The Kingdom of God, pp 8, 9

4 April

. . . The Jews could not get rid of their fixed idea that . . . they were bound to get into the Kingdom. On this point they clashed with Jesus again and again. When he reminded his hearers in the synagogue at Nazareth that God had shown mercy to a Gentile widow and a Gentile general, they were so angry that they would have killed him there and then if they could (Luke 4:23-30).

Jewish teachers sometimes compared the Kingdom to a banquet at which their race would sit down with the patriarchs and prophets while the Gentiles, shut outside, wept and howled and gnashed their teeth. Jesus took hold of that piece of imagery and turned it against them (Luke 13:24-30; Matthew 8:11, 12). Inherited privilege would not get a man into the Kingdom of God. The only passport was this break with the past, this new start expressed by the term 'born again'.

Now no one must run away with the idea that Jesus was for the Gentile but against the Jew, or for the Jew but against the Gentile. The Master was against no man. His invitation was to all who were weary and heavy-laden. When he found faith in Israel, he commended it—and when he found faith in a Gentile centurion, he praised it unreservedly as well. . . . The Kingdom was open to all who sincerely desired to do the Father's will. . . .

Now read Galatians 6:15, and thank God daily that you can belong to a Kingdom where a man is treated as a man, and not damned in advance because his skin is coloured or his nose hooked.

The Kingdom of God, pp 9-11

5 April

. . . The gospel of Matthew records Jesus as saying that 'two sparrows' were sold for 'a farthing', and Luke as 'five . . . for two farthings'. . . . During the reign of the emperor Diocletian the retail price of sparrows was fixed (in our coinage) at 10 for one-and-a-half pence. In Jewish reckoning five was much the same as our half-dozen—a familiar shopping figure. A housewife taking five would have the odd one thrown in free. Yet Jesus confidently declared that God cared for every such bird—sold 'in the cookshop' as Tatian added. 'Not a single sparrow falls to the ground without your Father's knowledge,' as J. B. Phillips's translation of the gospel puts it.

This is the picture language of the East, vivid and

arresting in its concreteness. Yet the truth itself is not less real, but more, than the figure of speech employed to describe it.

The personal care of God for the individual is not diminished because we ourselves are painfully conscious that we live in a world where great suffering is a consequence of great sinning. The believer cannot close his eyes to the fact that nowadays a particular kind of missile dropped, for example, over Oxford, would not only blot out the city completely but the county as well to an extent of 80 square miles. . . .

But no less in the days of Jesus were men at the mercy of forces which they knew not how to control. . . .

Jesus and our Need, pp 36, 37

6 April

. . . The discovery of atomic power is no more wrong in itself than James Watt's discovery of the power of steam. But if men turn their discoveries into weapons of mass destruction then men must repent—or suffer them. But no less in the days of Jesus were men at the mercy of forces which they knew not how to control. Buildings collapsed (Luke 13:4). Storms swept the seas (Acts 27:14). Drought bred hunger (Luke 15:14). Floods led to loss of life and property (Matthew 7:27). Sickness brought on poverty (Mark 5:26) and death (Luke 7:12).

Nor was man's inhumanity to man any less in intention then than now. The world in which Jesus spoke of the Father's care was one in which crucifixion was a legal method of carrying out the capital sentence and a gladiator's death agony was an accepted part of an afternoon's sport in the arena.

Today our increasing knowledge of the vastness of the universe in which we live is a further challenge to our belief that God cares for the individual. Challenge it may be, but we must not hide away from new knowledge. No life can be well founded on falsehood. We can accept the fact that God's creation is now known to be unimaginably greater than even some of the Bible writers supposed. But that only means that he who called the universe into being and who daily sustains it must be by that measure greater also.

Jesus and our Need, pp 37, 38

7 April

. . . The cry that the Kingdom of God was at hand constituted good tidings of great joy. . . . Jesus employed all manner of friendly and familiar illustrations to make this plain.

It was, said he in effect, like a wedding feast coming unexpectedly in the middle of a famine. Walk up! Walk up! And what was more, the feast was specially for those who could hardly remember when last they had enjoyed a good meal—the vagrants and penniless who lived in the ditches and under hedgerows. It was open house for them and they could eat their fill (Luke 14:16-23).

Or again, said the Master, the Kingdom is like a merry party thrown by a bridegroom for his friends on the eve of his wedding (Luke 5:34). Are there tears? Crocodile tears maybe. Are there condolences? Another good man gone west. But mock condolences. Every one is really feeling on top of the world.

Elsewhere Jesus said that the Kingdom was like a father welcoming home a long lost son, with both parties feeling that this was a far, far better thing than either of them had ever done before. So much a better thing that the father staged a feast with fatted calf as the principal dish (Luke 15:11-32), followed by a dance with all hands joining in, the boss leading off with the kitchenmaid, while the local fiddler nearly sawed his arm off. And if you tell me there were no fiddlers in Galilee, I shall retort by reproaching you for lack of imagination!

The Kingdom of God, pp 31, 32

8 April

Now this is what the Kingdom is—astoundingly good

news that demands to be told; news that one cannot keep to oneself; news such as might make those who cannot share it a trifle envious. Jesus said as much to his disciples. 'Many prophets and kings have desired to see those things which ye see, and have not seen them; and to hear those things which ye hear, and have not heard them' (Luke 10:24). But those who have seen and heard must surely tell. How can they do otherwise? So some ardent fellow might come rushing up: 'Congratulate me, my dear chap. I've just got engaged to the most wonderful. . . .' And he goes burbling on, as if he did not know that in such circumstances every Cinderella is a princess and any girl looks the most wonderful ever!

Now these are only human hints which suggest what the good news must have sounded like to those who first heard it. Here was promise to mortal man of triumph over those two ancient enemies—sin and death. Now men could know what they had never fully known before—how to live right both with God and man. And what the first believers felt about it all is shown by such phrases in the Acts of the Apostles as: '. . . did eat their meat with gladness', '. . . filled with joy and with the Holy Ghost', '. . . great joy in that city', '. . . rejoicing that they were counted worthy to suffer'.

This is what the good news of the Kingdom should mean to us and, when it does, we shall not be able to keep quiet about it!

The Kingdom of God, pp 33, 34

9 April

. . . Luke records the Master's disappointment over his own people's unwillingness to accept him as Messiah. 'O Jerusalem, Jerusalem, which killest the prophets, and stonest them that are sent unto thee, how often would I have gathered thy children together, as a hen doth gather her brood under her wings, and ye would not!'

Such a cry makes it clear that Jesus must have appealed to the capital more than once, but men did not want to be any different. Those who knew better—like the priests and the Pharisees—also knew that if the people followed Jesus they would lose all their influence over them, so they listened only to contradict. The Sadducees were concerned to preserve their privileged position as the group through whom the Romans governed the land, so they took no notice until they felt that Jesus had become too powerful a threat to be ignored any longer.

And the people themselves, burdened with the day-to-day cares of living, had little natural taste for a message so demanding as that of Jesus. Mostly they wanted to be left in peace. So what with those who could have listened but would not, and those who did not because they could not, the invitation of Jesus to share in the Kingdom which he had come to establish fell on deaf ears.

Jerusalem went her own way. . . . The people knew not the things which belonged to their peace. . . . Blind, they followed leaders who were blind, and the ditch into which they fell became their common grave.

Jesus and our Need, pp 75, 76

10 April

Jesus was sometimes disappointed with individuals—the story of the rich young ruler is one such instance. Here was a promising recruit if ever there was one—and one who did not wait to be called like Andrew and Peter, but who came running to hail the Master. This young man had money and came from good stock; he was such an attractive character that Jesus loved him. Yet for all his prepossessing ways the final test of discipleship found him wanting. The record says that he went away very sorrowful. That may be; but how much more sorrowful must Jesus have been. The disappointment in the Master's heart must have been doubly sharp because of the affection which he felt for this young ruler.

Such an experience was repeated many times over with Jesus. He must have been disappointed with the disciples who turned away when his words offended them (John 6:66); disappointed with those of the twelve who forsook him and fled; disappointed that Judas failed to respond to friendship's last appeal—the dipping of the sop in the common dish. Yet no disappointment, however piercingly felt, turned the Saviour from the Father's will.

The longer we work for God the more frequently are we likely to be disappointed. . . .

Jesus and our Need, pp 76, 77

11 April

As servants of the Kingdom we work for the conversion of men and of history—and men are desperately slow to learn the lessons of history. . . .

Perhaps this generation cannot realise how high were the hopes of men at the close of a war which had been announced as one to end war. Lord Curzon, moving the Address to the Throne after the Armistice in 1918, expressed the desires of many when he quoted Shelley's lines:

> The world's great age begins anew,
> The golden years return.

No golden years have returned. . . . The dreams of men have not come true. What then? Shall we retreat into our pleasures, concern ourselves with our private interests and let the world go to the devil if it wants to? Or, like Jesus, shall we keep on appealing whether men hear or forbear, and continue to proclaim the will of the Father that all men should live in fellowship with him and with each other? There is no doubt what Jesus would have us do. . . .

The thing to do is to take our disappointments to the Lord in prayer. He will understand for he passed along that sorrowful way in the days of his flesh. He who is touched with the feeling of our infirmities will give 'grace to help in time of need'.

Jesus and our Need, pp 77-79

12 April

The fourth gospel does not record any agony in the

Garden. The equivalent is: 'Father, save me from this hour' (12:27, *AV*). The triumph which followed is expressed in the phrase: 'Father, glorify thy name' (12:28, *AV*).

Thomas Kelly wrote:

> The head that once was crowned with thorns
> Is crowned with glory now.

But this 'glory' was not a species of decoration posthumously awarded for wearing the thorns. Not so! Christ's passion was his glory. These two are one and the same. His obedience unto death was his coronation. The Cross was his throne and he still reigns from the tree. That he should thus die was neither defeat nor disgrace. Had his death accomplished nothing at all it would still have been his finest hour. Death for him was not dishonour. If he had cursed his enemies, or had been so preoccupied with his own pains as to be deaf to the piteous cry of the dying thief, that would have been defeat. But to die as he died was triumph. Death was swallowed up in victory. The Son glorified the Father and the Father was glorified in the Son.

Jesus said: 'If any man serve me, let him follow me' (John 12:26, *AV*). He who hears and obeys his Master's voice cannot avoid the suffering of the Cross, but that trial will prove to be his crowning glory.

In Good Company, pp 9, 10

13 April

Three times the fourth gospel reports the Master as repeating this phrase—'The hour is come that the Son of Man should be glorified'—once when certain Gentile converts to Judaism, who were in Jerusalem for the Passover, asked to see him; again when Judas 'received the sop' and again in the self-revealing prayer of dedication recalled in John 17. . . . Each saying is so closely linked with the Cross that we would not have been surprised had the leading word been 'crucified'. That was the event present in the mind of Jesus when he spoke. But no; the word is 'glorified'.

Now when two people call the same thing by a different name, plainly they do not think the same way about it. . . . So if what I call 'being crucified', Jesus describes as 'being glorified', here . . . are two hearts which do not beat as one. . . . I do not yet speak the language of that Kingdom of which he is the chief cornerstone. I may be one of its citizens, but I am either so immature or so dull that I flounder over every sentence I try to utter because I am not familiar enough with the new vocabulary, and still think in such terms as are current in the city of destruction whence I am supposed to be fled.

If I keep on saying 'crucified' where Jesus uses the word 'glorified' it is sure evidence that I have not mastered the speech employed in Zion sufficiently well to know what the world calls 'loss', I should translate 'gain'. . . .

The Officer, March 1948

14 April

. . . In private life Pilate was a fair average Roman, happily married, holding the extremely difficult office of Procurator in Judea for longer than any one before or after him. He knew that Jesus was innocent and thrice sought to set the Master free. But what brought him finally to heel was the threat: 'If thou let this man go, thou art not Caesar's friend'. . . . Pilate knew that he did not stand too well with the Emperor as it was, and he could not afford to risk the imperial displeasure still further— even for the sake of. . . . So Pilate called for water and washed his hands.

Is there any wonder that the first believers regarded the world, and the spirit of worldliness, as the foe most to be feared when they remembered what it had done to Jesus? And today, whenever that spirit prevails, the Son of God is crucified afresh.

This being so, it is an error to suppose that worldliness is one of the prime temptations of youth. In reality it is one of the most subtle temptations of age. . . . Youth has its faults, but these are more often due to reckless generosity of spirit. The failings of age are more self-

83

regarding. The urge to hold what we have and to add thereto, no matter at what sacrifice of principle, is an evil pressure which is hardest to withstand in middle life.

The Officer, September, October 1950

15 April

We . . . know those days when it seems as if the Lord said, 'My face shall not be seen.' Without reproaching ourselves with imaginary transgressions, we have to accept that clouded days are as much a part of the spiritual order as they are of the natural order. . . . But I bless because, however dense and chilling the mists, experience will prove that he was close at hand even when I could not see him.

The supreme example of this is to be found in the Cross when Jesus cried out, 'My God, my God, why hast thou forsaken me?' However we understand that outcry, or whether we reverently conclude that here are depths we cannot plumb, it certainly looked to friend and foe alike that, wherever God was amid the darkness which covered the land from the sixth hour to the ninth, he was not with him who hung upon the Cross. Yet later, reflecting upon the finished work of Christ, the apostle saw that this was just where God was, never more truly with his beloved Son than in his act of atonement. 'God was in Christ, reconciling the world unto himself.'

And God will be with us in our hours of spiritual darkness. . . . If he says 'no' to all we want, he will yet give us what we need, and 'in the cleft of the rock' will graciously reveal enough of his might and mercy for us to know that he lives and loves us still.

In this assurance I find sweetest rest!

Essentials of Christian Experience, pp 50, 51

16 April

'Public enemy Number One', said Principal J. S. Whale, 'is neither ignorance, nor stupidity, nor defective social environment, but sin, which is the deep mysterious root of all these evils.'

'Certain it is', wrote Winston Churchill, 'that while men are gathering knowledge and power . . . their virtues and their wisdom have not shown any notable improvement. . . . Under sufficient stress—starvation, terror, warlike passion or even cold, intellectual frenzy, the modern man we know so well will do the most terrible deeds, and his modern woman will back him up.'

'I have seen him (General Bramwell Booth) illustrating sin, taking a handkerchief from his pocket, would turn it over, look at it . . . then seek a hiding place. At last he would find a dark corner, perhaps inside the piano, and there he would thrust in his "sin". . . . Then he would turn to his audience and talk about the uneasy stirrings of buried wrongs . . . finally bringing the matter to a climax by thrusting his hand into the hiding place and crying, "Here it is, Lord. Here is the hindrance".'

'Today thou shalt be with me in paradise.' Forgiveness was instant and complete. His (the dying thief's) sins which were many, were all forgiven.

International Company Orders 1944

17 April

Some years ago I had the privilege of preparing for the press a series of extracts from the diary of a Salvation Army officer who was interned in Macassar from Whit Sunday 1942 to September 1945 . . . against all rules of course. . . . But days and dates were accurately filled in so that one entry read:

April 1 1945, Easter Sunday. Attended divine worship. Text: 'The Lord is risen indeed.' Air raid alarm, 9.45 am. A wild scramble to take cover.

To some it may seem that an entry about an air-raid makes a mockery of Easter Sunday. In one sense I couldn't agree more. There is nothing whatever in common between the means of destruction and the Son of Man who came not to destroy men's lives but to save them.

Yet in another sense there is no incongruity at all. For here was a testimony that the presence and power of the risen Lord could not be set at naught even when all hell was let loose. Easter is our annual witness to the truth that love is stronger than hate, that life is stronger than death. The resurrection of Jesus is the unanswerable demonstration of the undefeatable power of God.

Faith in the Resurrection was no late addition to the creed of the Church; it was there from the beginning. The earliest chapters in the Acts of the Apostles declare that 'with great power gave the apostles witness of the resurrection of the Lord Jesus'.

The truth of Easter is that Jesus is not someone who has risen, but who *is* risen. He is not someone about whom we may read, but someone whom we may meet. We are not limited to a study of his life; we can know his living presence. 'The Lord is risen indeed.'

The War Cry, 17 April 1966

18 April

Fear intimidates more than one lad or girl—and older person—today. That fear draws no ponderous bolts and fastens no material doors, but the fear of not conforming to a social pattern can imprison a man in a mental attitude where the sin of sins is to be out of step. It is just at this point where Jesus can break into that self-made prison and stand beside us to impart his own courage to our failing hearts.

Christ is not outside the walls of those fears and inhibitions of ours which surround us like a prison. He is on our side of the barriers. As with Paul in his Jerusalem cell we can say: 'The Lord stood by me.' And by virtue of his strengthening presence we can burst the fetters of those fears and stand free men.

If fear bolts some doors against Jesus, sin bolts many more. Habits would persuade us that we must remain the kind of men we have allowed ourselves to become. We are bound who should conquer, slaves who should be kings.

We resign ourselves to a fourth-rate—fifth-rate or tenth-rate—place in the school of manhood. We are at the bottom of the class and—God pity us!—have lost the desire to rise. Wretched men that we are, who shall deliver us?

The New Testament has an answer to that question. It consists of two words. 'God can!'

The War Cry, 17 April 1965

19 April

Any conversation can be a conversation with him when our hearts burn within us. At every meal he can make himself known to us in the breaking of bread. On any road the scales can drop from our eyes and we can recognise our unknown companion as the living Lord. . . .

Some years ago Sir Alexander Paterson, at the time the leading British authority on prison reform, paid a visit to the French penal colony in Guiana.

'When I stepped ashore at Cayenne on Good Friday (he said) there seemed to be every suggestion of Calvary . . . but no thought of the Resurrection. Walking down the main street on Easter Sunday morning I came face to face with an officer of The Salvation Army. We spent the day in his little homestead. He apologised for the simplicity of his hospitality. He gave me all he had—a slice of cake and a drink of lemonade. It was an Easter communion I shall never forget.'

The risen Lord was present in their midst—as he can be in your home, or with you on the street, or wherever you may be reading this page. Speak to him now, for he hears—and your voice will join in the cry of astonished joy: 'The Lord is risen indeed!'

The War Cry, 9 April 1966

20 April

'Doubting Thomas' became a byword. Our fathers in the faith used to sing with great abandon, 'Is there anybody here like doubting Thomas?'—and then wait for so unbelieving a spirit to purge his fault by casting himself at the mercy seat along with weeping Mary and sinking Peter.

Thomas called Didymus seems to have been handled more gently. For one thing, his friends did not wash their hands of him. They had good news for him. 'We have seen the Lord' (John 20:25, *AV*) they said. They knew that by temperament he was prone to believe the worst—and they felt he should hear the best as well. . . .

What crowned the day for Thomas was that Jesus greeted him like a long-lost disciple. He knew that if anyone could fling the book of rules at him, that one was Jesus. Here he was doubting the Resurrection . . . but here was Jesus offering of his own accord the evidence which alone could set his disciple's unquiet mind at rest. 'Reach hither thy finger . . . reach hither thy hand . . .'. We do not know whether Thomas accepted the invitation and touched the wounds which the sins of men had inflicted on his Lord. Maybe the testimony of the senses was no longer needed. The overwhelming generosity of Jesus had banished the last vestiges of doubt from his mind. 'My Lord and my God,' he cried.

In Good Company, pp 25, 26

21 April

He would be a bold believer who would claim that one particular Christian doctrine is of greater importance than any of the rest, but this is what the apostle Paul seems to have done when writing to his converts in Corinth. 'If Christ has not been raised from death, then we have nothing to preach and you have nothing to believe' (1 Corinthians 15:14, *GNB*). The faith which Paul proclaimed stood or fell by the resurrection of Jesus. . . .

To save myself unnecessary disappointment I need not expect to discover any first-hand account of the Resurrection itself. . . . No one actually 'saw' the Resurrection. . . .

Nevertheless my questionings can—in part, at any

rate—be answered by taking note of some of the results of the Resurrection. . . .

The New Testament is one such result. Every word in each of the 27 books was written by a believer in the Resurrection. Every Christian place of worship in all five continents owes its existence to men and women who in their lifetime believed, or who now believe, in the Resurrection.

Every Sunday is a weekly celebration of the Resurrection. . . .

Most significantly of all, the Resurrection gave birth to that fellowship of men and women of every race and tongue and colour and nationality who acknowledge Jesus as Lord.

In Good Company, pp 22, 23

22 April

. . . The Ascension does not mean that he laid aside that humanity which he assumed when he 'took upon himself the form of a servant'. What he learned by the things he suffered he never unlearned. We who are his followers can count ourselves blessed that he who returned to the Father shared our lot, and he who shared our lot is now and ever one with the Father. . . . With the God and Father of our Lord Jesus Christ there is no sorrow common to man which he has not shared.

Take a fact so ordinary, and yet so bitter, as family squabbles. Jesus knew the sadness of these, for at one time even his brothers had thought of him as beside himself, and his mother had sought him out to bring him home.

He also knew what it was to lose his friends. At the tomb of Lazarus he wept so bitterly that even the onlookers remarked: 'Behold, how he loved him.'

He felt as well the equally sharp tooth of the general gracelessness of men and women. On one occasion, of ten men whom he had healed, only one returned to give thanks. . . .

The ascended Jesus never forgot what it was to be man.

In Good Company, pp 28, 29

23 April

The Acts of the Apostles might well have been entitled 'the Acts of the Holy Spirit', for the growth of the Christian Church was born of the Spirit of God himself. The Cross—much as we adore that symbol of shame, now our glory—was not the last act of God in his work of redemption. Our faith rests on the fact, not that Jesus lived, but that he is now living. Yet even the Resurrection—by itself—would not have furnished the disciples with power sufficient for their needs. Jesus recognised that fact, and told them to wait in Jerusalem until 'the promise of the Father' should be fulfilled.

The Holy Spirit of God did not come into the world for the first time at Pentecost. Jesus himself was 'full of the Holy Ghost' (Luke 4:1 and Matthew 12:28). By him 'the prophets wrote and spoke'. Pentecost made this difference—that thereafter any man, according to his capacity, could be filled with the Spirit of God. Jesus said that this divine event would be worth so much to the disciples that they might well lose him in order that the Spirit should come. . . .

The fruit of the Spirit is not to be found in noise and excitement, although strongly expressed emotions may well accompany a spiritual revolution. But Paul wrote that the marks of the Holy Spirit in any life were 'love, joy, peace, long-suffering, gentleness, goodness, faith, meekness, temperance'. The Holy Spirit may foster many good gifts 'but the greatest . . . is love'.

International Company Orders 1939

24 April

Probably on no subject is there such confusion of thought as upon the person and nature of the Holy Spirit. When we speak of the Trinity, we must not try to imagine three persons who are separate by nature and independent in action as, for example, a father, a mother and a child. When Jesus spoke of the Godhead as one (John 17:22), he implied that there were no watertight barriers of individuality between the Father, Son and Holy Spirit. God, the Father, is self-existing. He is the Source of Divine energy and power. The Son is begotten of the Father; the Spirit proceeds from the Father and the Son (John 1:18; 15:26). But the Father, Son and Holy Spirit share every act of knowledge, love and will.

. . . The best analogies from human experience fall short of any satisfactory explanation of this divine mystery. We may say, however, that the Holy Spirit is God himself present within the regenerated soul of man. He whom Jesus revealed as Father can be experienced as a personal indwelling Power. He is God in action in and through converted people. All who are saved have some personal experience of the Holy Spirit, for his is the power which brings about the new birth. The disciples themselves had some knowledge of him prior to Pentecost. 'Ye know him; for he dwelleth with you, and shall be in you' (John 14:17). The Holy Spirit came to them in greater measure after Christ's Ascension in order to give them power for the work which they had to do.

International Company Orders 1939

25 April

. . . The Spirit was needed to quicken the 120 waiting disciples into newness of life. This was done almost unceremoniously—as is evident from Luke's account of events on the day of Pentecost.

There was 'a violent blast of wind' *(Moffatt)*; 'a blast of violent wind' *(Barclay)*; 'the rushing of a violent wind' *(J. B. Phillips)*; 'The roaring of a mighty windstorm' *(The Living Bible)*. Believers spoke 'in languages they didn't know' *(The Living Bible)*; 'in foreign languages' *(Goodspeed)*. Onlookers were 'bewildered' *(NEB)*; were 'beside themselves with perplexity' *(Knox)*. Some of them present 'made sport' of the believers *(Basic English)*. Another group looked on 'contemptuously' *(NEB)*. 'Others treated the whole affair as a jest, "They are full of new wine," they said' *(Barclay)*. In such a situation today

91

there might even have been arrests for a breach of the peace. . . .

It is an error of judgment to associate the power of the Holy Spirit only—or even principally—with the unusual and the bizarre, as if the strangeness of an experience constitutes an authentic sign of the divine presence. . . . The message was made clear and plain, appealing to human reason and directed at the human conscience with such good effect as to evoke the instant response: 'Men and brethren, what shall we do?'

In Good Company, pp 33-35

26 April

The Spirit of God came to take the place of the inspiring presence of Jesus who was God made manifest within the limitations of human life. Under the conditions of space and time, only a few people could know Jesus intimately. He could not be everywhere at once. His death ended all that. Through the Holy Spirit, who would 'receive of mine and . . . shew it unto you', believers everywhere were able to have fellowship with the eternal Christ. The bonds of time and space were broken. Thereafter, wherever men sought to know him, he could be found of them.

. . . The Holy Spirit is described as the 'Comforter' and as the 'Spirit of truth'. The first title comes from a Greek word meaning 'one called in to aid'. The term has a legal origin, and the idea is that the Holy Spirit will champion the disciples in their struggle against what would otherwise be overwhelming odds. They are not to be left like 'orphans' to face the storm alone (. . . Wycliffe actually translated 'comfortless' as 'fatherless'). The Holy Spirit will be their 'stand-by', their 'strengthener', their 'consoler'.

The 'Spirit of truth'—the second title—was given because the Holy Spirit would help the disciples to understand the meaning of divine events after Jesus had left them. For example, the Holy Spirit enabled Paul to perceive that the Cross of Christ was not a symbol of shame but a means whereby the redemptive love of God reached down to man. . . . The Holy Spirit helped Catherine Booth to stand for the right of women to preach the gospel. . . . The promise . . . is as much for us as for the first disciples.

International Company Orders 1939

27 April

Pentecost was known in the Old Testament as the 'Feast of Weeks' (Exodus 34:22), the 'Feast of Ingathering' (Exodus 23:16), and the 'Day of Firstfruits' (Numbers 28:26). Fifty days after the Passover came the harvest feast when the corn was gathered in. As a token of thanksgiving, two loaves of bread made from the new wheat were 'waved' (ie, offered) in the Temple. Following this service, each worshipper would bring a freewill offering according to his means, and then a free meal was given in the Temple grounds to the poor, the stranger and the Levite.

We need not suppose that Acts 2 describes all that happened on this memorable day. The historian (Luke) has fastened on the most important facts, as, for example, his summary of Peter's speech around the apostle's three main points: that the new age foretold by Joel had begun, that Jesus was raised from the dead by the power of God, and that their risen Master was now with the Father, proof that his mission to men had been in accordance with the purpose of God.

. . . Concerning the attitude of this early band of believers we may note their complete obedience, their eager expectancy, their unity of purpose. . . .

International Company Orders 1939

28 April

In any attempt to understand what happened to the band of 'an hundred and twenty', we must note that Luke does not say that there was fire, but 'tongues like as of fire'. Similarly—not wind, but a 'sound . . . as of wind'. A more accurate—if less widely understood—translation would be the use of the Scots word 'sough' for 'sound'. Luke uses the most powerful forces of nature to describe what took place when the assembled company felt themselves in the grip of the Holy Spirit of God. Their bands were broken. Their repressions were shattered. They were released, confident, exultant, intensely aware that it was God who had done this thing, and eager to speak about it (verses 4, 6 and 11).

Peter repudiated the mocking suggestion that they were drunk so early on a sacred festival day (verse 15), and proceeded to explain that this event—so puzzling to onlookers—was born of the purpose of God. His remarks were based on three Old Testament quotations. . . . His reasoning, though perhaps somewhat foreign to our ways of thought, was convincing to his listeners, as might well be the simplest utterances of anyone whose words were clothed by the power of the Holy Spirit. . . . The upshot was that some 3,000 persons accepted Jesus as 'both Lord and Christ' that day—a company which soon grew so rapidly as to include 5,000 men.

We may ask whether such spiritual results can be achieved—at least in some degree—today. . . .

International Company Orders 1939

29 April

We may ask whether such spiritual results can be achieved—at least in some degree—today. They are— when lives are Christ-centred, Christ-controlled. Whenever God's people throw off the sloth and selfishness which so easily beset us all, then the Spirit of God works in and through them. Here is an illustration from chapter three of *Kingdom Come* (Redwood):

> Once, in the twilight, Peter Rawlings talked with two ministers . . . in neither of whose 'successful' churches (success was a matter of congregational numbers) did anything ever happen. . . . Three men prayed round an office table that night. . . . Jesus at last became real to them. . . . Here is part of a letter which Peter received on the following Monday:

'I have lived in that atmosphere of last Tuesday almost ever since. How much yesterday's services were influenced by that evening I cannot tell, but I experienced what was undoubtedly the greatest day in my ministry. God was never more manifestly present than last night. . . . No fewer than 20 people of all ages came out to the front, some as an act of reconsecration and others in decision. . . . It just all happened as though it were the most natural and the most expected thing in the world.'

'The promise is unto you . . . and to all . . . even as many as the Lord our God shall call.'

International Company Orders 1939

30 April

What had brought about this change? The events at Pentecost supply the answer. . . .

Mary Slessor, when asked how she succeeded in transforming so vast an area in Africa, replied that her heart was often in her throat, and that frequently her courage seemed to take wings and fly away. Only a sense of the presence of God kept her calm and strong. Otherwise, she was too nervous to cross a Glasgow street. So Peter did not take this bold stand in his native strength. Out of weakness, the Holy Spirit had made him strong.

Has there been any like change in our own lives? At the moment we may be crippled by long-standing habits of wrongdoing, or cursed by a fatal hesitancy when it comes to witnessing for our convictions. In the hour of crisis we are fearful and timid as was Peter in the courtyard of the High Priest. Our irresolute condition will be cured when we yield our lives to the will of God. Then his Spirit will flood us with power.

Here I was much abused, because of my religious scruples, by some rough school-fellows, who did not stop short of physical torment, with the result that I received injuries which accounted for a good deal of ill-health in after years. My school life did help me at least in this one direction, that there I received the world's first blows and learned to bear them. I was soon nicknamed 'Holy Willie' and treated with almost every kind of indignity that the rather cruel mind of a certain type of boy could suggest. . . . But I cannot say that it has ever hurt me greatly to be laughed at on account of my religion.—General Bramwell Booth.—*These 50 Years.*

International Company Orders 1939

1 May

. . . When we think of Pentecost we must not suppose that this was the moment when the Holy Spirit came into existence. God is eternally Father, Son and Holy Spirit, and the three persons in the Godhead share every act of thought, will and feeling. . . .

The Holy Spirit is actively at work in the world today. It is wrong to think of him coming at Pentecost and then somehow fading out. As he has been active from all eternity, so he is active today. We beg of him to come, but he is here. We ask him to fall on us, but he is ready to do so long before we have ever thought of offering such a prayer.

Do not picture the Holy Spirit as distant and aloof, One who has to be besought very earnestly before he will answer your prayer. Think of him as you think of the ocean which surrounds this small island called Great Britain. The sea enters every estuary, fills every creek, floods every pool to which it can gain entrance. Let there be a vacant hollow on the coast line and in flows the sea. The task is often not to invite the sea in but to keep it out.

Yet . . . we can build dykes of complacency and selfishness around our hearts and say 'thus far and no farther'. Against those walls the Holy Spirit beats in vain.

Jesus and our Need, pp 32, 34, 35

2 May

The work of Jesus and the Holy Spirit are intertwined. In Jesus we see what the Holy Spirit can do with a human life. John the Baptist declared that he who was to come would baptise with the Holy Spirit, and at the Jordan the

Spirit indeed came upon Jesus. Led by the Spirit he went into the wilderness. In the power of the Spirit he returned preaching and teaching. To the presence of the Spirit he testified in the synagogue at Nazareth. God gave not his Spirit 'by measure' unto him; that is to say, all that Jesus did was by virtue of the Holy Spirit.

Before the Master's death he spoke of the day when, having ascended to the Father, the Holy Spirit would take his place. The disciples had looked to the historic Jesus, had learned of him, had depended on him. Now the Holy Spirit would be to them what Jesus had been in the days of his flesh, and they would look to the Spirit for strength and direction as formerly they had leaned on Jesus.

In turn the Holy Spirit fulfils his office by relating all he does to Jesus. He convinces men of their sin and consequently of their need of Jesus as Saviour. He shows men what true goodness is by reminding them of Jesus. Finally, he makes plain the meaning of judgment; we shall stand or fall by our likeness to Jesus. . . .

The Holy Spirit is actively at work in the world today. . . .

Jesus and our Need, pp 33, 34

3 May

The life of the Early Church in Jerusalem was marked by four main features. The believers were eager to learn, . . . eager to be friends with each other, . . . eager to worship together, . . . eager to share.

The Holy Spirit taught them that they could no longer hold their possessions for their sole personal benefit. Those who had wealth must use it for the common good. This idea was not put forward by any particular apostle, but appears to have been a spontaneous action prompted by the Spirit of God. There was no compulsion upon any one to give anything at all. There was no law—save that of love—to say how much any believer ought to give. But many sold their possessions and placed the proceeds at the disposal of the apostles. . . .

Examining one day at Headquarters the returns of sub-scriptions received during a given period, I noticed a frequently recurring item of one shilling and fourpence under the same name. . . . The sender was a widow and a soldier at one of our country corps. . . . I directed that an officer should go and see her with a view to discovering something of her circumstances. . . .:

'I live alone since my husband died. He worked at the factory . . . and . . . they kindly made us an allowance of two-and-six a week, and we had the old age pension for one of us. . . . So I always reckon to save the money for one loaf each week—I call it my "Jesus loaf"—and I send the money each month to Headquarters. You see, both I and my husband were saved in the Army.'

Such gifts must bear fruit unto God out of all proportion to the money values by which we identify and record them.— Bramwell Booth, *Echoes and Memories*.

International Company Orders 1939

4 May

Without reserve, they belonged to Christ. They had no private ambitions, no secret hopes, no barriers which stood in the way of an unreserved surrender to Jesus of themselves and all they hoped to be. They obeyed the Master's final commands to the letter, and returned to Jerusalem there to continue 'with one accord in prayer and supplication'. We salvationists may not be prone to make the same mistake as many earnest and intelligent seekers— that of discussing religion instead of obeying its keen-edged commands. Talk is always easier than action. But sometimes we are tempted to allow personal prejudices and rivalries to interfere with the full surrender of our lives to the will and Spirit of Christ. Our lives must be Christ-centred if they are to be Spirit-filled. . . .

Their whole attitude was charged with faith. They expected that Jesus would be as good as his word—and he was. The Holy Spirit came to men and women who had prepared themselves to receive him. He will hardly come unsought to the bored or listless believer. We need not complain that our lives are powerless if our use of the recognised means of grace is only occasional or haphazard. It is not that the Spirit of God is unwilling to come in fullness to everyone's life. He is positively anxious to do so. But if we either refuse or are too indolent to prepare our hearts for his coming, then our consequent weakness is our own fault.

International Company Orders 1939

5 May

The apostles continued to hold public meetings 'in Solomon's porch' which was part of the large open court of the Gentiles. . . . They were arrested . . . but Peter's defence of himself and his comrades so infuriated the Sadducees that they 'took counsel to slay them'.

The apostles offered no resistance. . . . They respected the Sanhedrin as the organ of national authority, although they had defied its commands.

Peter's defence was bold as it was astute. To the first part of the accusation he declared that, in any clash of loyalties, the commands of God came before those of men. . . .

In Millais' picture 'The Huguenot' two lovers are saying goodnight in a Paris garden on the eve of St Bartholomew. Word has gone round that the Protestants are to be massacred the next day. The girl ties a white scarf—the badge of the Catholic party and the sign of safety— around the lad's arm. Gently, but firmly, he unwinds the scarf. Inwardly, honour has battled with affection, and honour has won. Like that of the cavalier of Lovelace's poem, the action implied:

> I could not love thee, dear, so much,
> Loved I not honour more.

. . . In any clash of loyalties, Christ must come first.

International Company Orders 1939

6 May

Philip . . . was probably a Greek-speaking Jew of broad outlook and warm heart . . . free from racial

99

hatreds . . . and religious narrowness. . . . He was utterly absorbed in his message and his mission, and acutely sensitive to the pressure of the Holy Spirit of God. . . .

God does still guide men. Instances of this in Army literature alone are many and varied. One of the closest parallels to this incident was the finding . . . of suitable premises for the Abbey Street (London, UK) Goodwill Centre:

After months of vain inquiry, the Slum Secretary decided on a change of method. She put the position before one of the members of the Slum Brigade who had just reported for duty, lent him a motor van and driver, and invited him to make the finding of a new centre his appointed task. . . . How it came about was narrated by the discoverer at the opening ceremony.

'For some reason or other I came to the City that morning with my thoughts full of Tabard Street, in the Borough. . . . We went round to the far side of it, to see what might be there. Instantly, we both knew that we were "under control". . . . That is the best way I can describe the feeling which took possession of us. We found ourselves in a long, straight street—neither of us had ever seen it before—and we traversed it slowly, he looking to the right, and I to the left, for what we somehow knew we should presently find. . . . Some 300 yards farther on, the driver applied his brakes suddenly, even before I had time to tell him to do so. We were there.'

Within a few hours negotiations were opened for one of the most important posts in the country.—Hugh Redwood.

International Company Orders 1939

7 May

For centuries the Jews had thought of themselves as 'a peculiar people'. This idea was of God in its origin, but they had made their divine election a cause for self-regarding pride and narrowness. They were God's *only* children. The rest of the world mattered neither to him nor to them. Throughout the whole of life they drew a line dividing the 'clean' from the 'unclean'. . . . Even to touch an unclean thing or person was to become unclean. The very dust of a heathen land was regarded as defiling. Milk drawn from a Gentile cow, bread and oil touched by Gentile hands, were impure. No Jew would sit at table with a Gentile. . . . Jewish Christians can hardly be blamed for sharing these prejudices. That was how they had understood the law of God since the days of Moses. The Holy Spirit had to work what was nothing less than a mental and spiritual revolution. . . . Peter was taught that no man—and no food—was common or unclean in the sight of God.

. . . The centurion faced Peter with the same question that the Ethiopian had put to Philip. Was there any reason why he should not be accepted into the fellowship of the Christian Church? Hitherto the aim of the believers had been to Christianise the Jews. Peter was now trying to adjust his mind to the amazing fact that God wished them to Christianise the world. . . . Peter and the brethren with him gladly welcomed Cornelius and his Gentile friends into the classless brotherhood of the Early Church. . . . Just as the Holy Spirit bridged that difference in the first century, so God is now calling us to a brotherhood of love in which no man will find himself branded as an alien, nor excluded as a stranger. The Salvation Army, in which many races co-operate for the establishment of the Kingdom of God, is a miniature of what the world might be, if only men opened their hearts to the grace of God.

International Company Orders 1939

8 May

Frequently we speak of prayer that 'changes things' and prayer which 'moves his arm'. The truth in these phrases must not delude us into treating prayer as a method of inducing God to do what we want. Any concept of prayer as a slot machine which must yield a return when a penny is inserted—else the mechanism is out of order—is not prayer 'in the name of Jesus'. The promise expressly is that 'whatsoever ye shall ask the Father *in my name,* he will give it to you'. Asking in his name means to ask in the spirit of him who gave the promise. He prayed that the

Father's will, not his own, might be done, even when his life was at stake. The measure in which a prayer is granted is the measure in which it agrees with the wisely-loving purposes of God.

This does not mean that identical prayers from two different men will be answered in identically the same way. Assume that both Peter and James prayed that their lives might be spared. We must not infer that God heard Peter, but not James. Since all men are different God cannot treat any two alike. The very fact that he gives to one, but withholds from another, is proof that he cares for his children as individuals. Each case—as we say—judged on its merits. That is a cause not for repining, but for gratitude. . . .

Others of the Twelve doubtless sought safety by leaving the capital. They would continue to tell of Jesus wherever they went, so that the king's plan for crushing the Church only led to growth just where growth was most desirable—in the wider Gentile world. . . . Good comes out of evil when men—refusing to lie down beneath calamity—face it in the strength of the Spirit of God. As a bird cannot fly except in a resisting medium, so to rise we require the opposition of some hardship to be overcome.

International Company Orders 1939

9 May

The hallmark of the Holy Spirit's presence is not to be found in any spiritual excitements, but in the activity of love which Paul placed first in his 'harvest of the Spirit', and which Jesus continually exemplified in his life and work. This may be the clue which some of our people are seeking. The fruit of the Spirit does not ripen in a brief hour of unusual rapture so much as by the constant practice of the sturdy virtues of righteousness. The gifts of the Spirit leave their most permanent impress upon a man's character rather than his emotions. The Spirit's work is to enable those whom he indwells to manifest that love which is the fulfilling of the law. This is his sign manual—not a boisterous temperament, nor a happy-go-lucky disposition, nor a capacity for easy denunciation. There can be a great and mighty wind and the Lord not be in it.

To be filled with the Spirit is to be filled with holy love which, according to the New Testament, is not merely an emotion and certainly not to be confused with liking. To love is disinterestedly to serve God and man—and by such living alone is Jesus glorified.

It was—and is—ever the work of the Holy Spirit to glorify Jesus. He speaks not of himself but he makes known the truth about the Saviour of men. . . . He seeks no exaltation for any save him who sitteth at the right hand of God. . . .

The Father gives the Spirit who glorifies the Son, to whom—ever one God—be praise and dominion now and eternally.

The Officer, May, June 1950

10 May

. . . We are most often perplexed about ourselves, our own slow growth in grace, our seemingly unending struggle with our own ingrained faults. There is a good and a bad side to this sense of spiritual discouragement.

The bad side is that too much indwelling upon our imperfections can confirm us in those very faults we are seeking to eradicate. Indeed, such constant introspection can be a form of egoism. We are dwelling upon ourselves instead of looking unto Jesus who alone can deliver us from ourselves. There is great wisdom in forgetting the things which are behind for only in so doing can we free ourselves to reach out for those things which are before. . . .

Of course, there is a good side to our perplexity over our spiritual shortcomings. Our refusal to be satisfied with ourselves as we are is a sign not of the absence of the Holy Spirit, but of his presence. To be spiritually discontented is a mark of grace, not a cause for further self-despisings. . . .

103

We are perplexed because at times it would be hard to recognise a picture of the Master in some of our thoughts and actions. That is all to the good. Perplexed we may be—but not unto despair—for while Jesus lives and grace is flowing we can yet become men and women after God's own heart. And this, not because we are sufficient in ourselves, but because our sufficiency is of God.

Essentials of Christian Experience, pp 56, 57

11 May

'I wish'—I once overheard an officer say—'I understood what this "religionless Christianity" meant.' 'Me too,' I echoed privately and feelingly, if ungrammatically. We cannot escape the climate in which we live, nor entirely avoid the phrases which bespatter the pages of our favourite religious weekly. I am the last one to say that [salvationists] should be ignorant of current movements of thought, but no one should be led astray by what C. S. Lewis once called the chronological fallacy—that is, of supposing that the last phrase to be coined in a paperback or newspaper article is, for that reason, the one most surely to be believed. . . .

For my part I have no quarrel with new insights into the meaning of the word of God, nor with new ways of expressing old insights. However, the vogue of 'religionless Christianity', now dying away, is a warning of how a phrase can be mouthed without meaning. Not only with this phrase, but with all other theological catchwords, we should do as the climber does when reaching for a new handhold or foothold. He gives it a thorough testing before letting go his present grip and committing his weight wholly to the new one.

There is wisdom in the words: 'Test everything' (1 Thessalonians 5:21, *RSV*). This is not: reject everything. But prove all things. And in all your questionings never give way to the despair of unbelief. The Spirit of truth is ours to lead us into all truth.

Essentials of Christian Experience, pp 53, 54

12 May

The image is all important. According to this gospel, what sells an article , . . is the image which speaks to the prospective buyer in depth, arousing instinctive feelings of admiration or dislike. . . . So the image of one brand of soap is built around the pure innocence of the unspoilt mother/daughter relationship, while the sale of another variety is cultivated by use of the glamorous appearance of the sophisticated socialite. Here is a faith which would prefer to sell a mountain rather than cast it into the midst of the sea. Much more preferable to dispose of it at a profit. Given the right image all things are possible. . . .

The premise admitted, it is not a far cry to the deduction that a man's image can sell (or ruin) the man. There was some kind of minor inquest after a recent presidential election in the United States to discover why the image of one of the candidates had not come over successfully on television. And it is openly admitted in traditional Britain that one political leader has a poor image on the screen to the possible detriment of the fortunes of his party. If these things are so we should have a concern for the image of the Army lest what we really are should be spoiled by what we seem to be. Or is this logic standing on its head? Is the projection of our work in the public mind more important than the work itself? . . .

The Officer, June 1965

13 May

Let the work of the soldiery be generously appreciated by the officer. Much is said nowadays about the function of the layman in the church, but much that is now said as if it were new was said to the salvation soldier more than a century ago. 'I want', said William Booth on his sixtieth birthday, 'to see The Salvation Army reach such a degree of perfection that the charwoman who gets saved on a Sunday will find her proper place and have her work set out for her by the Monday night that follows.' That was setting the laity to work with top speed. If no church can function adequately without its lay people no Army can fight without its soldiers. They are greatly to be praised, for the faithfulness of the many far transcends the limitations of a few.

But the soldier must also generously value the work of his officer who has set aside commercial rewards and recognised working hours in order to be a shepherd of the sheep. We can all do with some encouragement, even the most austere of us, and maybe some young lieutenant would thank God and take courage if you told him last Sunday morning's holiness meeting had been a great blessing to you. If it was not, would you inquire within yourself how much this was due to your personal inattention rather than the officer's inexperience?

The Call to Holiness, pp 88, 89

14 May

Let everyone unite to welcome most generously into our Salvation Army fellowship the men and women who kneel at the mercy seat.

Converts may be neglected on two counts. In a large corps they can be lost to sight amid the multifarious activities of the sections. Indeed, those who leave the Sunday night prayer meeting before its conclusion may not be aware that there have been any seekers at all. In a small corps a solitary convert may be too prominent. He stands out to his own embarrassment amid the few.

Never forget that in entering into a new fellowship with God a convert has to find a new fellowship with man. In breaking with his sinful ways, he has broken with those with whom he shared those ways. . . . A man needs friends—none more so than the new convert. It is not enough to shake his hand and say 'God bless you' at the hall door. His old companions would do more for him than that. He would be welcome till turning-out time at the *Dog and Dart.* Should not the generosity of our welcome exceed theirs?

They [believers in Rome] were to present themselves to

106

God a living sacrifice. But by the same mercies of God ought we not freely to present ourselves to every convert in salvation fellowship. The generosity of heart and mind which makes this possible is . . . a fruit of the Spirit.

The Call to Holiness, pp 89, 90

15 May

It was in the juniors where most of us first learned that a parable was an earthly story with a heavenly meaning. The definition sufficed at the time, though now we have put away childish things, we might advance a stage in understanding and define a parable as any everyday incident seen through the eyes of Jesus. . . .

The parable of the sower is a key parable—'a parable of parables' it has been called—and is no exception to this rule. It is a slice of life seen through the eyes of Jesus and provides us with at least two surprises, the first of which is rather damping. It seems as if Jesus was pouring cold water on our immature enthusiasms. In your work for God, says this parable, be prepared for disappointments. Three parts of the sower's efforts were virtually wasted. The seed which fell by the wayside, on the stony ground and on the thorny soil came to nothing. Three-quarters of the sower's eager toil was love's labour lost. Three out of the four soils produced nothing for the harvest. In other words, don't take it as anything unusual if a good deal of your work goes down the drain. That is to be expected. You will spend much of your nerve and spirit and energy all for nothing.

To which the understandable comment is: then why go on? . . . We would not mind weeping with fatigue if only we returned bringing our sheaves with us. But sheaves— and in the plural! The fact is that to hide the nakedness of the land . . . we are tempted to pass off stubble as sheaves!

Such feelings of disappointment are not strange to Jesus for he himself shared them. . . .

The Officer, January 1948

107

16 May

The parable of the sower is not a poet's analogy, told with a poet's perfection of language. It was born out of the Master's own anguish of spirit. He was the Sower who went forth to sow. His own nation was the field. . . .

He knew what it felt like to have his appeals fall on stony ground or thorny soil. What harvest was there with the rich young ruler who, though stirred emotionally, jibbed when it came to selling all that he had?

Or what harvest with the Samaritan village which refused to receive him because his face was set towards Jerusalem, graceless treatment for One who made a Samaritan the hero of what was to be one of his best-known parables?

Or what harvest was there in Nazareth, the country village which scornfully turned her back upon her most illustrious son?

Or what harvest was there with the disciples who, after months of association with him, could still quarrel about place and position?

If that is how it was with the Master, can any servant expect to be immune from like wastage and disappointment?

The Officer, January 1948

17 May

'Jesus, being full of the Holy Spirit, returned from Jordan', but that did not save him from bonds of afflictions. The most dedicated spirit cannot escape a proportion of wastage—and a heavy proportion at that. This seems to be the law of the universe. It is certainly present in nature where much is wasted that a little may grow. Says the old farming couplet:

> One for the mouse, and one for the crow,
> One to rot, and one to grow.

As in the parable of the sower, three-fourths has to be

written off as dead loss so that one-fourth may ripen in harvest.

But the second surprise in this parable is as encouraging as the first was sobering. The small proportion of seed which does germinate produces such an amazing crop—thirty, sixty and one hundred fold—that it is worthwhile to continue working for God though so much does go to waste. Truth is usually a balance of opposites, and it is so here. While disappointment often attends our work for God, it is abundantly worthwhile going on because no one can tell when he will strike a patch of good soil and then the harvest will both amaze and reward him.

The Officer, January 1948

18 May

This . . . is one reason why our work confounds the person who lacks a sense of vocation. He is not prepared for the dismaying wastage of effort, and he also staggers at the promise of God through unbelief. Having seen so much go for nothing, he cannot believe that the harvest from so little can be so plenteous. So he has the worst of both worlds and often turns with relief to the less demanding fields of secular enterprise.

Yet in both these aspects of divine truth, Jesus is the supreme illustration. At his death the harvest looked sparse enough in all conscience—a few faithful women and still fewer men about the Cross. But now the seed has become a tree so large that all the nations can lodge in the branches thereof. . . .

So our sense of oneness with the Master in this work to which he has called us is very close. He is as much one with us in our failures as in our successes. . . .

It may be that we do not at all points closely resemble him who is both Saviour and Pattern. Indeed, the longer we gaze at the Pattern, the more dismayed do we grow over our botched copy. But if our very weariness born of our work for him is a point of resemblance to him, we may be thankful that at times we are o'erdone. For if the choice has to be between being tired with Jesus, and fresh through not sharing his toil, we may prefer to be weary. That, at least, will be accounted unto us for righteousness. It will be one point where we resemble him. And to be like him even in the smallest detail is surely our joy and our crown.

The Officer, January 1948

19 May

The word recreation itself gives a clue as to how leisure may be best employed. That pursuit or pastime is good which re-creates a man's power of body, mind and soul. These three go together. Man is a trinity in unity and no part of him can be treated by itself as if the other two did not exist. What might benefit the body is barred if it would harm the soul—and so with the mind. What blesses one must bless all. Man is a balanced being and he must maintain that balance. All human powers, whether of brain or brawn, belong to God and a man will have to account for the use of them all. The salvationist will therefore not allow himself in any leisure pursuit which would hinder his spiritual progress, conflict with Salvation Army principles, or lead to the neglect of accepted duty. Leisure and work can alike be regarded as God's good gifts to man, but neither should be used to separate God from man.

This means that the salvation soldier will not engage in any so-called pastime which is morally wrong. . . . In the second place, he will not engage in anything which might lessen the effectiveness of his own personal example, nor increase the pressure of temptation upon others. . . . Thirdly, there are recreations which are ethically sound and physically beneficial but which, if carried to excess, would prevent the salvationist giving due time and attention to duty. Here again he must exercise a discerning restraint, and on this point a right understanding of the meaning and use of Sunday is essential. . . .

IHQ Archives

20 May

. . . Thirty centuries ago, in a nomad community, the Jews were taught the worth of one no-work day in seven—a rule observed by the orthodox of their race to this day. In the time of our Lord, though the Jews were scattered in small communities around the Mediterranean—there were more of them outside Palestine than inside—they still put away their work at the Friday sunset, lit the lamp and, the following morning, while the Gentile world around them was busy getting and spending, made their way to the synagogue, there to worship the God of their fathers. Indeed, Sabbath observance formed one of the grounds of their exemption from military service in the Roman army. Jews were not summoned to courts of law on the Sabbath, and if a charitable distribution of money, bread or oil was made in Rome on the Sabbath, a portion was set aside to be handed to needy Jews on some other day.

Now the Christian observes Sunday as the equivalent of the Sabbath. There was no Sunday at all until Jesus rose from the dead. As he arose on the first day of the week, his followers ever since have kept that day as a weekly commemoration of his triumph over the tomb. . . .

Certain work may be unavoidable. . . . But I beg you long to ponder whether we should go beyond the barest minimum. . . .

Sunday is the time for rest because—and my whole argument hinges on this point—it is the time for worship.

In the Dinner Hour, pp 16-18

21 May

Let us recall that those two great upsurgings of the human spirit—the French Revolution in 1789 and the Russian in 1917—both of which have permanently affected the course of history, at first dispensed with Sunday as the day for worship and rest. . . . But both movements, after a period of experiment, restored Sunday to its pride of place. What a Marxian state has had to respect, let a nominally Christian country honour!

. . . Do not lend yourselves to the ridicule of what is mis-called Sabbatarianism. If you do, you will be cutting off one of the branches on which you are now sitting. . . . If Sunday is merely a matter of man's convenience, a human arrangement which we find useful to observe, then what man has ordered, a stronger man can set aside. Reflect, I beg you, how two or three men, clutching at power, have nearly pulled the whole house of civilisation about our ears. I repeat then, that if Sunday is but an agreed convention regarding the number of hours that we shall work, that what man has proposed, another may well be able to dispose. But if Sunday is divinely instituted a day for worship, for rest and—I add, lest it be taken selfishly—a day for service of our fellows, then man will do well thus to accept and rightly to use that which God has planned for his eternal good.

In the Dinner Hour, pp 18, 19

22 May

There is no reason why sex should not be discussed in a perfectly natural manner, but, at the same time, be spoken of with reverence because it enables men and women to act on behalf of God in the creation of children. . . .

. . . As the sixth commandment protects human life, so the seventh is designed to safeguard family life. Put baldly, the commandment means that a man must not misconduct himself with another man's wife, nor a wife with another man's husband. There is no loophole, no suggestion that if you are unfortunate enough to be at-tracted to someone who is married already, then your love is so noble and glowing a thing that an exception should be made in your case. Whether we like it or not, there are no exceptions.

A hard law? For some, I agree—for there are always those who marry in haste and repent at leisure—but a law infinitely in the best interests of all who take seriously their responsibilities as parents; and certainly in the best interests of the children, who are all too often the unfortunate sufferers by any attempted dissolution of the marriage tie.

In its direct application the seventh commandment is one for married people. . . .

In the Dinner Hour, p 27

23 May

In its direct application the seventh commandment is one for married people. Does that mean the authorities expect folk to misbehave, but propose to save them from the physical fruits of their folly? The fundamental objection to Regulation 33B is much the same. Its very existence tends to create the impression that 'infectious' contacts are being carefully rounded up and that promiscuous intercourse is being made medically safe.

Such an idea is a thoroughly insecure foundation upon which to build the so-called better world. I do not need to quote Christian teaching to prove that nothing weakens any nation more than moral laxity. Secular history does that. Not without cause did Blake cry out:

> The harlot's cry from street to street
> Shall weave old England's winding sheet;
> The winner's shout, the loser's curse,
> Shall dance before dead England's hearse.

Well, what do you think? Are these arguments Puritanish, the prejudices of a killjoy? Hurl such verbal brickbats, if you will. I will seek the shelter of a final quotation on this matter of morals, giving the author's name at the end of his words.

> Of course thirst cried out to be quenched. But will a normal person lie down in the dirt on the road and drink from a puddle? Or from a glass with a rim greasy from many lips?

If men will not hear Moses and the prophets, will they listen to—Lenin?

The Officer

24 May

Religion, instead of being—as is wrongly supposed—a 'pie in the sky when you die' kind of affair, is deeply concerned about what happens here and now in this life to flesh and blood men and women.

The eighth commandment is an illustration of this concern, for it establishes a man's right to own property. . . . It establishes a man's right to what is his own.

. . . This truth is double-edged. If it safeguards my right to what is necessary for a full human life, so it does for my neighbour, my acquaintance, my enemy. I cannot deny my opposite number the consideration which I claim for myself. If he must not rob me of what is necessary for what the American constitution calls 'life, liberty and the pursuit of happiness', neither must I steal those essentials from him. And to that word 'steal' I give the widest possible meaning, embracing such rosy-coloured equivalents as 'scrounging', 'finding', 'winning', 'lifting', 'scrumping'.

. . . But the verb 'to steal' has still a wider application. If I am paid one pound for a job, I must put twenty shillingsworth of work into it, else I am a thief. On the other hand, if I have put twenty shillingsworth of work into a job, I should be given one pound, else the man who underpays me is a thief. So to give short weight, to mislead by advertisement, to 'put it across' another man in a personal deal, breaks the eighth commandment. This rule applies to every transaction—whether a deal running into tens of thousands of pounds or the matter of pence across the grocer's counter.

In the Dinner Hour, pp 30-32

25 May

Of course honesty is a good policy. We don't return to the shop where we are not given value for money. We don't keep on dealing with the firm who puts it across us in business. Even the mug does not stand twice in the seaside saleroom where a persuasive auctioneer cajoles him into parting with a five-pound note for what, seen from the back of the crowd, looks like a gold watch, a set of silver teaspoons, a handsomely engraved coffee-pot and, as a gesture of goodwill from the vendor to the buyer, a diamond tie-pin thrown in. Once bitten, twice shy. Honesty is good policy.

How I wish that those who quote this saying would go on to complete it. It was coined by Richard Whately, one-time Archbishop of Dublin, and ended: '. . . but he who is governed by that maxim is not an honest man.' That is to say, honesty is to be the rule whether it is good policy or not.

This truth is silently recognised by all decent citizens. . . . We can thank God that the eighth commandment has been driven deep into the conscience of many, and resolve—by precept and practice—to help make it the common rule for all.

In the Dinner Hour, pp 32, 33

26 May

. . . Serious as may be any transgression of the eighth commandment, the ninth forbids an offence which, according to Shakespeare at any rate, is even more vicious still.

It was the wretch Iago in *Othello* who, by his base use of high moral standards, roused the Moor's jealousy of his wife's good name. Hinting at what Desdemona was doing, he said:

Who steals my purse steals trash; 'tis something, nothing;
'Twas mine, 'tis his, and has been slave to thousands;
But he that filches from me my good name
Robs me of that which not enriches him,
And makes me poor indeed.

. . . I am not guilty of exaggeration when I say that decent folk, who would be disgusted by any breaking of the seventh or eighth commandment, frequently transgress the ninth in so far as they originate or repeat innuendos about other people; catty, gossipy half-truths about friends; and by them the latest scandal—however little foundation it may have—is relished as a choice morsel to be shared with their cronies. Of course, it's all 'off the record', not for publication, told as between friends. None of it may be actionable, but to say what we know is only partly true, or to repeat a statement of whose accuracy we are not certain, is to bear false witness. No wonder the child's rhyme prophesies dire punishment for the slanderer:

> Tell tale tit,
> Your tongue shall be split,
> And all the dogs in the town
> Shall have a little bit!

And there is good theology in many a nursery rhyme!

In the Dinner Hour, pp 33, 34

27 May

Lies are told for different reasons. Some are born of fear. The results of speaking the truth may be personally unpleasant. Others are born of pride. A lad repeats what he knows is not true just to keep his end up before the gang. Occasionally lies are due to genuine forgetfulness—which is always pardonable. But so far as is in you, let it always be the truth, the whole truth and nothing but the truth—no colouring, no false emphasis, no touching up of the highlights or darkening of the shadows: just the truth. . . .

In 1898 war broke out between Spain and the USA. The match which set the fire alight was the destruction of the US battleship *Maine* in Havana harbour. It was stated that the Spaniards had blown her up and, on these grounds, the USA declared war. The *Maine* was subsequently raised by US engineers who then discovered that the ship had been sunk by internal explosion. Her loss was not the work of Spanish agents, but the result of her own ammunition igniting and blowing her up. That false report cost Spain fifty per cent of her men in certain battles, and the USA fifty per cent of her troops stricken by disease in other tropical areas.

These days are shadowed enough without adding to the

distress of men and nations by falsehoods which often harm the innocent most of all. Said Paul: 'Speak every man truth with his neighbour; for we are members one of another.'

In the Dinner Hour, pp 35, 36

28 May

Let me run up my colours at the start and say that my own convictions on the matter of total abstinence are part of my total Christian convictions. This is not solely an inherited or traditional conviction, though it was one always followed in my own home by my parents who were officers of The Salvation Army before me. It is a conviction against which I rebelled for a time but to which I subsequently returned, making what I had been taught a matter of personal acceptance.

This I realise is the conviction of a minority, which fact is ever before me as, at the call of duty, I attend many private and public functions, both religious and social, of which eating and drinking are inseparable parts. And as few among us honestly relish being odd man out, we may occasionally be tempted to debate within our own heart whether our lone stand is justified. . . .

It has always been the strong suit of the Trade, and with those allied thereto for social or commercial reasons, to represent drinking as a constituent part of the only acceptable and agreeable way of life. The argument is that this is how the normal man conducts himself. Cranks and faddists, like the teetotaller, will be ever with us, but they belong to that lunatic fringe who are never happy unless they are making a nuisance of themselves on the outer edges of community life. . . .

The War Cry, 11 February 1967

29 May

Let me disarm a possible criticism by saying that *I do not brand drinking as the worst sin in the calendar.* If I am asked to itemise in any sort of order those evils which at the present moment do so sorely beset mankind, at the head of the list might come the clash of colour—too often reduced to terms of white versus black whereas it is really white versus the rest.

Then would come war as an instrument of national policy, for this today derives increasingly from the clash of colour. For while we in Europe have learned the hard way that to toss a bomb into our next door neighbour's house means blowing the tiles off our own roof and the glass out of our own windows, this fact of life is not as yet appreciated so acutely in other continents.

Immediately behind stalks the spectre of world poverty, and, in close attendance, those social evils which are variously styled the crime rate, the divorce rate, the delinquency rate, the accident rate—and in each of these drinking is a contributory factor making a bad situation worse. Leaving alcoholism out of the picture for the moment, it is drinking as a contributory factor to our social woes which forms the reverse side of that 'gracious' living which at a city banquet will advise me to take Pouilly Blanc Fume with my scampi, Chateau Batilly with the grouse and Graham's 1955 with the stilton. . . .

The War Cry, 11 February 1967

30 May

'It would be hard to say why historians have not rated the effect of strong drink as the significant factor in 19th century history which it was. Its importance stands out on every page of the contemporary record. The most prominent factor in every disputed election was bestial drunkenness, which the candidates were expected to subsidise by expending what were, considering the cheapness of liquor and the smallness of the population involved, very large sums. . . . In the background there was always the degradation and the cruelty—particularly to the weak and defenceless—which resulted from drunkenness.' (*The Making of Victorian England*—G. K. Clark.)

118

And in the 20th century, no less than the 19th the havoc wrought by alcohol in its many forms persists in breaking through despite every effort made to disguise it as a minister of sweetness and light. This emerges in individual lives, and as a factor in public health. . . .

If the social glass is no danger, why have the majority of airlines a fixed rule that no intoxicants shall be taken for eight hours before take-off? . . . What applies to air safety applies to road safety. . . . 'The results of the study of the effect of alcohol upon driving performance reveal that . . . there is progressive impairment in skill, judgment and reaction time from the first drink onwards. And the drinker himself becomes progressively less able to detect his own impairment.' . . . (Medical Research Council Memorandum 38).

The War Cry, 11 February 1967

31 May

. . . In the matter of total abstinence every vote counts, for your witness determines how you spend your money and where you spend it; the character of your home—the influence which goes out of your home and what your friends find there; the values which your children learn by your example. So whether the church of your choice takes any stand on the drink question or not, you make your personal stand.

But let it be made with clarity—of which accuracy is an essential part. The cause is far too valuable to be ruined by generalities or inaccuracies. And let no one allow himself to become involved with isolated texts of Scripture which may or may not support his stand. Our convictions on this matter arise out of the second of the two great commands of Jesus that we should love our neighbour as ourselves. I cannot therefore allow myself in any practice which would directly or indirectly, by short range or long range effect, work to the hurt of my neighbour.

But however rooted and grounded our convictions on this or any other matter, they should always be stated with clarity. However irrational or abusive any opposition may become, we ourselves must never be less than charitable in our judgments and courteous in our responses. Our cause requires this of us for it is part of the redeeming purpose of God. This finally is why, in spite of the odds against us, I continue to believe in the triumph of righteousness in this and every other realm where Christ is destined to reign as King.

The War Cry, 11 February 1967

1 June

Just over a hundred years ago the working people of Manchester, and of south Lancashire generally, were suffering great hardship because of the blockade exercised by Union arms over the Confederate ports during the American Civil War. Denied imports of raw cotton from the cotton-growing South, Lancashire mills closed down and operatives and their families went hungry. Nevertheless in the depth of the winter of 1862/63, 6,000 Manchester men and women urged Lincoln to maintain his policy until slavery had been ended—and this though they themselves were among the hardest hit by that policy.

Lincoln replied on 19 January 1863, 'I know and deeply deplore the sufferings which the working men of Manchester . . . are called to endure at this crisis. In the circumstances I cannot but regard your decisive utterances on the abolition of slavery as an instance of sublime Christian heroism which has not been surpassed in any age or any country. . . .'

In the same spirit of dedication let all who share our convictions serve without counting the cost until victory over the drink traffic in all its forms has been won.

The War Cry, 11 February 1967

2 June

Associated with most sporting fixtures is the practice of gambling, and many an otherwise clean game is spoilt by the money which changes hands over it. . . .

Here there is but space to clear up one major confusion—that there is nothing wrong in a man having a shilling on a horse when he can afford it, but everything wrong in having many shillings on many horses when he cannot afford them. One great church went so far along this line of faulty reasoning . . . as to say: We hold then, that it is not wrong . . . to play for stakes, even for large stakes, provided the players can easily afford it.

The honest salvationist instinctively recoils from such casuistry. So to argue is to make morality dependent upon riches. What is right for a wealthy man becomes wrong for a poor one. This is the death of morals. Carried to its logical conclusion, the argument implies that the wrong in gambling consists in losing. This is on a par with the idea that the wrong in stealing lies in being found out.

Gambling is evil in itself, whatever the stakes. It is the worship of luck, which is a denial of the loving providence of God. It is the exploitation of chance, which is the negation of skill. . . . An action does not become ethically justifiable just because it is financially profitable. If that were so, burglary would be a highly moral profession.

As General Albert Orsborn said: '. . . The Salvation Army has always regarded gambling as wrong in principle and harmful in practice.' From that declaration no salvationist will wish to depart.

IHQ Archives

3 June

. . . Their history [ie, that of the Children of Israel] began with Abraham. That was where Stephen commenced when defending himself before the Sanhedrin. 'Men, brethren, and fathers, hearken; the God of glory appeared unto our father Abraham, when he was in Mesopotamia.' Let the exiles then look to the rock from whence they were hewn and the quarry from which they were dug. . . . Spelled out more fully this meant: look at what God has done and then look at what man can—and should—do. Is not this what the Spirit is saying to us at this point in our own history?

Let salvationists look to the rock whence they were hewn and the quarry from which they were dug. Our

Abraham and Sarah are called William and Catherine. And look to them, not to suppose that we are merely of human origin but to mark how true it is to say: he was but one when I called him, but I blessed him and made him many. I gave him this unimagined increase—The Salvation Army.

What was it made our Abraham the greatest of them all? The completeness of his dedication. 'I early resolved that God should have all there was of William Booth.' And likewise our Sarah. 'I know not what he is about to do with me, but I have given myself entirely into his hands,' she said.

Their response, like that of Abraham, was unqualified. . . . What he would have you do, do quickly.

Essentials of Christian Experience, pp 58-62

4 June

To look to Abraham means first to look at what God did. For God's action preceded Abraham's response. Without God's call the patriarch would never have left his country and his kindred for a land he knew not of. Any wandering nomad of that day moved from well to well, from oasis to oasis, driven on by nothing more significant than physical need—the need for his flocks for water and of himself for food. What set this man apart from the desert tribesman of his day was that his movements were God-guided and therefore God-blessed.

So to look to Abraham is to be reminded of what alone gives significance and purpose to life. It was God's call in his heart and God's hand on his shoulder that made Abraham's life so meaningful. It was the outworking of God's purpose which blessed him and made him a blessing.

Yet there are those who almost fear the hand of God upon their life. They are near to dismay at the thought of what he may ask them to do or where he may tell them to go. But . . . 'the land that I will show thee' may be nearer than we think. But the call to go and work there is as

122

genuine a call from God as came to any character in Scripture—Old Testament and New Testament alike. . . .

Essentials of Christian Experience, pp 59, 60

5 June

As with Abraham, God is calling us from the familiar to the unfamiliar; from the known and customary to the unknown and strange; from a settled routine to some new adventure in his service. There is no knowing how God will use, or where he will send, the man upon whom he has laid his hand. But far from this truth provoking hesitancy or fear, it can be a source of supreme confidence. If God guides I can never be lost—not even if I am in a land I know not of. If all I do is as he directs, then there is no moment and no situation in which he cannot work for the furtherance of his redeeming purpose.

One holiday weekend some years ago one of our Australian bands was travelling by coach to a country engagement when a mechanical breakdown brought them to a halt near a bridge over a dried-up creek. No band wants to be late for any fixture, and while repairs were being effected, the men did a spot of hymn tune practice. Then from under the bridge crawled a hobo, looking very much the worse for wear. He had been sleeping rough overnight and the music awoke him. It transpired that he had been a salvationist—a bandmaster—himself, and it was not long before the drum became a mercy seat around which the men knelt to pray.

Is it not an exhilarating experience, one without parallel in any other field, to be working within an economy where even a mishap can be turned into a means of salvation?

Essentials of Christian Experience, p 60

6 June

To look to Abraham also means to look at what man can—and should—do.

'He went out not knowing whither he went' is one New Testament comment on Abraham's answer to God's call. That is to say, his was total obedience. . . .

It is sometimes said that if only we had this or that early-day warrior with us again, what victories would not be ours once more. To such an observation I listen with respect for I yield place to none in my admiration for our fathers—and mothers—in the faith, the latchet of whose shoes we are not worthy to unloose. And yet is there not a measure of unreality in that desire? Those giants of the past cannot return. . . .

I become uneasier still about this kind of talk if the inference is that without their return we cannot hope for a renewal of those blessings which were given in their day. . . . This is really to limit the Holy One of Israel.

And I am still more ill at ease, almost to the point of doubting the sincerity of the speaker, if his expressed wish becomes his excuse for retiring to the sidelines. The present is nowhere near as good as the past, so I pray thee have me excused. . . .

What he would have you do, do quickly.

Essentials of Christian Experience, pp 61, 62

7 June

Now why is it so necessary that creed and conduct should agree?

To begin with, the man in whose life deeds and words do not tally is self-deceived. In the parable of the two houses, he is the one who built his dwelling on sand. He thought it was safe enough and it looked as secure as his neighbour's home—until the storm undeceived him and his place caved in about his ears.

Now this kind of self-deception which fondly imagines that the difference between words and deeds is of small consequence is to be found in all walks of life.

For example, there is the man who can be heard voicing his views any summer's day at Old Trafford, . . . telling the world what should or should not be done by the batsman at the wicket. . . . 'If I'd been aht i't middle, I'ahd 'ave late cut that spinner for fower!' . . . His second cousin is to be found in the front row of the gallery of many an Army hall when a musical festival is in progress. . . . 'Now if I'd been taking that cadenza. . . .' And it may well be that he thinks he could have done something wonderful with it.

But ask the one to bat or the other to play. . . . Their boasting recoils on their own head. . . . 'Shooting a line' . . . is a tragedy which discredits the doer and breeds cynicism in the hearer. . . .

The Kingdom of God, pp 37, 38

8 June

. . . The man whose words and deeds do not agree hurts the cause he intends—or pretends—to serve.

For example, an election address may contain promises of a good time to be had by all, but the longer those high-sounding declarations remain unfulfilled, the greater the discredit on the party making them. Those fulsome sentences do them more harm than good. . . .

Even a bad man will prefer consistency in conduct—and how right he is. That was why the behaviour of Ananias and Sapphira was so blameworthy and was dealt with so drastically. It was the first recorded instance of in-consistency in the Early Church. Those two people pretended to give all they had to the work of God, while keeping back some for themselves. To want the security which a nest egg is supposed to provide was not in itself wrong, though it compared unfavourably with the generosity of those who had given all they had. But the sin of this married couple lay in the fact that words and deeds did not match. And if such inconsistency had been allowed to pass unchecked, who knows where the rot would have ended?

Finally, the man whose deeds do not agree with his words betrays the Kingdom from within. . . .

The Kingdom of God, pp 38, 39

The Christian faith has never been permanently set back by outward opposition. It is an anvil which has worn out a good many hammers. Be assured that, despite all you read in scare columns or hear in wild conversations, no 'ism that ever was, or is, or shall be, can destroy the Christian religion. But that faith has been betrayed time and time again by those who claim to be its friends. Whenever the gates have been opened to the enemy, they have been opened from within.

A known disciple of Jesus led the Master's enemies to the place where they could arrest him. Neither the world nor the devil can harm the Kingdom, but we can. That is one of the frightening privileges of friendship with Jesus. We are put in the place where we can sell out on him. It is those who have 'tasted the good word of God' and 'fall away' who 'crucify the Son of God afresh, and put him to open shame.'

How can we watch that we do not fail Jesus in a peculiarly distressing way?

The answer is that if we love Jesus enough we will keep his commandments. But if we do not, we will not. The truth is as simple as that—and as uncompromising. . . .

The Kingdom of God, pp 39, 40

. . . If we do not love him we cannot keep his commandments, for only love will prompt us to do so. Love is the source of obedience. Love and obedience are two parts of the one relationship between a man and his Saviour, but there is no doubt which comes first. To try to obey Jesus without first loving him is to have an engine without steam, a car without petrol. Love comes first, for it is when we care for Jesus sufficiently that we will obey him whatever the cost. It is 'love unquestioning' that follows, dares, triumphs.

. . . Love Jesus enough—and you will obey him. . . . To love Jesus is simply to belong to him—and to go on doing what you know he wants you to do whether you find the prospect thrilling or not.

Doing his will consistently like this will keep you continually in his presence and, continually in his presence, his love will fill your life. In return you will come to serve him not because you must, but because you want to. Loving him, you will keep his commandments and, keeping his commandments, you will abide more securely in his love.

The Kingdom of God, pp 40, 41

11 June

Of all the visits which Jesus paid to the Temple at Jerusalem, none make more striking contrast than the first and the last—the one dating from the time when he was a boy of twelve, the other when he was a man fully matured.

'Beautiful for situation, the joy of the whole earth is Mount Zion' was a line from the Jewish hymn book which Jesus knew well. . . . In point of size the Temple could not but impress any lad seeing it for the first time. In ground area the building was larger than either St Paul's or Westminster Abbey. . . . The western approach to the Temple was by a bridge over the Cheesemaker's valley which, at its highest point, was 225 feet above the ground. Our imagination may be helped by recalling that the Clifton Suspension Bridge . . . is but 20 feet higher. So far as design and size were concerned, the Temple was built on the grand scale.

. . . Marble shone and gold glittered wherever the eye cared to wander. Eight gates rich in primary colours and overlaid with precious stones gave access to the ground. The ninth, made of Corinthian brass, we know as the Gate Beautiful.

Most moving sight of all was the dense cloud of smoke rising in the still morning air, sign that once again the daily sacrifice had been offered according to the prescribed ritual. . . . The burnt offering consumed, the visitor was free to listen to the instruction given in the surrounding courts by Jewish rabbis to their pupils. . . . We know how Jesus joined in this . . . so wholeheartedly that time was forgotten, and not until three days had passed did his sorrowing mother find him. . . .

The Officer, October 1946

12 June

Twenty years passed, and Jesus stood for the last time in the Temple. On this occasion his feelings were those not of delight but of disgust. . . . Seeing the trafficking which was going on in the Court of the Gentiles, he cried (quoting from two of the prophets): 'It is written, my house is the house of prayer: but ye have made it a den of thieves.'

This was no flourish of words, no extravagant epigram. . . . He was speaking sober truth as his hearers knew—the guilty parties most of all, for, by this time, the Temple had become not only a place of worship but a storehouse, a bank and a market. . . . In his sight mammon, not his Father, was being worshipped in the holy place.

Of course, this trafficking had gone on for years—indeed, for so long that the ordinary Jew had grown accustomed to it, cynically resigning himself to what was beyond his power to alter. Though there is no mention of these malpractices in Luke 2, they were certainly in existence when Jesus came to the Temple for the first time. But what the boy saw was not what the man saw. There must have been with Jesus a steadily growing disillusionment with the organised religion of his day, until at last he denounced that which had been his delight.

Most of us, like Jesus himself, were brought up under religious influences. . . . My brother and I grew up in the faith that ours was a glorious movement not having spot or wrinkle. . . . Should we be missing of an evening, there was but one place to look—in the Father's house. . . .

And now how has the pendulum swung? . . .

The Officer, October 1946

13 June

And now how has the pendulum swung? If in youth we saw nothing but the virtues of our movement, in age we tend to fix our eyes on its imperfections. No good purpose would here be served by itemising them; they are such as are common to most forms of community life. This does not mean that we should turn a blind eye to them. Indeed, the more we love the Army, the more will they be our concern. But in an attempt to steer a true course between a cynical indifference and a zeal which ignorantly wrecks rather than reforms, I look to the example of Jesus in this particular situation.

Two actions of his stand out—one spectacular, the other quieter; one the work of minutes, the other the labour of a lifetime; one capable of accomplishment maybe by a lesser man in a burst of anger, the other possible only to him in whose heart burns the charity of God.

First of all, Jesus expelled from the holy place those who were trading in the name of religion. But the record adds a second thing: 'And he taught daily in the Temple . . . for all the people were very attentive to hear him.' That is to say, he stood amid the moral wreckage of what had been, prior to his coming, God's best thing, and went on proclaiming the gospel. . . .

Whatever happens, the bush must burn and remain unconsumed. It shall not profit us, either as a movement or as individuals, if we gain all technical competence in our various . . . duties, and yet lose that first love for whose dear sake we left father and mother and brethren. . . .

He who is one with Christ in the sacrificial task of taking away the sin of the world shall see of the travail of his soul and be satisfied.

The Officer, October 1946

14 June

After Jesus had defeated the tempter in the wilderness

129

he returned to Nazareth, and then occurs in the gospel of Luke this significant statement: 'He went into the synagogue *as his custom was.*'

. . . The synagogue at Nazareth had been his spiritual home as a boy. Here he had heard the praises of God and listened to the record of his dealings with his people. As a young man Jesus may have frequently read one or other of the appointed Scripture portions. Here he had joined in the prayers hallowed by centuries of usage, and would have listened week by week to an address given by the synagogue president or some visiting rabbi. . . . So with Jesus the habit of public worship was formed as a boy and he did not neglect it when he became a man.

We salvationists must learn to treat the public worship of God with equal care. . . . In our meetings God's presence is invoked, his word preached, his forgiveness offered, his grace received as freely and fully as where the air is charged with incense. . . . All that we need for the nurture of our souls is to be found in our meetings.

Now, if we take this high attitude toward our Army meetings, we must respect them accordingly. . . .

Jesus and our Need, pp 71-73

15 June

If our public worship of God is one of the major ways in which he strengthens us to do his will, then we must not neglect it. If we are bandsmen, we will not go to the hall only when the band is on duty, staying away when it is not. It is always our duty to seek God and his grace. Nor will we be more keen to go to the hall when a 'special' is present than when there is not. There would be few special visitors to a hill country village like Nazareth. But Jesus went *as his custom was.*

Sunday morning should not be the time when we catch up on all the odd jobs left over from the week. . . . We all have time to do what we want to do. The sportsman always has time to cheer on the local team on a Saturday afternoon. . . . The film fan always has time to see the latest MGM. . . . If we want to join in the worship of God we will find time to do so. . . .

. . . If Jesus thought it right and helpful regularly to attend the house of God, so should we. None of us would claim to know better than he did.

Jesus and our Need, pp 73, 74

16 June

Children in the market place in the days of Jesus played at weddings and funerals, and the Master had the right word for both occasions.

We can never be thankful enough that he could comfort in sorrow. He fought death for the sake of others even before he vanquished the last enemy himself. To Jairus he restored his daughter; to the widow of Nain her only son; to Martha and Mary their brother. But do not think that only in sorrow can Jesus be of help. If he was ready to weep with those who wept, he could also rejoice with those who rejoiced. . . .

Two out of every three weddings in Britain are still celebrated in a place of worship. . . . And in the local paper the paragraph looks good which reads, 'The bride, who was given away by her father, wore . . . and the hymns, the bride's own choice, included. . . . The bride also wore . . . a gift from the bridegroom's mother, and additional interest lay in the fact that the bride's parents were themselves married in the same church a quarter of a century ago.'

But there's much more than a paragraph for a hard-pressed reporter in marriage as a religious ceremony. . . .

Jesus and our Need, pp 54, 55

17 June

First of all, Jesus made it plain that marriage is God's intention for men and women. . . . While it is true that the Jew of the first century regarded all life as coming under the rule of God and so no act was ever merely secular, in the Gentile world of that age marriage was largely a civil arrangement. Lifelong faithfulness to one partner was the exception rather than the rule. . . . In the second place, Jesus made marriage a lifelong institution. 'Man must never separate what God has joined together' (Mark 10:9, *J. B. Phillips*). . . . Whatever the civil law may allow when a marriage has broken down, there is no doubt that Jesus taught that it ought to last 'till death us do part'.

The third thing that Jesus did was to make men and women equal in this happy partnership. Said he of God's creative purpose, 'Male and female made he them.' [This] means an equality of status before God and the world, and that we owe to Jesus.

These three privileges are safeguarded in Christian marriage . . . one where Christian grace is sought that the Christian purpose of marriage may be fulfilled.

Jesus and our Need, pp 55, 56

18 June

Discussion about the nature of marriage is no new thing. In the first century, as in the twentieth, the character of marriage was frequently a matter of public debate. And in the first century, as in the twentieth, there was no unanimous opinion as to whether there were justifiable grounds—and, if so, what these were—for the termination of marriage. It was in this setting that Jesus proclaimed marriage as a lifelong union. The context shows that to a direct question he gave a direct answer.

As a Christian community we are concerned to practise and to maintain the sacrament of Christian marriage. This does not mean that we regard as less worthy, or any less binding, the vows which may be taken by any two contracting parties before a civil registrar. We also realise that practising Christians are somewhat of a minority and this means we cannot impose our views, however dearly we hold them, upon society if a majority of that society refuses to live by them.

Nevertheless, we are entitled to testify to our convictions. Indeed, we are in duty bound to do so. . . . Within the fellowship of practising Christians it is our concern to see that we follow our Lord in all our relationships. Nowhere is this more essential than in that personal and intimate relationship known as marriage. . . .

Essentials of Christian Experience, pp 21, 22

19 June

. . . What lad takes his girl to the altar but on the assumption—unspoken at times but nevertheless deeply cherished—that this is for good and always? And what girl goes to the altar but in the assurance that this is for keeps?

. . . This is where the majority of our young folk begin. . . . To those young folk . . . the Christian Church says: How right you are. We are with you. This is the Christian way—and we want to help you to keep it.

How can this ideal be maintained?

Here Christian grace comes to the help of Christian teaching. Oneness in mutual affection can be undergirded by oneness of dedication to God.

We who are salvationists are at some advantage here. . . . Our religion is not a one service on a Sunday affair. Our faith enters into every relationship of life. It enables us to make a discriminating use of our leisure. It guides our conduct in business. It sets the foundations of our home life. And our faith cannot be kept out of our wedding— one of the most crucial moments in any life. If our religion means anything to us at all, it must have some bearing upon our attitude to marriage. If it can be ignored here, it can be ignored anywhere. If it is dismissed as irrelevant here, it is irrelevant everywhere. But for us our devotion to one another is expressed within the context of our dedication to God.

Essentials of Christian Experience, pp 22, 23

. . . Unity of devotion, expressed in a unity of dedication, is sustained by a unity of supplication. Two people live together. They serve God and man together. They pray together.

Those who have read *Triumph of Faith* will know that the late Bandmaster George Marshall and his wife, Jenny, had made a habit of praying together once a day ever since their wedding and, as an extra, George would repeat Psalm 23. In the early hours of a January morning, shortly before his promotion to Glory, the bandmaster woke up under the impression that they had forgotten to pray as was their custom before retiring.

'Of course we prayed,' said Jenny. George Marshall was not entirely convinced. 'Let's go through the twenty-third psalm again,' he replied. So this devoted husband and wife repeated: 'The Lord is my shepherd. . . . Yea, though I walk through the valley of the shadow of death, I will fear no evil: for thou art with me. . . .'

To pray together is to be shielded from evil, not only from the perils which beset the body but also from the dangers which assail the soul.

Like all other Christian relationships, Christian marriage calls for Christian grace. We cannot obey the commands of Jesus without the help of Jesus. But that help, when sought, is never denied. Nor will it be refused to any who seek the happiness of the home of which Christ is the Head.

Essentials of Christian Experience, pp 24, 25

21 June

. . . Jesus never denied the honest questioner the proof for which he was asking. When the Pharisees demanded 'a sign' they were given none because they did not really want to be convinced of the truth of the Master's claims. 'A sign', if provided, would only have turned them into reluctant disciples at the best. . . .

Do not think your heart evil or your experience feeble

beyond the rest of your comrades if, like Thomas, you long for certainty before committing yourself. In all probability there are already several specific truths which you fully accept. Then act on those. . . .

Never allow what you don't know to disturb what you do know. There is a time in life when we imperiously demand to know all the answers. We call upon the universe to stand and deliver up all its mysteries. Later on we begin to realise that if we knew all the answers we should be as God! Thereafter we speak more softly.

Remember, too, that life will not stand still while you spend time amassing voluminous evidence upon the basis of which you intend to make up your mind for or against the Christian faith. In any given situation I have to do the best according to the knowledge I may at that moment possess. If I do not come to a decision of my own, life will decide for me. . . .

Jesus and our Need, pp 60, 61

22 June

Life requires that we shall act according to the best we know at the moment when action is demanded. The lad who deferred asking his girl to marry him until he knew all about her would never ask her at all. And the girl who determined never to accept any suitor until she knew him equally thoroughly would go to her grave a spinster. Hamlet's trouble, you recall, was that he could not make up his mind. 'The native hue of resolution' was 'sicklied o'er with the pale cast of thought'.

No man on earth but sees through a glass darkly. This goes for the wisest and the saintliest alike. Now 'we know in part, and we prophesy in part'. But the believer is most often given light enough to see by. The distant scene may be hidden but the next step is always clear.

. . . Jesus would not have us rock our minds to sleep. He himself was a great lover of questions. He was asked questions and often answered them by asking others. He was out to make people think. Look how question marks pepper his conversation. 'How think ye?' 'Whom say ye?'

135

'What shall it profit?' 'What shall a man give?' 'Are ye so
without understanding?' 'How much more?'

Questionings are not wrong so long as you ask them in
his company. And if the answer seems long in coming,
don't make the outsize blunder of leaving his side. Keep
close to him whatever happens. Better walk in the dark
with him than travel alone by sight.

Jesus and our Need, pp 61, 62

23 June

Augustine's well-known saying, 'Either God cannot
prevent evil or he will not; if he cannot, he is not all-
powerful, if he will not, he is not all-good' . . . sounds like
one of those unanswerable posers which silences argument
for all time. In reality it overlooks the simple truth that
God is not the author of evil. One who is wholly good
cannot be the source of anything but good. What God has
done either in creation or redemption cannot be other than
good. At the sight of the beauty of creation the morning
stars sang together (says one of the inspired poems in the
Bible) and all the sons of God shouted for joy. That good
work man has marred. Much of the suffering which causes
us such heartbreak is the result of human sinfulness, past
and present. We may ask why God ever allowed man to
sin; the answer is because he desired him to be free.

This perilous gift of freedom was needed if man was to
become fully man. Man rises to the stature of manhood
only as he possesses and exercises the power of choice.
Without this, man would be reduced to an automaton or,
at best, to a superior kind of animal. He would certainly
not be man capable of loving, agonising, failing,
triumphing. Without personal freedom, man could know
neither tears nor laughter. A robot cannot fall in love.
Would you prefer to be a robot?

This freedom of choice, which must leave a man open to
choose the wrong if he so wishes, is one—though not the
only—source of human suffering. . . . The prodigal son
had only himself to blame for his empty belly. . . .

Jesus and our Need, pp 63, 64

24 June

But our difficulties arise not so much over suffering in general as that suffering which is undeserved. When a bad man comes to a sticky end we feel that a kind of rough justice has been done. For example, we shed no tears over the closing years of Herod the Great. A ruler who had three of his own sons executed and, on his death bed, tried to arrange for a wholesale massacre of Jewish leaders in the hippodrome at Jericho so that his own funeral might be a time of genuine sorrow, seems to deserve all that came to him—and more. . . . But we are sick at heart over the Massacre of the Innocents which he ordered. We join Rachel in weeping for her children. These young babies had done nothing amiss. It is the undeserved suffering of the innocent which seems to challenge the goodness of God.

This problem is as old as time. The book of Job is one long tortured wrestling with this very point. Job, who was blameless in character, suffered the loss of family, wealth and health in successive strokes. His wife could only tell him to curse God and die. His friends brought him the cold comfort of their involved arguments, all of which were intended to prove that Job must have sinned else he would not have suffered. This the old chieftain would not have. He protested his innocence. At the last day, he declared, he would be vindicated. His friends went on arguing but they had no satisfying answer.

Indeed, the Old Testament has no wholly satisfying answer to the undeserved suffering of the innocent—except that one prophet speaks of a particular Man who will accept such suffering in a way that will be used for the salvation of many. . . .

Jesus and our Need, pp 64, 65

25 June

. . . The Old Testament has no wholly satisfying answer to the undeserved suffering of the innocent—except that one prophet speaks of a particular Man who will accept such suffering in a way that will be used for the salvation of many. But that was the only light which shone through the gloom—and men turned away even from that.

So that when Jesus came he was rejected of his people because God allowed him to suffer. If he was the Christ, so they said, he would have come down from the Cross. To them suffering was a sign of divine disapproval. God's curse must be on a man who had to endure a cross. Of all people he who hung thereon could not be the Messiah. He cannot have been God's Anointed else why was he suffering there? Yet, far from rejecting Jesus, we now see that God was with him in his suffering. That was the inspired comment of Paul on the mystery of the Cross. God was there, at the very heart of this sinful deed, in Christ reconciling the world to himself.

. . . The Christian faith does not give us a cut-and-dried explanation of the origin of human suffering but offers us something much more relevant to our need. . . . Grace given to bear what comes our way to the glory of God can be an aid to Christian character. . . . A cross, willingly accepted, can become a means of grace to ourselves and to others, just as the Cross, willingly accepted, has become the means of that divine help which we call salvation. . . . This is one more way in which we can join in his redemptive work for the salvation of the world.

Jesus and our Need, pp 65, 66

26 June

Sometimes a person will betray himself by an 'idle' word which is an indecent word—or as near indecent as he can make it. In public he is on guard; at ease among his intimates, out it comes. . . . 'Let there be no foul language', wrote Paul to the Ephesians (4:29, *J. B. Phillips*). Give the man short shrift who, in your hearing, tries to be funny at the expense of decency. . . .

The warning of Jesus about the 'idle' word does not mean that we are to be dumb, hardly daring to open our mouths lest we say the wrong thing. What is needed is a mind so stored with things lovely and of good report that our speech will carry the same appetising savour. Goodness is not the enemy of wit. To think so is to fall for the idea, carefully fostered by the world, that only evil can be interesting. That is just not true. 'I had heard', said Mme de Stael when she came to England, 'that Mr Wilberforce was a religious man, but I did not know he was one of the wittiest.'

Jesus and our Need, pp 43, 44

27 June

The Greek adjective translated 'idle' (Matthew 12:36) used to mean 'unemployed' in the sense that the thing so described was without purpose. It was idle. The 'idle' word is the purposeless word which escapes me when I am off guard. Such a single word can give me away more thoroughly than any set speech. The 'idle' word discloses what I really am. When certain others are listening I may watch what I am saying, but what when I am at ease? The 'idle' word reveals my true character and by my character I shall be judged.

This is one reason why we salvationists should be accurate in our speech. Of one politician it was rather unkindly said that his most brilliant orations were composed of half a fact and a couple of rumours. . . . Clever maybe, but meet for a salvationist? Is not the more excellent way to let your yea be yea and nay be nay? . . .

Of certain dedicated people in the New Testament it is said that 'they spake as the Spirit gave them utterance'. . . . The Holy Spirit gave them both thoughts and words; ideas and the means whereby to express them. And he still does that in personal witness and in public testimony for those who seek his aid.

Jesus and our Need, pp 43, 45

28 June

Centuries ago a prophet in exile spoke of [God] as so infinitely great that all nations were as dust in the balance before him. Yet in the same breath the prophet added that no man should suppose that because of this his way was hid from the Lord. The everlasting God had his steadfast eye on the faint and the weary and all who called upon him would renew their strength. This truth still holds good.

Remember that two words, often on our lips, are not to be found in the New Testament. They are 'fate' and 'luck'. Jesus never used them. They are heathen words anyway. 'Fate' was originally the spoken word of Jupiter, father of the gods, and was deemed unalterable. . . . And as for 'luck', scholars are not sure themselves where that word came from. . . . Some have suggested that it was a gambling term which crossed the Channel from the Low Countries. At any rate it never was, nor is, a Christian word. Neither fate nor luck have any place in the economy of grace.

. . . Jesus never said that the sparrow does not fall. What he said was that no sparrow fell to the ground without God knowing about it. . . . In Jesus God entered once for all into human life. He took upon himself the seed of Abraham. He knows our frame. It is for us to trust this truth and to obey his will. 'To those who love God', as Paul said, 'everything that happens fits into a pattern for good.'

Jesus and our Need, pp 38-40

29 June

We salvationists should generously appreciate the work of all other followers of Jesus Christ. This does not require us to undervalue our own movement nor to suppose that we lack any of the necessary means of grace. On the other hand, we need not be in the least perturbed should any, concerned with the ecclesiastical letter which killeth rather than the Spirit which giveth life, question whether we belong to the true Vine. The answer to that is to show that we belong to the Vine by bearing the fruits thereof. Such evidence puts the matter beyond dispute. But if we appeal to the work of the Holy Spirit as proof that we are part of the Body of Christ, we must not hesitate to acknowledge his presence and work elsewhere. . . .

We salvationists are accustomed to hearing our work commended. We have almost come to expect this as a prescriptive right. Let us not be slow generously to acclaim all good work everywhere and, as we appreciate the Christian service of others, learn how better to do our own.

Let us also be generous with one another. We must give the lie to the cynicism that one potter cannot bear to hear praised another potter's pots. . . . The children of light must not show themselves more small-minded than the children of the world.

The Call to Holiness, pp 87, 88

30 June

. . . The Founder would undoubtedly have agreed with the sentence which was a favourite quote of Mr [Aneurin] Bevan: 'A society which limits its idea of civilisation to the accumulation of material abundance, and of justice to their equitable distribution among its members, will never make of its cities anything that differs in essence from a group of ant-hills.' This is but to say in many words what our Lord said in a few: 'A man's life consisteth not in the abundance of the things which he possesseth.'

The obligation to turn men from this darkness to the light rests not upon them but on us. Error will not correct itself. Lost sheep do not return to the fold of their own accord. The lost coin could not find itself. . . .

I recall now travelling along a dirt road in the outback of New South Wales and overtaking a solitary sheep whose fleece was thickly coated with brown dust and knotted with thorns. The creature was plainly lost, but with its head down it was trotting on uphill in a most determined way, but every step a step in the wrong direction. Sheep, coins and men cannot find themselves. They have to be found. And upon us who have accepted

Jesus as Saviour and Lord there rests the perpetual obligation to share his redeeming ministry. To this task he still calls us.

Essentials of Christian Experience, pp 38, 39

1 July

. . . No one present would subscribe to Henry Ford's alleged dictum that 'history is bunk'. To be fair to him, he did explain that history was bunk 'only to me. I did not need it very badly,' he added. But we need it. Indeed we cannot do without it, because without a sense of history our movement would become both rootless and direction-less. We would be ignorant both of our past origins and our future destiny. . . .

That our past is mainly seen through a glass darkly is not the fault of the younger generation—save where they themselves have deliberately turned their back upon avail-able knowledge. If fault there be, the older generation is blameworthy if our history has not been writ in large letters so that, in the language of *The Living Bible,* 'anyone can read it at a glance' (Habakkuk 2:2). . . .

. . . The better our story is known the more will it be clear that our fathers in the faith were possessed solely of a single-eyed desire to draw men closer to God and—as a direct consequence thereof—closer to one another. The two great commands of Jesus cannot be separated. Nor will they ever be superseded.

From a paper read at the fifth annual conference of the Territorial Historical Commission in New York in September 1978.

In Good Company, pp 70, 72, 75

2 July

The date was 2 July 1965. Salvationists from every continent and speaking many tongues thronged [West-minster] Abbey, overflowing into the cloisters and filling the neighbouring parish church of St Margaret's. The flag of The Salvation Army—seen at countless nondescript street corners—had been borne from the west door to the steps of the Sanctuary where it was received by the Sacrist and set up against a background of crimson and gold. The climax of the gathering was the unveiling of a bust of William Booth in the chapel of St George and then, as the congregation dispersed, the joyous music of the Abbey bells could be heard above the sound of London's weekday traffic as the flag with the star in the centre flew from the Abbey tower.

One hundred years earlier, on the same date, William Booth held the first of nine Sunday evening meetings in an ancient tent lit by naphtha flares and pitched on a disused Quaker burial ground between Vallance Road and Fulbourne Street, E1. Such was the zeal of the missioner and his few helpers that, of the motley company gathered on the hard, backless benches, some professed conversion. But the days of the tent were already numbered. New patches on the old canvas had only made the existing rents worse. So after the last Sunday in August the unusable remnants thereof were removed to an undisclosed destination at an overall cost of ten shillings.

How come that a work with so hazardous a beginning in Whitechapel was so honoured a century later in Westminster?

No Discharge in this War, pp 9, 10

3 July

In the spring of 1865 Mrs Booth was invited to conduct a mission at Rotherhithe, and her success confirmed her husband and herself in the conviction that London, and not the provinces, should be the centre of their activities. William found a house for his wife and family at 31 Shaftesbury (now Ravenscourt) Road, Hammersmith—then separated from Knightsbridge by open fields and cattle grazing under the elms.

One June evening in that same year a gospel meeting was about to conclude outside the Blind Beggar—a public house which still stands on the north side of Whitechapel

Road and a few yards west of the present Cambridge Heath Road. Some of the participants belonged to the Christian Community—an association first formed in the seventeenth century by Huguenot refugees. Others were attached to the East London Special Services Committee—an undenominational group formed to lighten the darkness of that area. The leader of the open-air meeting inquired whether there was anyone else who would like to speak. William Booth, who was passing by and had stopped to listen, did not need a second invitation.

Within a matter of days John Stabb and Samuel Chase, two members of the Special Services Committee, called on him to ask if he would accept temporary oversight of the mission whose principal 'building' was the decrepit tent pitched on the disused Quaker burial ground. The missioner who had been engaged had fallen ill.

Temporary? William Booth, as he was to tell Catherine, had found his destiny!

No Discharge in this War, pp 16, 17

4 July

Early in May the annual printed report of The Christian Mission was being prepared. . . . The heading at the top of the page ran: 'The Christian Mission under the superintendence of the Rev William Booth is a volunteer army. . . .

. . . William's pen hovered over the word 'volunteer'. He was not overfond of it, for the Volunteers—a part-time citizen army constituted in the reign of George III— had long been a stock music hall joke. So 'volunteer' was crossed out and above it was written 'salvation'. The change from the indefinite to the definite article completed the new name which appeared for the first time in the text of the editorial page of *The Christian Mission Magazine* for September 1878.

. . . Now by eastern as well as western windows, by northern as well as southern, the land looked bright. The year had seen an increase of 21 stations, of 57 evangelists and of over 1,300 members. Still a Gideon's army, maybe.

144

A total of 50 stations, 85 evangelists and 4,400 members was not a multitude—but it was an army on the march.

One commentator was to describe the alteration in name as fortuitous. If it was, William Booth altered better than he knew. The Christian Mission was now in deed and truth an Army of Salvation. No word is more biblical than salvation, and no army richer in resources than a detachment of the army of the living God.

No Discharge in this War, pp 34, 35

5 July

The country had to admit, almost against its will, that a new and effective army had appeared, seemingly out of nowhere, to fight the battles of the Lord. The scoffers might scoff—the *Punch* of that day among them—but more serious people looked for a serious explanation. *The Contemporary Review* for August 1882 invited a rising star in the Anglican Firmament, Randall Davidson, then resident chaplain at Lambeth, to say what these things meant. His explanation was fourfold—(1) that nothing succeeds like success; (2) that this new movement put its converts to work without delay; (3) that the personal testimony of those converts was an effective method of evangelism; and (4) that preaching and teaching were given in the language of the people.

Randall Davidson was right with his last three observations; the first overlooks those years when The Christian Mission was fighting for its very life. At the same time, none of these factors, taken either singly or together, any more account for the growth of The Salvation Army than a study of the economic, political and religious state of the first-century Mediterranean world accounts for the growth of the Early Church. The only adequate explanation of the rise of Quakerism in the 17th century, and of Methodism in the 18th, is that there is no merely rational explanation. Of each it may be said: 'This is the Lord's doing, it is marvellous in our eyes.'

God was again at work in the 19th century. . . .

No Discharge in this War, pp 36, 37

6 July

Into this unrelieved drabness came an Army whose flag was woven of primary colours—yellow, red and blue, and surmounted by the sacred symbol of their faith. . . . This was the good fight of faith which injured none but could bring happiness to all.

The flower girl in *Pygmalion* behaved like a lady when she was treated like a lady. The converted though still semi-literate labourer, slowly spelling out in his recently acquired copy of the New Testament: 'Unto him that loved us . . . and hath made us kings and priests unto God . . .' felt himself lifted to a station and clothed with a dignity he had never known before. A king and priest! Then he would behave like such, even though he still lived in a slum. The theological content of the phrase was doubtless not fully understood by him. But he sensed its practical implications. He was no longer a dogsbody—to be pushed around. He was dear to God. That fact was enough to set a man firmly on his feet. Nor was this truth to be dismissed as another variation of pie in the sky. A man's common sense told him that a faith which could not come to terms with the reality of death as well as life was not worthy of the name. This new calling invested his present life with a sense of worthwhileness. This was no postponed dividend, payable only when the mortal should have put on immortality. 'Present pay I now receive' sang the convert—and in these new riches he could invite others to share.

No Discharge in this War, pp 37, 38

7 July

Bands of varying sizes and degrees of musical skill began to make themselves heard. They were not always welcome. 'Are you one of those who yesterday were turning Hull into hell?' asked an irate resident of Captain Edward Higgins, later to be the Army's third General. The question was possibly justified for not all these musical pioneers possessed a zeal which was according to know-ledge. . . .

The outcry which arose concerning the setting of religious words to secular tunes . . . and the horrified charge of blasphemy raised by some undoubtedly sincere people, overlooked the fact that in the Arian controversy in the fourth century rival theological views were discussed over shop counters and set to the popular tunes of the day. Luther unblushingly advocated the use of 'the common songs of our own people for use in our churches'. Even Paul Gerhardt's moving words, 'O sacred head, sore wounded' have been forever wedded to what was originally a sixteenth century love song. . . . And today an accepted hymnal like *Songs of Praise* discreetly hides the secular tune behind some such innocuous description as 'Gaelic air', 'English traditional melody' or 'From a Dresden song book'.

In this matter William Booth may now feel himself vindicated as one born out of due time. What is called 'the people's musical vernacular' is now cautiously welcomed rather than wholly condemned. Even the twenty-fifth anniversary service of the World Council of Churches held in St Peter's Cathedral, Geneva, included a psalm setting in contemporary idiom—guitars, drums and all! Shades of the once maligned Joystrings!

No Discharge in this War, pp 42, 43

8 July

. . . It is not unfair to say that all churchmen were not longing to see red guernseys in the pews and—was it even thinkable?—the sound of tambourines to the music of the organ. Both parties had to wait till 1965 for that. Some personal qualms now raise a wry smile; others were much more serious.

For example, when R. W. Church was Dean of St Paul's, Bramwell Booth approached him on the possibility of arranging a service in the cathedral for salvationists. No Army personality would take part. Sufficient for them to be in the congregation, but perhaps the service could be conducted by Lightfoot who, in his diocesan charge of 14 December 1882, had commended the literature of The Salvation Army to the attention of his clergy, and maybe the sermon could be preached by Liddon who had already attended two or three Army gatherings. Dean Church was cordial—but uncertain. Were not salvationists mostly working people? Bramwell Booth agreed. And would not most of them be wearing hobnailed boots? Again Bramwell Booth agreed that some, perhaps many, might be so doing. In that case the Dean felt that as St Paul's had recently been repaved at no small expense, he could not risk any scratches to the marble. . . .

No Discharge in this War, p 99

9 July

If not the most important, at least one of the more picturesque of [Evangeline Booth's] activities was her visit to the Klondyke in 1898. Gold had been discovered and in Skagway—a boom town where public order was not always maintained—a group of salvationists held an open-air meeting on the corner between the Pack Train saloon and Soapy Sam's Place. Soapy Sam—he answered to the unromantic surname of Smith—had been chased out of Denver, but now he and his gang, all of whom were quick on the draw, had been establishing themselves in their new home town. But Soapy had been listening to Evangeline, then little more than 30 years of age. All the same, salvationists could not conceal their alarm when they saw Soapy and a small bodyguard approaching.

'Leave him to me,' said Evangeline. Supper was over, she told Soapy, but they could talk over a cup of cocoa. Believe it or not, cocoa it was! Soapy explained that if he surrendered to the authorities it would mean death for him, whereat he was told of a salvation which meant victory alike in life and in death. Then there was prayer together—but not long after Skagway wearied of Soapy. In the shooting which followed he was badly wounded and, though a surgeon worked on him in the hope that he might live to be hanged, Soapy cheated the gallows.

Like father, like daughter, like William, his cherished Evangeline believed in salvation for all.

No Discharge in this War, pp 56, 57

10 July

. . . As with the roll in the eleventh chapter of the Epistle to the Hebrews of those who lived by faith, time would fail to tell of them all. . . . There was Herman Martinsson who was accepted for officership at fifty years of age after having been an actor for a quarter of a century, both playing and writing his own plays. It was a piquant situation when he was announced to conduct Salvation Army meetings in a town where one of his plays had been billed the week previously. . . .

. . . Vilhelm Andreas Wille, when in his forties left his well-established medical practice in Køge for Semarang in Java where, with his wife and four children between five and eleven years of age, he lived on the frugal salary of a Salvation Army missionary doctor until his retirement in 1931. He opened the William Booth Memorial Eye Hospital in June 1915 and for his services was appointed by Queen Wilhelmina as Officer of the Order of Oranje-Nassau, by King Christian X a Knight of the Order of Dannebrog, and by General Bramwell Booth as one of the first admissions to the Order of the Founder. Such a life would, almost by itself, justify the word of Professor Cronfelt of Odense that 'in its youth the Army was "the ugly duckling", but it has become the beautiful white swan, the beating of whose wings can be heard over the whole world'.

No Discharge in this War, pp 63, 67

11 July

Take, for example, the scandal of home industries which led to the exploitation of unfortunate children by their equally unfortunate parents, driven to this extremity because of their own low wages of loss of employment.

Work would be brought from the factory to the home, completed there overnight, and returned to the factory in the morning. As an illustration, the finishing off of ladies' belts, made mostly of strong elastic to which buckle, clasp and slide had to be sewn, was paid at the rate of five farthings a dozen. A mother, or elder sister, after working a ten hour day, would bring home twelve dozen belts to be finished overnight. In this particular instance another family occupied each of the three other rooms in the house, and one child from each would be enlisted for the work. This would include an older girl who had already done a day's work, another somewhat younger who had been making matchboxes in her own home, another two—younger still—who between school hours had been looking after the smallest of the children, or else carrying to a nearby tailor pairs of trousers which her mother had been finishing off. Supervised by the oldest of the number, the group of five fell to work and by half-past ten had finished the gross of belts for which the payment was fifteen pence, or three pence per person. . . .

Paper bag making at home yielded the unbelievable return of three farthings per gross large brown bags, and three half-pence per thousand for small sweet bags. . . . One child would fold . . .; another would flick on the paste; a third would count and stack the finished bags. As likely as not a school inspector might call and find the children gainfully employed, but the fierce logic of the harassed mother was that if her children did not help her both she and they would starve. And if they starved, what use was schooling?

Bread for my Neighbour, pp 94-96

12 July

The plight of the unskilled female match workers was brought to the attention of the public by the successful strike led by Annie Besant in July 1888. William Booth made his own inquiries into their need and, encouraged by his experiment in setting up a mini-bookbinding factory to provide employment for young women taken in the Army's rescue homes in London . . ., resolved to establish a match factory where hygienic conditions and better wages would be the order of the day. . . . The factory rule was to be 'fair wages for fair work'—and this slogan appeared upon two of the earliest varieties of match boxes. Other labels read: 'Love thy neighbour as thyself'; 'Bear one another's burdens'; and 'Our work is for God and humanity'. These are now collectors' pieces. . . .

From her home in Staffordshire the Duchess of Sutherland let it be known that 'the earnest ladies of the district are banding themselves together to bring the *Darkest England* matches into common use. I am giving them a fair trial at Trentham, and am very satisfied with them up to now.'

Despite all this enterprise, however, there was a sense in which the match factory failed, for it was taken over by the British Match Company on 26 November 1901. But William Booth had never sought big dividends. What he had done was to accomplish his threefold objective and make an effective protest against sweating; raise the wages paid to the workers; and demonstrate that in the match industry human lives need not be placed at risk. . . .

Lamprell Street was not a big business success story but, what was more important, William Booth was able to provide another demonstration of the truth that the social consequences of industry could not be ignored.

Bread for my Neighbour, pp 110-114

13 July

A leader in *The Social Gazette* declared: 'A man has a right to demand that his country shall supply him with work or food; the General's proposal is that he shall be supplied with both.'

In this matter William Booth was not a pioneer. London had seen soup kitchens in operation in the 18th century. . . . At first this was solely a winter activity but, when the cold was severe and prolonged—as at the beginning of the reign of William IV—three shelters were opened providing for more than 6,000 people. There were also night refuges—known as strawyards—in Victorian times. Possibly the oldest and largest in London was in Cripplegate, but later moved to Banner Lane, where the dormitaries were heated by an outsize communal fire.

Yet even the worth of these was questioned. To have a place in which to sleep at night would encourage the idle and profligate to haunt the public house by day! Beside, were there not workhouses and casual wards for the homeless and starving? There were—but the principle of deterrence ruled with an iron rod in the kingdom of poor relief. . . . The workhouse was deliberately made 'wholesomely repulsive'. . . .

James Lewis, labourer, was charged with failing to break seven hundredweight of stone in return for food and shelter in the casual ward of the Stroud workhouse, and was sentenced to fourteen days' imprisonment with hard labour. . . . A female pauper who left the workhouse dinner table before the appointed time because her suet pudding was uneatable, was given fourteen days' hard labour for insubordination. . . .

Bread for my Neighbour, pp 115, 116, 85

14 July

Official figures reported 48 deaths from starvation in London in 1898; 39 in 1903; 42 even in 1910. . . .

James Theade, aged 62, journeyman bootmaker, who was found lying in the New Cut on 28 December 1898, at 1.50 am . . . told a constable that he had sought admission to the local casualty ward, but because he had fourpence in his pocket he was not allowed in. He then tried for shelter in a common lodging house, but it was full. He died in the Lambeth Infirmary at 6 am the same morning. The cause of death was given as acute congestion of the lungs, due to exposure and want.

At the inquest on James Greaves, carman, living at Vine Court, Whitechapel, his widow stated that he had been out of work for some time and they had little food in the house. The deceased became so ill that she obtained a parish order and took him to the infirmary. The Medical Officer deposed that death was due to influenza and pneumonia, aggravated by want of food.

A widow, Eliza Topping, died three-quarters of an hour after admission to the infirmary. The coroner's officer testified that she and her two sons lived in a top floor back room measuring 12 feet by eight, containing one broken chair, two old cans, and one two-foot nine-inch bed in which all three slept. Her body was in an advanced state of emaciation. There was no fat anywhere on what was virtually a skeleton, and the deceased could not have eaten for the previous four days.

Nor were these isolated instances.

Bread for my Neighbour, pp 39, 40

15 July

In the summer of 1905, 450 unemployed men tramped the 100 miles from Leicester to London to plead their cause before the Prime Minister. . . . Mr Ramsay Mac-Donald . . . asked the Army to feed the marchers while they were in the capital.

. . . Of wider coverage still was the assistance given to a group of unemployed men who determined to march the 180 miles between Manchester and London in the late winter. They carried with them what was described as a 'Petition to the King'. . . . The marchers had been warned in advance that they would have to take pot-luck with beds and meals, but at Hanley their leader made his way through the winter fog to the officer's quarters, only to find that he was leading a meeting in the Army hall. . . . The upshot was that the whole company enjoyed Salvation Army hospitality overnight and the officer, who had slept with them, provided them with a hot breakfast in the morning.

The next day's tramp brought the men to Stafford where . . . the two single women officers . . . offered the shelter of the Army hall overnight. At Birmingham the men again fell back upon the Army, but at Coventry arrangements had been made for their reception. At Northampton, however, the Chief Constable appealed to the corps officer. . . . Supper was ready in the Army hall . . . by the time they arrived, and a liberal covering of clean straw was spread over the floor of the young people's hall. 'The softest bed we've had for a week' was the general comment. Then some of the Northampton bandsmen turned up with bandages and ointment for blistered feet and weary limbs. Not quite the oil and wine of the Good Samaritan, but as near as made no difference.

Bread for my Neighbour, pp 123-125

16 July

The winter of 1905 was a sorry one for Britain. In London 8,000 starving men demonstrated their plight by marching from the City to the West End. Every night between two and three am 1,000 homeless men were given a hot supper at the Army's food kitchen in Wych Street. The last hope of a job for an unemployed man was at the dock gates around which hundreds would gather before dawn broke, and each weekday morning Salvation Army officers would distribute upwards of 600 breakfasts. Queen Alexandra inaugurated a National Fund for the unemployed with a personal gift of £2,000, her one stipulation being that £1,000 of this should be placed at the disposal of The Salvation Army. The Mayor of Northampton made a personal gift of £900 for the needy of his town, and the local Salvation Army officer was one of the two agents commissioned to undertake the distribution of this charity. Speaking that winter in Penzance, Lord Rosebery, the Liberal leader, said that if he were dictator he would take General Booth into his counsel, for he had the knowledge and the machinery to deal with the residual problem of the unemployed and the unemployable which seemed to be beyond the resources of the state. It is hardly credible that barely a dozen years had passed since William Booth had agreed to an independent inquiry into the financing of his social schemes in order to demonstrate to the sceptical that he had not been privately profiting from his public appeals.

No Discharge in this War, pp 137, 138

17 July

In the now vanished Imperial Russia the work was begun almost by holy subterfuge. . . . A calculated risk was taken in opening the first corps without any government approval, but on 20 December 1914 an enrolment of eight soldiers took place in Petrograd. . . .

Then came March 1917, and the Kerensky revolution. . . .

One day a group of soldiers surrounded one of their street meetings and . . . insisted one of the cadets should accompany them to their local headquarters. . . . Standing against the wall he cried out: 'Listen before you shoot. I am not afraid to die.' Baring his breast as he pulled up his Army guernsey he continued: 'I am saved and will go to Heaven. . . .' The execution was postponed, then suspended, and finally abandoned altogether. . . .

Hopes rose and fell according to the vagaries of government officials but then, due to an unguarded remark by a young woman salvationist, one officer after another, together with several local officers, were arrested. . . . There was one more false dawn in April 1922, when against all expectation an appeal to the government secured official sanction for the Army's work and for several further months public meetings were allowed. But as suddenly as the sky had cleared it darkened again. . . . The Salvation Army was finally proscribed. . . .

But the Founder's song 'O boundless salvation' is still to be heard in some evangelical churches in Russia. . . .

The History of The Salvation Army Volume 6, pp 42-46

18 July

Two major relief operations were undertaken by the Army at this time (1937). One was the care of 1,400

Basque children, part of 4,000 of school age who were brought to England at the time of the Spanish civil war. . . . Some of them had lost both their parents either in the actual fighting or in air raids which were destined to be a prelude to the saturation bombing of the Second World War. . . . The beat of an Army drum provoked some of the more nervous to near panic. It resembled too closely the sound of the shot which had killed a brother or wounded a father. . . .

In her autobiography *A Life for Education* Dame Leah Manning refers to what she calls 'the outstanding contribution' made by the Army to the care of these children. She writes:

> On the Saturday after the children arrived I went rather diffidently to ask if I might make arrangements for them to go to the nearby Catholic church to attend Mass on Sunday. The officer in charge smiled as he replied: 'That's all arranged for. The priest will be here at eight o'clock on Sunday morning to celebrate in our own hall.' I was not astounded! A display of such ecumenical understanding is what I would have expected from so compassionate and kindly a movement. . . .

A letter was received in August 1940 by Brigadier John Martin, an officer who had been associated with this work, from a Spanish girl who had been cared for at Clapton. 'I wish to offer you my home. My husband and I now have a place of our own, and there will always be room for you.'

The Better Fight, pp 143-146

19 July

The other major relief operation was in China where . . . though war was not officially declared until December 1941, within two years Japanese forces occupied many of the Chinese seaports and most cities as far west as Hankow.

Several salvationists lost their lives in this indeterminate fighting. Lieutenant Wang Kuan-lung, who had been commissioned for only four months . . . was seized, stripped of his uniform and bayoneted to death. . . . A woman local officer of the Pao Ting Fu North Corps was also killed and for over a year her husband searched for her body. Finally he found it in a ditch a mile out of the town, and identified his wife by the Home League badge still attached to fragments of her clothing. . . . Thousands of Chinese were saved from slow death through starvation by the devoted efforts of many. . . .

Though cut off from his regional officer, Captain Shtien of the Tientsin North Corps housed men refugees in his hall and women in his quarters. His action so impressed the authorities that they placed at his disposal a more commodious building where he fed 2,000 people daily. Similarly, Captain and Mrs Ch'i Ke-shun of the Central Corps housed 400 refugees in their hall and later fed over 1,000 people a day from a makeshift kitchen set up in a local school. This work developed so far beyond its hasty beginnings that in the spring of 1939 the *Peking and Tientsin Times* could report three refugee camps under Salvation Army supervision. . . . Many of the refugees returned to their own villages each with a gift of seed for the next planting. . . . When this work was at its height there were 36 centres feeding over 40,000 people at any one time.

Two facts shine out amid this chaos and distress. One was that the Army's evangelical work was maintained. New corps and halls were opened. . . . Training for officership, with a two-year session, continued. . . . The other was that Chinese and Japanese salvationists remained on Christian terms. . . .

The History of The Salvation Army Volume 6, pp 146-149

20 July

When the distinguised Japanese salvationist, Commissioner Gunpei Yamamuro, was promoted to Glory on 13 March 1940, his passing and his funeral were reported in the Army's Chinese papers, as was the message of condolence sent by the general secretary in Peking. . . . When Commissioner Benwell, the Territorial Commander for North China, curtailed his homeland furlough and hurried back to Peking in the late autumn of 1937 because of the increasing gravity of the situation, his journey via Yokohama and Kobe was facilitated by Salvation Army leaders in Japan.

In January 1938 when Colonel Yasowo Segawa (by this time chief secretary in Japan) was in northern China, he was able to smooth the way for approximately 100 refugees in the care of Adjutant Yin Hung Shun who were returning from Tsinan to their homes along the Tsin-Pu railway. At Su Ch'iao, half-way between Tientsin and Pao Ting Fu, the Army captain greeted the Japanese soldiers who entered the village with a copy of the Chinese *War Cry* and a gospel portion, and received from them a promise to respect the Army hall. In like manner, among the troops who entered another Chinese village was a salvationist from Tokyo who was on the staff of the officer commanding this particular detachment. As soon as he met the Chinese corps officer he arranged that a notice should be posted on the street gate of the Army quarters forbidding Japanese troops to enter. In this way many young women and girls were able to find refuge in the Army officer's home. . . .

Among the cadets of the second training session in the [South China] territory were two nurses who first met the Army when they came to help in relief work.

The History of The Salvation Army Volume 6, pp 149, 150

21 July

As elsewhere in Europe the final months of the war brought great hardship to the Dutch people generally. The curfew, lasting with few variations from 8 pm to 4 am, curtailed all evening meetings, and the shortage of heat and light further hampered public work. Many men salvationists—officers and soldiers alike—were conscripted to serve in German labour camps, and rations for those at home became limited and uncertain.

But early on Monday morning, 1 May 1945, a small group of officers made their way to the territorial headquarters in Amsterdam. For four years the building had been occupied by the staff of the Labour Front but now the Director offered to show the visitors round the building. They had no need of his services however; they knew the place well enough themselves. Instead they covered a table with the Army flag and around this returned thanks to God for deliverance.

Next day they came back to hoist the Army flag on the roof-top when a couple of armoured trucks started to open fire on the people in the street. Members of the Dutch Resistance Movement answered fire with counter fire, and the officers on the roof-top found themselves caught between both. The Army flag was riddled with bullets and four went through the top floor windows of the building. But the uproar ended as unexpectedly as it had begun. White flags appeared; the two hostile trucks vanished and, on the following morning, when Canadian troops entered the city, the blood and fire flag was flying from the roof of Prins Hendrikkade, 49-51.

The once liquidated Salvation Army had again hoisted its colours!

The History of The Salvation Army Volume 6, p 181

22 July

In the autumn of 1946 the band of the Rotterdam I Corps . . . visited the Regent Hall Corps. . . . Travel so soon after the war could still be more of a penance than a pleasure. Private hospitality was still a drain on family rations. Both the visitors and their hosts had known the hazards of armed conflict. . . . But if an ordeal shared is an ordeal halved then those two groups of salvationists were able to encourage one another in the Lord. It does not detract one iota from the superb musicianship displayed by the Tranås Band . . . when they visited London and the home counties during Eastertide 1947, to say that their compatriots from Huskvanna . . . were true encouragers of the brethren when they visited Bremen, Hamburg, Hanover and the Ruhr over Easter, 1948. Most of the men brought their rations with them and then left extras for the scanty cupboards of their hosts.

But perhaps the most electrifying of these exchanges was the visit of the Coventry City Band . . . to Germany in June 1950. . . . The name Coventry meant on the continent—in the words of a Berlin paper: 'the hate-filled, victory-assured symbol of absolute destruction by bombs of an enemy city'. But when after having visited Hamburg, Kiel and Hanover, these English Midlands bandsmen arrived in Berlin at 7 am one weekday, the capital's Philharmonic brass orchestra, led by Hans Steinkopf, were on the station platform to greet them. Enthusiasm reached such a pitch that extra police had to be summoned to control the estimated crowd of 5,000 who made it difficult even for the bandsmen to reach their allotted places for the final outdoor festival. *Wiedersehen* was sung in such an emotional fashion that some of the Coventry men could hardly join in for their tears.

The History of The Salvation Army Volume 7, pp 33, 34

23 July

Sunday 25 June was the date when fighting broke out along the 38th parallel. Orders were issued for all western women and children to leave South Korea at once. By Monday morning Mrs Commissioner Lord and one other single woman officer were the only expatriate women left in Seoul. Late that evening they were told that they also would have to be evacuated, whereupon Commissioner and Mrs Lord had to decide whether they would once more be parted as they had been in 1942 when Singapore fell. The commissioner had received a cable from the General authorising him to delegate his authority as the Army's leader in Korea to the senior indigenous officer and to leave while it was still possible to do so. Word came from the US embassy that a seat would be reserved for him on the last plane due to fly out at half-past two in the afternoon. Herbert Lord elected to stay. He chose to do what no one could have compelled him to do.

He who accepts Jesus as Saviour and Lord will be willing to follow in his steps.

This principle, exemplified in Christ's death on the Cross, both illuminates the teaching of the Master and also provides the most powerful motive of all for the dedication of the believer.

In Good Company, pp 12, 13

24 July

As with the ministers of God, so with the Church of God, whose founder is the Holy Spirit. By his coming at Pentecost men and women were drawn into a new and living community of which Jesus was—and is—the Head. Where Christ is, there is the Church. Just as in the Old Testament Israel was a people peculiar to God—that is to say, his very own because it was his good pleasure so to choose them—in the New Testament the Church is the New Israel, a people redeemed from iniquity and zealous of good works. The Church inherits the promises. The Israel of grace takes the place of the Israel of race.

Wherever there is present the love of God, the grace of the Lord Jesus Christ and the fellowship of the Holy Spirit, there is the Church. Priest may be absent or present. Prayer may be free, liturgical or silent. The singing may be plainchant, the psalms of David in metre, or a brisk Salvation Army song. The essential is not order but faith. Where men and women are gathered in love to God and to each other, there is the Church, the Church which exists to preach the gospel. That is the right priority. The gospel does not exist for the Church.

But wherever the gospel is made known in its own native spirit and power, there is an undeniable part of the community of Christ which no man can excommunicate. If he does, he may be found—as Gamaliel once warned his colleagues—even to fight against God himself who so often acts exceedingly abundantly above all that men can think.

To that Church William Booth belonged. . . .

The Salvation Army Year Book 1958

No one need stand aghast as if the vigorous life of God in his people was going something amiss in breaking out in new ways assuming new forms. When a stream is in full spate old banks inevitably disappear. The new life cuts its own channels, irrigating ground hitherto untouched and making barren places blossom like the rose. Is this to be bewailed? Where there is life there is growth, as every parent knows. How can ecclesiastical garments which fitted in the first century, and possibly in the tenth, be deemed the only adequate attire for the twentieth? The law of adaptation is not a sign of the absence, but of the presence, of the Holy Spirit.

'We must not simply look at what was done of the apostles,' said Beza, 'but have respect to their end and purpose, and that manner and form now to be used that may best bring that to pass.' The purpose of the apostles was the salvation of men, and what accomplishes that end is truly apostolic in spirit.

Was not this what John Wesley himself discovered? 'God powerfully called him forth', declared the Conference address two years after his death, 'into the streets and open fields, and afterward raised to his assistance hundreds of men who never passed through the usual forms of ordination. . . . In all these things he acted. . . on the ground of unavoidable necessity or, which is the same to a truly pious soul, from the clearly manifested providences and will of God.'

Fully could this be said of William Booth and his first evangelists. . . .

The Salvation Army Year Book 1958

. . . William Booth and his first evangelists . . . preached as did certain men of Cyprus and Cyrene at Antioch. Was that ministry of prophets and teachers irregular? Had they any consecrated building save the unknown dwelling house where they met? Did there then exist a threefold order of bishops, priests and deacons? And ought not hands to have been laid upon Saul of Tarsus and he be not sent forth until there was?

'The true apostolic succession,' wrote Hort, 'means nothing more or less than the continual call of men to service by Christ himself. No ceremony avails to effect it. The ministry of the New Testament is one of mission. "The true succession", to quote Cromwell, "is through the Spirit."'

It therefore follows that officership in The Salvation Army is not to be regarded as of inferior grade in the ministries of God. For, to quote General Bramwell Booth . . ., 'our officers are, equally with them all, ministers in the Church of God, having received diversities of gifts but the one Spirit, endowed by his grace, assured of his guidance, confirmed by his word, and commissioned by the Holy Spirit to represent him to the whole world.'

Here then are the terms of a commission wide enough to embrace every young man and woman possessed by a sense of vocation, and demanding enough to stretch to the full all who embrace it. . . . Most officers do indeed lead their congregations at least twice every Sunday in the praise of God and in the declaration of his saving truth. But the same men and women . . . may on Monday be helping to clean up a sick room, on Tuesday be listening to a story of a missing son, and on Wednesday be concerned with the needs of an unmarried mother. In this is to be found the true democracy of the Spirit. . . .

The Salvation Army Year Book 1958

27 July

In this is to be found the true democracy of the Spirit. On the one hand it is true that there is hardly a professional qualification which cannot be used in Salvation Army service—surveyor, accountant, doctor, teacher, printer, cashier, social worker, editor, nurse, book-keeper, translator, architect, radiotherapist, farmer, composer. All that is required is that these several skills be

163

fired with a sense of mission and be used in God's service without thought of conventional rewards.

On the other hand it has pleased God to employ men with few gifts. The work of the Army has been furthered by many such in days past. Loyal to the New Testament and true to its tradition, the Army does not refuse the lad or girl who has little more to bring than a pair of willing hands and a loving heart. That was all of which William Booth could boast at his beginning. His formal schooling ended when he was thirteen. His further education was gained across the pawnbroker's counter or learning the bitter lessons of a year's unemployment. Yet his early resolve that God should have all there was of him demonstrates that human usefulness is not finally determined by human capacity but by human consecration clothed in divine power.

'I do not desire the pastor's crust without the pastor's call,' wrote the 21-year-old William to a Nottingham friend. The call came, born of the plain need about him. That was before he stood before a crowded chapel in Hull and testified to the faith that was in him. And in an age of human possibilities and perils such as William Booth never imagined, man's manifest need of Jesus remains a call.

Let your immediate dedication match the urgency of this call. The altar will sanctify the gift.

The Salvation Army Year Book 1958

28 July

. . . If there were at one time some who would have stoned William Booth, the present danger is that he be canonised and the cutting edge of his deeds and words be blunted by the deadweight of the larger than life monument which we raise to his honour. It would be ironic—which God avert!—if this soldier-prophet became a piece of Victoriana, an historical curiosity who, having served his day, fell on sleep, which example it is suggested by some that his soldiers would do well to copy.

That this is no hypothetical danger comes home to me

every time a reporter or interviewer leads off with the remark that the social conditions which galvanised William Booth into action have disappeared from our common life. Must not the movement which he founded be therefore something of a Victorian anachronism and should it not, like its Founder, now pass from the scene of action?

In reply two comments should be made. The first is that it is quite true that the obvious mass poverty which disgraced the mid-nineteenth century has disappeared. When William Booth, just out of his teens, first came to London . . . C. J. Blomfield, then Bishop of London, could speak of 'the immense population within a mile and a half to the east and north-east of St Paul's, living in a most wretched state of destitution and neglect.' . . .

But my second point is this—suppose our community needs were fully met, who says that it was these which first moved William Booth to action? . . . 'All our social service', was his oft-repeated remark, 'is the outcome of the spiritual life of our people.'

Essentials of Christian Experience, pp 36-38

29 July

It was Jesus who spoke in this way to Paul. 'I have appeared unto thee for this purpose. . . .' It was Jesus who spoke in this way to William Booth. And it is the same Lord who speaks to us in the same way today. He still gives his orders. 'Rise, and stand upon thy feet.' Let no one resent them. For if he cannot command us who are saved by his grace, whom can he command? And if we are not his soldiers to obey, whose orders are we willing to accept in lieu of his?

So far as the Christian gospel is concerned, this is what could be called the crunch. Even those who would reduce our knowledge of that historic Jesus to a minimum leave untouched the fact that he was the friend of publicans and sinners. That is to say, his ministry was a redeeming one. Now the work he has for us today is none other than the continuance of his own work in the days of his flesh. If his was a gospel of redemption, so must ours be. To preach any other gospel is, as the apostle said elsewhere, to be accursed.

But we are not left to attempt this on our own. We are neither thrown back on our own devices nor left to think up our own conception of what our work should be. As his work on earth was redeeming work, so must ours be also. But, confronted by such a call, none need hesitate. For those who are willing to follow his example will find that the grace of his presence will be all-sufficient.

Essentials of Christian Experience, pp 39, 40

30 July

For William Booth to mean anything to those who never knew him after the flesh . . . then two or three points must be singled out where by nature, or more possibly by grace, we come within viewing distance of him. So for this purpose let him be a man—of faith, of hope, of charity.

Of faith in God—else he would never have taken the crucial decisions which, though hid from his sight at the time—and from the sight of his contemporaries as well— were to determine the nature and course of his own future together with that of the movement not yet born.

. . . Whatever fears may have gripped the heart of the perplexed William Booth he cast himself upon the Lord whom he had accepted as Saviour in his teens, and committed himself to serve this same Lord in a land he knew not of. This was to step out on the seeming void and find the rock beneath. And this is what he went on doing—with his own life, with his own family, with the movement of which he was the Founder. Every step had to be taken in faith. He had not passed any of this way before. There were no precedents to guide him; no signposts to follow. But just as the highest form of courage is to know fear and yet triumph over that enemy, so faith can be assailed by doubt and yet continue to trust.

166

With such a beginning it is not surprising that William Booth's last coherent words were: 'The promises of God are sure—if you only believe.'

Address—2 July 1965

31 July

To his faith in God he added hope. . . . The New Testament speaks of hope as an anchor . . . fastened 'within the veil'. That is to say, Christian hope is rooted in the very nature and purpose of God himself. This divine hope which William Booth held—or, more accurately, by which he was held—enabled him to hope for men.

All his schemes for the improvement of society . . . centred around what God could do for man and in man and through man. . . . To turn man's self-centredness into a genuine concern for his neighbour, nothing less than the converting power of God was required.

This was a point which William Booth strongly pressed during a conversation which lasted for more than an hour with the then Mr Winston Churchill when Home Secretary in 1910. Prison reform was under consideration but, in the Founder's judgment, prison reform must go far beyond the reform of prison conditions to the reform of the prisoners themselves. . . . The word conversion occurred so often that, as the Home Secretary rose to his feet, he asked in his own inimitable way: 'Am I converted?' To which William Booth answered in his own inimitable way: 'No, I am afraid you are not. But I think you are convicted!'

Yet when it is recalled that the Salvation Army officer has now the freedom of the prisons of the nations from Surinam to Sydney via Singapore, that in the penitentiaries of the United States some 4,500 men now follow a system of Bible studies sponsored by The Salvation Army, that when the Republic of France decided in 1945 to close her penal settlement in Guiana, it was to the Army that this task was entrusted, then the world has been converted to the ways of William Booth far beyond his dreams.

Address—2 July 1965

1 August

To faith and hope he added charity . . . the outworkings of the love of God shed abroad in the human heart.

His was a love, like that of his Lord, for the world. His last conversation with his eldest son had to do with the needs of the world. 'Promise me', he said, 'to do something more for the homeless. The homeless in every land. Not just in England but throughout the world.'

And if one of his dying concerns was with the needy of the world, his other had to do with the unity of the world. 'I have been thinking of all the nations and all the peoples as one family,' he said, a dream toward which our sadly divided world is still struggling.

Lest anyone should confuse this with a Wellsian love for mankind in general which can go along with a distaste for the company of men as individuals, let there be recalled the occasion when, as so often, William Booth had been besieged by reporters. He ended the press interview by saying: 'Now, gentlemen, as I've given you half-an-hour of my time, I'll take a couple of minutes of yours.' And with that he prayed for the assembled group of pressmen. . . . This was the love of God shed abroad in his heart.

. . . As his testimony was, 'By the grace of God I am what I am', by that same grace we may become what God would have us be.

Address—2 July 1965

2 August

It was after four years of itinerant evangelism in provincial England . . . that an invitation to Catherine Booth to preach in Rotherhithe brought her to London— with William following later when he had completed his current engagement. And from Rotherhithe they went to Bermondsey and from Bermondsey to Deptford.

These were not areas beloved of any man who was first and last a careerist. If the hand of God had not been upon these two 36-year-old north-midlanders, with their young but ever-growing family, they could well have sunk without a trace. As it was, when they finally settled on Whitechapel as their parish, the Christian Revival Union—as William Booth called his first community—numbered but sixty members after a year's work. And as for material assets, their one piece of property—the tent where their meetings were held—soon became so weather beaten that William Booth paid a man . . . to take it away.

If this work had been one man's—or many men's—scheming to secure a place in the ecclesiastical sun, it would have contained within itself the seeds of its own swift decay. . . . As Gamaliel said to the Sanhedrin about the Early Church, 'If this counsel or this work be of men, it will come to nought: but if it be of God, ye cannot overthrow it.' Of this movement to which we salvationists are privileged to belong, we may humbly say: this is the Lord's doing and it is marvellous in our eyes. It is he who has made us and not we ourselves. We who were not a people he has made a people. We will rejoice and be glad.

But as every privilege is also a responsibility, exultation is the least of the emotions which should possess us. . . .

Address—St Mungo's Cathedral, Glasgow

3 August

The call of God is never to privilege but always to duty. God chose Israel as his own that they might be the people through whom he could reveal his will and character, so that in turn, by their righteous living and sense of mission, they might cause this knowledge of the true God to cover the earth as waters cover the sea. He had planned for them not ease but service. Of course, the service of God is always man's supreme honour. He can rise no higher than that. But it is also man's heaviest obligation. To whom much is given from him will much be required. . . .

It is no light thing to be a child of God, nor for any body of believers to think of themselves as the people of God. For to belong to God is to belong to One whose love is inexorable. From him we may expect the truth, the whole truth, and nothing but the truth about ourselves.

We always know where we stand in his sight. He leaves us in no doubt whether we are making the grade or not. . . .

If we wish to see what it really means to be singled out by God as his very own, and to be given a task which is part of his redeeming purpose, then look at him who was God's very own Son. . . . The mission of Jesus was to sacrifice, to suffering, to death. And this not in spite of his being the beloved Son but because he was. Those whom God calls to be his own are never given the soft jobs; always the most demanding and often the most unrewarding.

Address—St Mungo's Cathedral, Glasgow

4 August

Upward to God and outward to man—this is the divine word to us who are salvationists. . . . In all our thanksgiving that we who were not a people have been made a people, we must not forget why this great thing has befallen us. Certainly not merely to share congenial fellowship with such like-minded comrades and friends as gather with us in our halls on Sundays and weeknights. And certainly not merely to delight one another with our music and song, increasingly competent though we may be to do so. That would be to repeat the mistake of Israel when they acted as if God had made them his own for their private pleasure and not for the fulfilment of his divine purpose.

God's purpose for us, now as at our beginning, is to reach upward to him in devotion and outward to men and women everywhere with his salvation. This is why we who were not a people have been made a people.

Commentators and reporters sometimes ask whether The Salvation Army has not outlived its time. Has it any future? Is it not a Victorian anachronism which is inevitably on its way out? But as the changes are rung on that kind of question I recall a sentence from Shaw's *St Joan* to the effect that the Church is in the hands of God, not God in the hands of the Church.

We are in the hands of God, and while we serve his redeeming purpose none can pluck us from his hands.

Wherefore lift up your hearts and renew your dedication, and God will continue to be with you in power and blessing.

Address—St Mungo's Cathedral, Glasgow

5 August

The mission of The Salvation Army is very simple and can be simply stated. It is to take the Christian gospel to the people where the people are. This can be understood quite literally for we ourselves act upon it literally. Wherever people are to be found there we go with the only message that can change character, transform the home, redeem society and save the world. Consequently, those who raise their eyebrows never so slightly when a group of young salvationists makes an early-morning appearance at The Blue Angel, or holds street meetings in Soho late on Saturday evenings, cannot have understood our unqualified acceptance of the Saviour's command to preach the gospel to every creature, nor can they be aware of the example set by our salvationist fathers in the faith.

To the formative years of the Army belongs the story of Bramwell Booth, when still Chief of the Staff to his formidable father, the Founder, appearing in a Plymouth music hall as the twelfth turn. He was played on stage by the orchestra with 'For he's a jolly good fellow' and the house responded *en masse* when, at his appearing, a piping voice called from the gods: 'Now fire a volley!'

'I spoke that night,' wrote the second General, 'of every man's need of true friendship—above all his need of the friendship of God. As I left the stage . . . the audience rose and gave me quite an ovation.'

If to go with the gospel to the people is the mission of the Army, it therefore follows that we deem it not only allowable, but essential, to use every method congruous with the spirit of the gospel to make the gospel known.

With the spirit of the gospel, be it noted, for this can be somewhat at variance with the current conventional practice of the gospel. . . .

The Salvation Army Year Book 1965

171

6 August

For centuries it has been thought that public worship is properly held in buildings of recognisable design at stated hours on the first day of the week. This is agreed—so long as it is not then supposed that this provides the only pattern to be followed in preaching Christ and him crucified. Of course, men of vision have said this before—George Fox on the fells and John Wesley in the fields. It would be somewhat ironic if the Lord who was expelled from buildings erected for divine worship in his day should now be strictly limited to buildings and occasions so accredited. . . .

Partly from necessity but more from choice . . . William Booth found himself preaching in a tent which had been erected in the Whitechapel burial ground belonging to the Society of Friends, for the benefit of 'the poorer classes not in the habit of attending any place of worship'. The same 'employment of extraordinary means to make known . . . the love of God' (William Booth's own words) led him from the tent to hire Professor Orson's dancing academy in New Road, then to the Effingham Theatre, then to a wool store in Satchell Street—and so on.

These places were no more 'consecrated' than the lecture hall of Tyrannus hired by Paul for the space of two years in Ephesus, but where the converting Spirit of God is manifestly present any hierarchical blessing is unnecessary. . . . The means are sanctified by God to whatever end may please him.

The Salvation Army Year Book 1965

7 August

. . . In pursuance of this mission of going where the people are with what the people need—which is not of necessity the same as what they want—the Army, in common with evangelists of every school, has sought to share the people's thoughts.

'Get into their skins' was what William Booth said to Frederick St George de Latour Tucker when he sent the one-time Cheltenham public schoolboy to evangelise India. To look at life through the eyes of those whom we desire to bring to Christ is a skill coveted by the soul-winner.

Here again is an approach for which warrant can be found in the New Testament. And seeing that the apostle Paul has been quoted once, let him be quoted again, for there are few better authorities.

A Regius Professor of Divinity at the University of Oxford referred to the apostle's 'declared policy' to become 'all things to all men', and to adopt the language and presuppositions of those whom he sought to convert to Christianity, and to work in and through categories of religious thought already current. He was also a master of . . . the art of conducting a subtle, submerged polemic by using the terminology and ideas of his opponents in a different sense from that of their original writing.

This 'almost chameleon-like effort to identify himself with the position of his audience' . . . is a pattern which every would-be evangelist, consciously or unconsciously, tries to adopt. He moves over to sit where his hearers sit. He wants to see through their glasses. He begins where they are so that he may lead them to where he is. . . .

The Salvation Army Year Book 1965

8 August

. . . Reported the *Nonconformist* in 1867: 'Mr Booth employs very simple language in his comments . . . frequently repeating the same sentence several times over as if he was afraid that his hearers would forget. . . . Not a word is uttered by him that could be misconstrued; not a doctrine propounded that is beyond the comprehension of those to whom it is addressed.'

This ability to speak the language of the people was given by T. R. Davidson in *The Contemporary Review* in 1882 as one of the principal reasons for the success of The Salvation Army.

A like approach is made today in street meeting and in writing. Some time ago *The British Weekly* quoted an observer who had been listening to a Salvation Army 'open-air' held regularly in the heart of London's West End. The commentator noted that a salvationist speaker began his informal address with reference (without mentioning the name) to William James's description of conversion as occurring when '. . . a self, hitherto divided, and consciously wrong, inferior and unhappy, becomes unified and consciously right, superior and happy.'

Not a bad starting point for a religious appeal in a secular setting because inner strife, a sense of inferiority, a feeling of deep-seated unhappiness, is common enough among the crowds who throng our city streets on a Sunday evening. Few may be skilled at self-analysis but many know when a man speaks to their condition. That salvationist began where his hearers were. He was looking at life through their eyes. . . .

The Salvation Army Year Book 1965

9 August

The same approach is found also in *The War Cry*. . . . Denominationalism is eschewed like the plague and, while providing for the Army's domestic interests, this paper devotes its main pages to religious teaching couched in secular language. Its editorial offices—with apologies to Francis Thompson—are pitched between Heaven and Charing Cross. Its language is not of Zion though its teaching is. A contributor searching for the right word will, like Malherbe, deem it wisdom to listen to the dockers at Port-au-foin. This . . . weekly is beamed at the man who may know what conversion means on the rugby field but has little knowledge of its religious significance.

So to write is one of the most difficult forms of Christian endeavour, requiring both a sound grasp of doctrine and a firm sense of words. Colloquial so-called can teeter on the edge of bathos. While on the one hand there is nothing more off-putting than the pulpiteer whose main asset is an assumed breeziness, on the other there are forms of devotional writing which engulf the unwary reader in a morass of words. His sinking feet can find no firm foothold and he is slowly suffocated rather than illuminated. But at this time of day to produce a religious paper which irreligious men will buy—and read—is a feat of evangelism for which God should be daily praised. As Dr Finlay said in the episode from his case book entitled *The Hallelujah Stakes:* 'Some good stuff in this paper.'

Last of all, the success of this continuing mission demands that people are valued for their own sakes. Like the Church universal of which The Salvation Army is an integral part, we do not exist for our own benefit. . . .

The Salvation Army Year Book 1965

10 August

The Army came into being because a man and his wife cared for people as people. To William Booth people did not constitute a congregation on which he could practise his own eloquence. Far from enhancing his sense of self-importance, the increasing numbers who surrounded him but drained him still further of virtue. Such was his disinterested love for his converts that he tried to detach them from himself and send them to one or other of the historic churches. But when they refused to go the same concern for their welfare compelled him to provide them both with articles of faith and the ordered means of grace.

So . . . The Salvation Army is found with a stated body of doctrine, a trained and commissioned leadership and a disciplined world membership. What future changes may take place in its domestic structure is as God may guide. . . .

But more important is that this movement, the youngest among many brethren, shall share with its elders in the faith those divine insights which it has been granted.

For example: that saving faith in Christ and not any ecclesiastical ceremony is necessary to salvation; that holiness has to do with persons not with places; that obedience to Jesus as Lord is essential for all who would continue to know him as Saviour; that divine grace can be fully experienced without material aids; that men and women, single or married, can truly be ministers of God; and that the people of God—individually as well as collectively must be a missionary people else they cease to be his people.

For ourselves, we would seek to retain our original sense of mission to the unconverted, and thus find in our initial impulse our constant purpose.

The Salvation Army Year Book 1965

11 August

William Booth used to speak of stretching his arms wide enough to embrace the very rich on the one hand and the very poor on the other. This was a true catholicity of which his Lord would have approved. . . . But . . . The Salvation Army evidences a new catholicity—the ability to marshal within its ranks for effective Christian service a cross-section of society, at one end of which may be the Lord Lieutenant of a Scottish county and, across country via professional and managerial occupations, includes the council house family and the unskilled labourer.

Watch any Salvation Army band marching down the street. It may comprise . . . a baker, bank clerk, butcher, civil engineer, civil servant, company director, draughts-man, electrical fitter, electro-plater, litho printer, locomotive fitter, manager (hosiery), manager (textiles), manager (trainee), railway signalman, schoolmaster (BSc maths), schoolmaster (BSc physics), student of agriculture, student of music and wages clerk.

. . . What holds these men together—and such a group is the world Salvation Army in miniature—is their love for Christ, their loyalty to their faith and their devotion to the purposes of The Salvation Army. . . . To maintain and increase this open-ended association through the pro-clamation and practice of the gospel of our Lord and

Saviour is a lesson I shall never finish learning. But that is no cause for despair. Nothing is more stimulating to heart and mind alike than to continue in the school of Christ.

The Salvation Army Year Book 1967

12 August

. . . There has never been a shortage of prophets among the people of God quick to declare that the axe is already laid at the root of the tree. Spreaders of despondency and alarm are not slow to tremble for the arm of the Lord, forgetting that their prototype was an aged ailing priest who had already failed in his high calling and could not control even his own family. However, the cry of Ichabod is as handy as any, especially when other self-appointed judges join in the chorus that the glory has departed.

The Salvation Army has attracted its share of these harbingers of gloom, particularly . . . when William Booth was promoted to Glory. . . . The obvious fallibility of these prophecies has helped to disperse the gloom which they may at first have caused. Yet believers themselves sometimes provide these unreliable seers with aid and comfort by their readiness to belaud the past and to bewail the present.

Not to go beyond my brief, there are those whose pleasure it is to recall the days that are no more when there were salvation giants in the land. Shall we ever see again a group of uniformed soldiers laying on the floor of the House of Commons a monster petition carrying 340,000 signatures which, if unrolled, would have measured two statute miles? Or will there arise another woman like Catherine Booth who dared to importune the Prime Minister of the day when her daughter was imprisoned for preaching the gospel? Or will the Army, moved by social injustice, ever open another Lamprell Street factory where it was demonstrated that 'match-maker's leprosy' could be eliminated and the end product yet bear the label: 'Fair wages for fair work'?

The answer in each instance is no. . . . But no, simply

because the victory has been won over each of the evils which gave rise to each of these protests . . . small use fighting the wars of the past, even in retrospect.

The Salvation Army Year Book 1968

13 August

Small use fighting the wars of the past, even in retrospect. The battles of the Lord [today] are not those of 1912, much less those of 1865. New occasions teach new duties. A movement is in danger of breaking the second commandment when it begins to worship its own past. Ours to serve the present age.

If we must not worship the past we can still learn from the past, and one thing the record of the past can do is to save us from present dismay.

'Had not been the Lord . . . on our side, when men rose up against us: then they had swallowed us up quick.' That the Army lives on to share in the redeeming will of God testifies alike to his goodness and to the place which, in his mercy, we still have in his saving purpose. For we were born in obscurity, grew amid poverty, suffered public obloquy, encountered widespread unpopularity and, in two world wars, endured no small adversity. Suppression was our lot in lands of the East and West alike. And the peace, so-called, of the last 25 years has had her perils no less hazardous than war—as recent news bears witness.

Believers do indeed live dangerously amid the power struggles of the day. Yet while regimes rise and fall the work of God, even where hampered, standeth sure. . . . Far from being dismayed, we may rejoice and be glad that the current setting of the gospel increasingly resembles what it was when the New Testament was being written. . . .

The Salvation Army Year Book 1968

14 August

Little social advantage is to be gained nowadays by

church-going; perhaps even less by being known as a practising Christian. A . . . speaker in the Light Programme of the BBC said that because she was a Christian she was considered a freak by many of her friends. Among university-type people (she went on) it was more acceptable to be regarded as a humanist. Being a believer didn't go with being 'mod' or 'trendy' or even with the capacity to think. But this is not new—not to anyone who has read of the outright laughter with which the intelligentsia in Athens greeted what the apostle Paul had to say about the Resurrection. Nor what a Roman governor had to say on the same point. 'Paul, you are raving; too much study is driving you mad.' . . .

We should lift up our hearts rather than be dismayed that once again the gospel has to be accepted for its own sake. It stands or falls on its own merits. The man who accepts the Christian faith has to do so without hope of any fringe benefits. Church-going as an integral part of social climbing is out; praise be! In times past there used to be talk—exaggerated possibly—about rice converts. There is no current equivalent for this. Nowadays the Christian faith has nothing to commend it save its own inherent virtue. Jesus Christ must be acknowledged as Saviour and Lord for his own sake.

The Salvation Army Year Book 1968

15 August

'Too ill to take Good Friday meetings at the Clapton Congress Hall,' said William Booth in 1910, 'but seventy people came to the mercy seat. Praise the Lord (he added), he can do without me. This is a mercy.'

Which it is. It would be a disaster if the work of God stood or fell by any one man or any one church. No man and no movement is indispensable. But, by the same token, no man and no movement loyal to the impulse of the Spirit will be cast off by him. The faithful remnant finds that God is faithful to them.

The supreme ground of our refusal to be dismayed is that in Jesus of Nazareth God has visited and redeemed

179

his people. Love's atoning work is done and cannot be undone. Not all the follies of men can destroy the power of the spirit of Christ let loose upon the world.

It may be retorted that this is an act of faith. So what? I do not regard faith as a dirty word. Most men have a faith of sorts. . . . Could it be—to put it mildly—that the truth revealed in Christ is nearer the mark than one man's stab in the dark? And when it comes to standing up and being counted, I'd rather be wrong with Jesus (if wrong he is adjudged) than right with anyone else.

The Salvation Army Year Book 1968

16 August

The indignant protestors at this supposedly new and undesirable mode of evangelism could have forgotten that, before the century had begun until his promotion to Glory in 1944, such a well-known Army character as Brigadier Tom Plant had delighted congregations at home and abroad with music and song based on what was undoubtedly a lineal descendant of the biblical instrument of ten strings. At the international congress in 1914, and again in 1921 and 1925/6, a singing party from the West Indies had captivated their British listeners with their lilting melodies and haunting harmonies. And if the guitar was the principal stone of stumbling, it was that instrument, played by Jenny Svenson, which accompanied the singing of 'We're bound for the land of the pure and the holy' when the Army opened fire in Sweden in December 1882.

The first public appearance of The Joystrings—that is, apart from the release of their first 45 single, a Cliff Michelmore programme and a Jimmy Young *Saturday Special*—was at the Army hall in Lomond Grove, Camberwell. . . . Within the week the group received—and accepted—an invitation which provoked increased assent and dissent the world over. This was to appear as the third act in the cabaret show in the Blue Angel night club. . . .

The Canadian *War Cry* reported that Dr Billy Graham

expressed his regret that a Salvation Army musical group should have entered a night club. To this the 'stand no nonsense' Commissioner Samuel Hepburn replied that 'the Army had been going into saloons, tap rooms, pool rooms and dance halls for scores of years, playing their music and singing their songs. The Joystrings were following in the Founder's footsteps—with equally desirable results. . . .'

Well for The Joystrings that some of their comrades at the training college had set their alarm clocks for the small hours of the morning, so that they might intercede in prayer while the group played. . . .

The History of The Salvation Army Volume 7, pp 168-170

17 August

Truth is not always stranger than fiction—save when it is to do with the work of God, as one more story from the centenary year will demonstrate. Towards the end of the Second World War, Dr and Mrs J. Bennett Alexander were living in Walthamstow in north-east London—he busy with a suburban practice and she with her works of love and mercy which enrich the life of those who serve in Christ's name. An unusually frank observation by the officer in charge of the local corps brought the doctor to the Army hall where he renewed his committal to Jesus as Saviour and Lord. Change of scenery did not weaken his deepened faith so that, when practising in the Lake District some years later, the Alexanders welcomed the suggestion of a visiting Army officer that an informal meeting should be held in their lakeside home. This was to prove a turning-point in their life for, next morning at breakfast, they told their visitor of their call to full-time service with the Army.

Unknown to the three at the breakfast table the next issue of the international *War Cry* was to carry a letter from Lieut-Colonel (Dr) William T. B. McAllister, Chief Medical Officer at the MacRobert hospital at Dhariwal in the Punjab, and headed 'The single-handed surgeon'.

Chief medical officer he was, but this was a case of one chief and no braves—save the indomitable nursing and ancillary staff. Neither assistant nor replacement were in sight—save to the eye of faith—and homeland furlough was due in a matter of months.

To the Alexanders this was a Macedonian call which they could not refuse and on the evening of Monday 5 August 1965, as the Millom Band played softly outside the village hall, scores of folk from the fells gathered to pray godspeed to the uniformed Dr and Mrs Alexander who were exchanging the coolness of Cumbria for the heat of India. Before the centenary year was out they had arrived in Dhariwal.

The History of The Salvation Army Volume 7, pp 206, 207

18 August

Completely different again was the open-air rally at the site of the former Quaker burial ground in Vallance Park Road where, in July 1865, William Booth held his first London meetings in a nondescript tent which, by the end of August, came to the end of its useful life and cost ten shillings to be carted away. Commissioner Catherine Bramwell-Booth (R), the guest speaker, praised the choice of a sundial for the memorial to her grandfather for he was constantly reminding his hearers that, in the language of the anonymous hymn writer, 'time is earnest, passing by'. 'Behold, now is the accepted time . . . now is the day of salvation.'

The scene which followed could have been a flashback to any evening meeting in the high summer of 1865. A drunken man shouted: 'There is no God'. A salvationist who was attempting to counsel another young man had to turn disappointedly away. However, a third man, who proved to be a backslider, pushed his way to the improvised mercy seat, followed by an urchin who inquired whether he could kneel there as well, after which a uniformed lassie salvationist stepped forward in an act of reconsecration. The Founder would have felt that these were the best of all tributes to his life's passion—better even than the presence of the casket containing the certificate granting him the freedom of the City of London fifty-five years earlier, which was given a place of honour at the reception in the Guildhall hosted by the Lord Mayor, Sir Edmund Stockdale.

The History of The Salvation Army Volume 7, pp 119, 120

19 August

There was a time when any man in Salvation Army uniform was taken to be a reformed profligate. It was thought exceptional for him to possess any different background. . . . The centenary bore witness past all denying that the Army not only embraced all races but, what was acknowledged rather more hesitantly, included all classes. . . .

The outcome was that at all levels in all five continents the centenary was greeted with good will. The Speaker in the Legislative Assembly of Alberta announced that an unnamed peak in the Rockies should henceforth be called Mount William Booth. The Hammersmith council placed a seat in Furnivall Gardens to commemorate the fact that William Booth once lived in that area. The Academie Francaise was accustomed to award a *Prix de Vertu* to the person or movement giving outstanding service to the Republic and, on the recommendation of Academician Marc Boegner, this was presented to The Salvation Army. The Postmaster General in the United Kingdom issued two centenary stamps, the first time a white man and a coloured man had appeared symbolically together on a British stamp design. The United States Post Office printed 184 million stamps of their Salvation Army issue. The much-visited floral clock in Princes Street, Edinburgh, displayed the centenary design—a task taking three men three weeks to set out in all its detail. And if to be near to nature is to be near to God, then this may be the right place to mention that cathedral services of thanksgiving ranged from St Machar's in Aberdeen to St Paul's in Melbourne, travelling—to name a few ports of call—via St John the Divine in New York, St George in Jerusalem and St James in St Helena on the way.

The single-minded salvationist would simply say: 'Give to Jesus glory!'

The History of The Salvation Army Volume 7, pp 200, 201

20 August

However, these centenary gatherings were not held solely to glorify the past. They proved to be occasions when current needs were currently met.

One of the centenary issues of the international *War Cry* carried the story of an American serviceman who owned a double allegiance—an AC2 hailing from Ocala, Florida, presently serving in Taiwan, who was also a salvationist. Second-class airman maybe, but a first-class salvation soldier—for he had a dream of the good which might be done if the Army flag was unfurled in Taiwan. It had been once—but fell victim to the bitter chances and changes of world politics. So he wrote to the nearest Salvation Army leader of whom he knew—the officer commanding in Hong Kong. . . . In the meantime young salvationists in Florida had heard of Leslie's dream, and the corps cadet honour clubs in the state agreed among themselves to contribute 1,000 dollars to the project. Meanwhile . . . Leslie . . . help or no help had begun to hold meetings in the city of Tauchung with the knowledge and support of some of the local community leaders.

Living in retirement in England at this time were Colonel and Mrs George Lancashire. They had given a large part of their active service to the people of China, and had been praying for the mainland salvationists who had crossed the Formosa Strait to resettle in Taiwan. These dedicated missionaries did not hesitate to respond to this situation as a call from the Lord and, in its centenary year, the Army repeated its early-day history when youth showed age the way to a new field of service.

The History of The Salvation Army Volume 7, pp 204, 205

21 August

But at home there were events just as significant though they involved only the ones and the twos as against whole populations. A baby girl, little more than an hour old, was found in a parcel lying close to the statue of William Booth which stands at the front of the training college overlooking Denmark Hill station. Some young mother in distress must have left her there, counting on the strong probability that a salvationist would be the first to discover the child. So it turned out—and at the nearby hospital the baby girl was named Sally Ann by common consent.

Close to the same time a Glasgow paper described how the corps officer stationed in a Scottish county town was in the habit of taking up his post just before seven o'clock in the morning when prisoners were due to be released. If they agreed, Captain Ronald Johnson would take them home for breakfast before seeing them off by train. One of the captain's early morning guests later returned and said that he would like to talk—whereupon the two men walked along the road that ran by the side of the Tay. The ex-prisoner revealed that he made his living by burglary and had already collected enough keys to set up in business again. The conversation was long, slow, quiet and earnest—after which the man let the keys fall from his hand into the river. There was then further prayer to him who is happier over one sinner who repents than 99 good people who do not need so to do.

The History of The Salvation Army Volume 7, pp 205, 206

22 August

The summer of 1975 also saw two of the Gowans/Larsson musicals presented in quick succession in London. . . . These were the fourth and fifth of the musicals which began with *Take-over Bid* in 1967. . . . Contrary to the Preacher's words, it is not true to say that 'there is no new thing under the sun'. These musicals were. The co-authors struck the rock of biblical lore and Salvation Army history and there gushed forth a fresh and sparkling stream of popular salvationist song. In this setting popular does not mean cheap or puerile. A tune which demands to be sung is a work of art. And when the words match the melody the combination is a gift of God. That is why the musicals have already made their own contribution to the recognised body of Salvation Army song.

What is more, the musicals seen so far—and there are others to follow—give the lie to the notion that only the morose are holy. Part of the miracle of these productions is that the story line which raises a laugh also leads to the mercy seat. A sense of humour is recognised as a gift of the Spirit in which tasteless vulgarity has neither a lot nor part. It is not hard, for example, to imagine what some contemporary producers would have made of the story of Hosea—the decent country man whose wife tired of him and who shacked up with any corner boy who would have her. There would be nods and winks and salacious innuendoes galore. Not in this production, however. To those in the cast, and the larger number in the congregation, who had never read Hosea, chapters 1 to 14, the musical came as a revelation of the eternal love that would not let men go.

The History of The Salvation Army Volume 7, pp 309, 310

23 August

The on-going activity of the Army can safely be committed to the Lord who first called the movement into being. Discussing in his *Principles of Christian Theology* the need for the Christian Church to make a more effective impact on the contemporary scene, John Macquarrie´ . . . has said that 'we shall have to be more prepared to recognise the Spirit's working outside the usual ecclesiastical channels and . . . be willing to give to the laity more initiative and responsibility than they have usually enjoyed. Both these points can be illustrated by another mention of The Salvation Army. . . . Although it has no sacraments, we could not for a moment deny that it receives and transmits divine grace. Its Founder, William Booth, could be regarded as a pioneer of "secular" Christianity in the best sense.'

. . . The only truthful conclusion is that there is no conclusion. There is no discharge in this war. One generation of salvationists may succeed another, but the work of the Army does not cease because human need does not cease. Whatever government may be in power and whatever economic theory may be the current fashion, some homes will still break up; some marriages will come apart; some children will need care and protection; some men will find themselves cursed with an inner inadequacy; some youthful spirits will hurt themselves in their revolt against society; some social misfits must be accepted instead of being rejected; some soul in search of a faith has to be pointed to the shining light which leads to the wicket-gate. A quarter of a century ago there were those who supposed that the welfare state would be a mother bountiful, the universal provider of every need. All voluntary, religious and social enterprise would wither away because there would be no place for it. The very opposite has proved to be true. There are now more such agencies than ever. So long as man remains man he will need a faith and a Friend.

No Discharge in this War, pp 247, 248, 244

24 August

By long-standing custom the Sunday morning worship of The Salvation Army is called a holiness meeting. There is the word—holiness. But before the association of ideas leads anyone to think of a Holy Joe and, disliking that kind of person, switch over to some more congenial programme, let me first repeat some lines you know. If they could be sung to Schubert's music they might sound more attractive still.

> Who is Silvia? What is she?
>   That all our swains commend her?
> Holy, fair and wise is she;
> The heaven such grace did lend her.

187

So the word holy can be applied to Silvia as well as Joe! And, applied to Silvia, is one of the reasons why her admirers—and in the plural as well—rave about her. In their eyes this is a quality which adds to her attractiveness.

> She excels each mortal thing
> Upon the dull earth dwelling.

Perhaps we had better have another look at this supposedly unwelcome word. If it could be cited as one of Silvia's main charms we may have our ideas about holiness all muddled up. Indeed we may! One is reminded of the wise and witty musical critic who remarked that good music wasn't as bad as it sounded. With a better understanding of this good thing, holiness, we might not find it as off-putting as had been thought. Starting then from scratch, here are three observations about this word. . . .

Address—27 June 1965

25 August

First of all, it can be agreed that holy, holiness and such kindred words are religious expressions and have to do with religious experience. It is true that the word is sometimes linked with bricks and mortar—as when a church is called Holy Trinity; or with a church rite—as with holy water; or with an ecclesiastical state—such as holy orders; or with a hymn faintly remembered from a long distant church parade in the services.

> Holy, holy, holy, Lord God Almighty!
> Early in the morning our song shall rise to thee.

But there's more to the word than that. The terms holy and holiness have been in currency for centuries. Their roots go back to the beginning of the human story. Scholars have written long dissertations to explain their origin and meaning. And we ourselves, without their theological knowledge, tread more lightly when we enter Canterbury Cathedral or Westminster Abbey. . . .

The fact is that the cathedral or the abbey—and all similar buildings—remind us of the unseen world which is both beyond and yet so close to this world of time and sense. 'Turn but a stone and start a wing.' In such a setting it dawns on us that there may be a God. This could be his house. And one of the basic meanings of the word holy has to do with this sense of awe which arises from the awareness that God is near.

Address—27 June 1965

26 August

Many names are given to the doctrine after which our Sunday morning meeting for worship has long been named. But the second blessing, Christian perfection, entire sanctification, the blessing of perfect love, all stand for one and the same experience. They are varying descriptions of the same reality, though for present purposes we will keep to the words 'holiness' and 'holy'.

Both go back to the earliest days of the religious education of the people of God and, to begin with, applied to that which provoked awe.

A place could be holy. 'Put off thy shoes from off thy feet, for the place whereon thou standest is holy ground', was the word which came to Moses. . . .

When the children of Israel came to Sinai, bounds were set about the smoking mountain lest they should unwittingly trespass on that which was holy. . . .

Similarly, none but certain persons could handle the Ark for that too was holy in that it belonged to God. . . . Increasing holiness was denoted by increasing remoteness from the common man. . . .

It was only to be expected that this idea, current in Jewish thought and expressed in their religious architecture, should shape the lives of those who were most earnest about their faith. . . .

Essentials of Christian Experience, pp 11, 12

27 August

I can yield my forgiven life to God that he may bestow upon me as much of his Spirit as I am able at that moment to receive. That may take place at a moment of time. But the work of the Holy Spirit in my life will never be ended for it is the greatest of the saints who have been most conscious of their imperfections. Those who live closest to Jesus are most aware of how far they fall short of his glory. Yet that same Holy Spirit who was in him is in them. Their sense of their shortcomings is not due to his absence but to his presence.

Here then is the twofold work of the Spirit. He can purify, but he will reveal what more remains to be purified. He can provoke us to that disinterested service for God and man which is love in action, but he will make us long to serve more selflessly still. His work will never be done though his first coming may have been at a recognisable moment. Our separateness will not be a separateness from people, but a separation from sin unto God and a dedication to people.

Though the presence of the Holy Spirit does not guarantee immunity from temptation or exemption from failure, he will give us grace to grow

> . . . like him who my pattern shall be,
> Till in his beauty my King I shall see.

Essentials of Christian Experience, pp 14, 15

28 August

The Book of Common Prayer speaks of 'the deceits of the world, the flesh and the devil'. These three can be taken as representing the main sources of temptation.

Some have their origin in the world—that is, in our day-to-day contact with other people. We have to live in the world. The salvationist cannot wrap himself up in cellophane. The monastery is not a practicable alternative for him. Even if it were it would provide no guaranteed immunity. There is no packaging for human beings which is germ proof. Daily life itself is a breeding ground for temptation.

Then there are temptations which arise from within ourselves. An untruth looks like a present help in trouble. Another's success can provoke a surge of jealousy. Sometimes this kind of temptation has to do with our procreative instinct and can sweep over a man like a flood. . . .

No human instinct is in itself evil though all can be put to an evil use. The remedy lies in a true conversion to God, so that these powerful energies within us which, unchecked, could make for our undoing, controlled and redirected bless us and make us a blessing. . . .

But whatever their source, temptations first begin as suggestions. . . .

Jesus and our Need, pp 80, 81

29 August

There are . . . temptations which, in the language of the Collect, arise from 'the devil'. We need not necessarily picture him with a tail and fork (his disguises are much more subtle than that), nor do I ever give him a capital 'D'. That would be to place him on a level with God. But some of the temptations which assail men can be explained only as part of a larger struggle between the powers of good and evil—what a recent commentator has described as 'the invisible realm where sinister forces stand flaming and fanatic against the rule of Christ'.

But whatever their source, temptations first begin as suggestions. At this stage no one should hold himself personally responsible for such suggestions except in so far as he may have wilfully put himself in their way. . . .

Some temptations can be brushed off as easily as we do the merest of casual acquaintances. A nod of recognition and we pass on. But as there are more persistent people so there are more persistent temptations. Just as some folk cling like leeches so also do certain temptations, and each of us must recognise his besetting temptation for what it is. We must recognise it, which is not to say we must walk off arm in arm with it. But to know it when we see it is strength not weakness. . . . To be forewarned is forearmed.

But to be prepared beforehand does not mean that I am going to sit down in my room, think about my particular besetment from morning till night and work out what I shall do when it assails me. . . . To be prepared beforehand means to strengthen in advance your whole being—body, mind and soul—in goodness. . . .

Jesus and our Need, pp 81, 82

30 August

If wanting could make us better, we would be better. If wishes were horses—but more often they are broken reeds. If desire of itself could transform us into men after God's own heart, we would have been that long ago. We know our weaknesses and are shamed by them. Shamed so much that when in the sessions of sweet, silent thought we take counsel with our conscience, we say: 'See that thou tell no man. Keep it dark!' A man who has never known a touch of grace may be unaware of his deeper needs, but not those who have tasted of the heavenly gift. We might be more content had our eyes never been opened to the beauty of holiness, but we are dissatisfied because we have glimpsed what might be.

The forgiven soul cannot be content to remain forgiven only. When theologians declare that 'a justification which does not issue in sanctification is no justification at all' they are but stating in their own idiom what simpler believers instinctively realise. For the ideal of Christian holiness has a most disconcerting power. Once we have seen it we can never unsee. What happened to the rich young ruler after he went away sorrowful is one of the minor mysteries of the New Testament, but it may well be that thereafter he was haunted by the sight of a homeless carpenter who had no purse of his own yet possessed a beauty of character which no money could buy.

The Call to Holiness, pp 2, 3

31 August

The word 'holy' is one of the oldest religious words, and its roots stretch out far and away beyond the covers of the

Bible. So far as scholars can tell, the word was originally applied to the sacred as distinct from the secular. The root meaning was separate. That which was holy was set apart from common use and dedicated to the service of God. . . .

If, of the ten commandments, four dealt with man's relationship to God, half as many again had to do with his relationship to his neighbour. A god who was righteous expected his people to behave righteously. Upon this foundation the prophets built. A king, though he were a king, could not annex his neighbour's vineyard. A David, though he were David, could not arrange to have one of his mercenaries killed in battle so that he might possess his wife. A man of property was not thereby entitled to sell a debtor into slavery for a song, nor regard the poor as dust beneath his chariot wheels. He might go into the holy place and offer all the prescribed sacrifices but, in God's sight, he would remain unholy. To no purpose would be the multitude of his sacrifices if his hands were stained with blood.

Isaiah saw that he who was high and lifted up was different from mortal man not only in his majesty but in his measureless moral purity. The separateness of God was a separateness from sin—the thrice repeated 'Holy!' announced that fact. . . . So the prophet prayed that he himself might be purged from sin before he called upon his people to cry for a like cleansing.

The Call to Holiness, pp 22, 24

1 September

How can holiness be accepted as life abundant, which it is, if it is thought to be repression run riot. How urgent the need to keep a right pattern before us so that our heart's longings be not mocked nor our spiritual desires misdirected.

But more than pattern is needed—and more than pattern can be found when we look to Jesus. This ideal, when accepted, has a compulsive power enabling us to grow like him.

This becomes true of a man's thinking, for it is a mistake to think that the experience of holiness affects one particular habit only, leaving all other areas of personal living untouched. Such a piecemeal conception of holiness allows a salvation soldier to love sinners but, as in the poem of Flora Larsson, to have little patience with 'the awkward saints'. By the same token a soldier may manifest great zeal for duty but this is eclipsed by a still greater zeal that this duty should be seen and known of all. His thinking is not yet fully transformed. He is not wholly possessed by the mind of Christ. And for the mind that was in Christ there is no substitute or equivalent.

A man's thinking can be changed radically when he looks long enough, and searchingly enough, at Jesus—his thinking about God, his thinking about his neighbours, his thinking about himself.

The Call to Holiness, pp 18-20

2 September

. . . A man's conception of holiness is governed by the character of the God he worships. Like God, like worshipper. So that when Jesus came, enriching beyond measure our understanding of God, he also deepened beyond measure our conception of holiness. When Jesus said, 'He that hath seen me hath seen the Father' he made it clear for all time that the nature of God had been finally revealed in his life. And if the call to holiness is a call to resemble God, then to be holy is to be like Jesus. Holiness means Christlikeness, not only in the negative virtue of sinlessness but in the positive accomplishments of holy love. 'Be ye holy' is therefore best understood as it is translated 'Be ye Christlike'. And that adjective, far from weakening our thoughts of holiness, is a more demanding word. What was a vague noun is now given a sharply marked outline. An ideal has been made incarnate. We are confronted not with an abstraction which each man may define as seems him good, but with a figure whose example defies the touch of time and whose words brook no denial. To use this short and simple definition of holiness as Christlikeness is not to bypass any of its theological implications. It is not to water down a doctrine whose strength, with some past expositors, has seemed to lie in the exclusively Pauline language employed. But here the experience stands stripped of all verbiage and is set out in the plainest of language. Where Christ is enthroned, there is true holiness.

The Call to Holiness, pp 24, 25

3 September

Where a man is 'strengthened with might by the Spirit', there Christ dwells in his heart by faith. And where Christ dwells by faith is also known the power of the Spirit. The Holy Spirit can do no other than make us increasingly like to Christ. And when in any life there are the beginnings of Christlikeness, that must be the work of the Holy Spirit. How can it be otherwise? These two cannot work to conflicting ends. They are allies not rivals. Every claim to holiness stands or falls by its likeness to Jesus. Every gift of the Spirit which a believer may claim to possess must be judged by its power to produce a more Christlike character.

. . . What is taught in the New Testament and confirmed by our Army teachers can be verified in our own experience. For this likeness to Christ is no affair of external imitation. It has been well said that all imitations are bad—even the imitation of Christ. Holiness does not begin with an outward conformity of habit but with an inward receiving of the Spirit. To conform to a pattern is not difficult. We see that process at work in a school, in a community, in a union. Newcomers assume the colour of the group far more quickly than they assimilate its spirit. They conform and are accepted—and this is as true of a club in the West End as in Bermondsey. This process begins as a pressure working from without, but in Christian holiness the work is from within.

The Call to Holiness, p 26

4 September

Christian holiness is much more than poise, though he who knows Christ within will know a heart's repose. It is more than the cultivation of courtesy, though that is part of its outworking. We are not here concerned primarily with external manners but with inward change. This experience is nothing less than the final dethronement of self and the infilling of the surrendered life by the Spirit of him who is the summation of all virtue.

'O God,' prayed Socrates, 'make me beautiful within.' With a greater knowledge of sanctifying grace than that Greek philosopher could ever have conceived, we can utter the same prayer, knowing that to possess the Spirit of Christ within will transform us without.

That this is true holiness let the Army Mother bear witness, as in the concluding sentences of one of her outstanding addresses in the St James's Hall, Piccadilly:

> Sanctification does not mean that Christ comes and works a work in me, and then departs to Heaven to look on and see how I maintain it. No, he truly does a divine work in me, but he cleanses the temple for *himself* (her italics) for his use. . . . Then is fulfilled the promise: 'I will come in to him, and will sup with him.'

Even so, Lord Jesus, come quickly!

The Call to Holiness, p 27

5 September

'Be holiness my aim on earth,' wrote Richard Mant. . . . There is no shortage of texts to support this aim, but the experience itself does not depend on any single proof text so much as on the whole spirit and teaching of the New Testament which bids us bear fruit unto holiness.

This is a high aim; some think too high an aim. In the second play of the *Man born to be King* cycle, Dorothy Sayers puts this very thought into the mouth of John, son of Zebedee. With Andrew, Simon Peter and Philip, he is talking to Jesus.

> Master, what is holiness? Is it just to keep the command-ments and say the right prayers, and do the right things, and

196

pay the proper dues, as the priests tell us? Or is it something quite different? The preaching of John the Baptist has troubled our hearts . . . we are disheartened because nothing we do seems to be any good, and the righteous God is so great and terrible and far away. How can we rise so far above ourselves? What sort of heroic thing is holiness?

This is a superb phrase. But the question must not be quoted in order to daunt our spirits. None must take this as a reason for edging away on the ground that here is form of spiritual heroism beyond human attainment.

. . . After the First World War there was a unique parade in London in so far that everyone taking part had been awarded the Victoria Cross. As this somewhat mixed company marched down Whitehall an observer was heard to remark: 'They look a very ordinary crowd.' To which answer was made: 'But ordinary people are capable of great valour.'

The Call to Holiness, pp 28, 29

6 September

The life of holiness is not for spiritual supermen only. The God who was the God of Elijah was also the God of Jacob. The struggle under cover of darkness at Jabbok was no less significant than the victory won on Carmel in full light of day—for which thanks be to God as there are always more Jacobs than Elijahs. What matters is not our all too human weakness but our willingness to allow that weakness to be transcended by the presence and power of the Holy Spirit. On those terms, nothing is impossible. With the consent of the human will nothing is too hard for the Lord.

This means that the first aim which the doctrine of holiness sets before us is victory over sin, not immunity from temptation.

Of the promise of victory there can be no doubt. . . .

But victory is not immunity. Here more than one seeker has gone astray. There is a full surrender to the will of God at the mercy seat or at the quiet of a bedside, but instead of peace and tranquillity temptation comes in like a flood. The believer is discouraged afresh. 'Is this the happiness you told me of?' he inquires with Pliable. 'If we have such ill speed at our first setting out, what may we expect betwixt this and our journey's end?'

Immunity from temptation is nowhere promised. . . .

The Call to Holiness, pp 29, 31

7 September

The form of the temptation may alter but the fact of temptation remains. A converted drunkard may be so radically changed as to dislike the familiar smell of the saloon bar. He can now sell Salvation Army papers where once he was too drunk to stand, and the very thought of a pint be repulsive. But is that same man never tempted to think what a wonderful fellow he now is to be able to do all this? Unless he is 'kept low by grace' is he not in danger of being lifted up by pride?

We can no more escape temptation than we can escape being jostled by people during the rush hour. Of course, I do not need to go out during the rush hour unless I must. If I do put myself in harm's way, then my excuses are as lame as that of the negro servant found in the chicken run who protested that he was there testing his will power. But if my work, or my Army duty, or an errand of mercy, calls me out in the rush hour, then out I must go. My daily occupation or my service to God may expose me to temptation, but I am no more obliged to parley with it than I am to start up a conversation with a stranger on evil bent who accosts me in the street. I can choose with whom I will stop to talk even in the rush hour. And at any waking moment I can choose whether to toy with some sinful suggestion or to turn to Christ with a cry for help.

The Call to Holiness, pp 31, 32

8 September

The experience of holiness does not confer immunity from temptation. Nor need we be cast down or suppose we are out of God's favour when tempted. Brengle defined temptations as 'God-permitted opportunities'. In that sense we may rejoice with James and count ourselves happy when assailed by temptation. Here is a God-permitted opportunity for victory, and such opportunities will recur from our conversion till our translation to realms above. Not until Mr Valiant for Truth heard the final summons did he yield his sword to the one who was to succeed him on the pilgrim way. . . .

In our aim for holy living we are not promised immunity from temptation, God having provided some better thing—victory by his grace.

In making holiness my aim on earth, a further truth has to be kept in mind. The question is sometimes debated whether the experience of holiness is gained instantly or gradually. The answer is that the life of holiness is both a crisis and a process. Now this phrase is not mine. We owe it to the saintly Handley Moule, Bishop of Durham. . . . This is one more illustration of the many-sidedness of the experience of holiness, the deepest work of grace in the human heart. Here is richness which includes opposites and which makes those seeming opposites not contradictory but complementary.

The Call to Holiness, pp 33, 34

9 September

First there must be a beginning. There arises an awareness of personal need which draws a man on to an act of full surrender. The forgiven soul awakes to the truth that forgiveness is not enough. Blessed is the man whose iniquity is forgiven—but that act of divine grace arouses in him a longing to be like the One to whom he owes his forgiveness. The prodigal who has been welcomed back from his wild excesses in the far country feels his need to be clothed in the garments of holiness fit for his father's house.

Or the beauty of holiness as seen in another life may awaken this desire. Here is the magic of Christian love shining in other eyes and the light of Christian joy illuminating another face. What could be more inviting? Truth not only is good but looks good. Grace and charm are never far apart. Goodness is usually attractive. That was why John Donne could break into raptures over George Herbert's aged mother:

> No Spring nor Summer beauty hath such grace
> As I have seen in one Autumnal face.

Or it may be that we ourselves have come so far as to be forgiven for Christ's sake and yet not wholly to be possessed by his Spirit. . . . Despair seizes us in our vain attempts to resemble him. . . . The life that is wholly forgiven needs to be wholly possessed. And to be wholly possessed requires a full surrender.

The Call to Holiness, pp 35, 36

10 September

A full surrender is the beginning of the life of holy living; the end of that experience I do not—I cannot—see. Fanny Crosby sang of those 'depths of love' and 'heights of joy' which lie beyond the narrow sea. The end of holy living is lost in the white light which surrounds the Father's throne where those who are his will be presented before the presence of his glory with exceeding great joy. There's a long, long trail a-winding between start and finish. Any comprehensive view of the doctrine of holiness must have room for both. The experience can neither be explained nor lived without crisis and process. . . .

In grace as in wisdom 'hills peep o'er hills and Alps on Alps arise'. Spiritually there is always the glory of going on and still to be. . . .

An aged and devout reader of the Koran was being ridiculed by younger men for his devotion to what was to him the sacred text. 'You must know it by heart. Don't you get tired of always reading the same thing?'

'For me it is by no means the same Koran,' was the reply. 'When I was a boy I understood it as a boy. When I was a man in my prime I understood it as a man in his prime. Now I am old I understand it as an old man. Always for me it has something new.'

How much more is this so of the education of the Spirit where new light is continually surprising the believer as he thinks of what grace can do, and receives continually of that grace in his own life.

The Call to Holiness, pp 37, 38

11 September

What we learn by experience in this matter is also taught by Scripture. For example, no man was more certain than Paul that there was no condemnation to those who walked 'not after the flesh but after the Spirit'. The spirit of life in Christ had made him free from 'the law of sin and death'. Once for all the ding-dong struggle of the past had ended. In the old familiar phrase, this work of grace was a finished work. No more would he long for the good he could not, nor mourn the evil which he would not. That crisis point was past.

But no man was also more assured that he was only seeing in part and knowing in part. Late in life he wrote from imprisonment in Rome, 'I do not consider myself to have "arrived", spiritually, nor do I consider myself already perfect. But I keep going on . . .' *(J. B. Phillips).*

Every believer can rejoice in these allied truths. Let him hold to the one as firmly as the other. For here, in the true tradition of Salvation Army teaching, is the starting point. An act of surrender is demanded. The forgiven life must be wholly yielded to the will of God. There must be a resolve, as God may help, to part with all that is wrong. . . .

The Call to Holiness, pp 38, 39

12 September

. . . We can hear these phrases in dozens of our meetings as the invitation to the mercy seat is made.

But here am I also delivered from the peril of complacency, from any vain thought that a single act of surrender is enough. At no point is the believer ever as good as he can be. Ever must there be growth in grace, and every day of growth will prepare the way for days of further growth. Just as the longer a musician practises his art, the more sensitive becomes his ear to any untuneful-ness, so the closer a believer draws to Christ, the more sensitive will he become to anything unChristlike in his life. That is the reason why the greatest saints have ever been the greatest penitents. But their penitence has brought forth fruits meet for spiritual progress until glory has finally crowned what grace began below.

Such an ending in sight demands a beginning in faith. And the beginning will assuredly, under God, lead to so happy an ending.

We may be still more encouraged to make holiness our aim when we think of the experience as a privilege, not a burden.

There is the burden of doing. . . . There is the burden of giving. . . . There is the burden of being. . . . The poor man is nearly on his knees. It is as if our tenth article of faith was pitched in the minor key . . . 'the sad and almost unsupportable burden laid upon all believers'. . . .

Privilege or burden; which is true?

The Call to Holiness, pp 39-41

13 September

That religion is a burden, and an unnecessary one at that, is the view of many an unconverted man. He has his work cut out earning his bread and butter and keeping a roof over his head. Why should he add to his cares by supporting a religion which would, in the first place, rob him of things pleasant and, in the second place, require him to do things unpleasant such as going to church on a Sunday morning when all he wants to do is to read the paper and listen to his favourite disc jockey? So runs his reasoning. . . .

Righteousness may sound a forbidding word, but basically it stands for a right relationship with God. Is that not a desirable privilege? An unconverted man may not think so, but then he is no judge for he does not know what it means. But we do, and when we do not enjoy that right relationship with God we are of all people most miserable. No person is so unhappy as the heart back-slider. The old world is not for him. He has seen through its shams. He is not to be deceived any more by its catch-penny tricks. He has discovered for himself how chilly is its painted warmth and how false its surface smiles. . . . But some miserable sin has come between him and his Lord so that he enjoys neither the spurious consolations of the world nor the solid comforts of his faith. He might be more content had he never been saved at all. . . .

The Call to Holiness, pp 41, 43

14 September

The life of holiness is not a burden, not a deadweight. Our doctrine is never closer to the heart of Scripture than when it describes this experience as 'a privilege'!

To cover the length, the breadth, the depth, the height of this privilege is, as Doddridge said of grace, 'a work so sweet, a theme so high' as to require eternity for its exposition. Here we can but sum up this privilege as 'righteousness, and peace, and joy in the Holy Ghost'. . . .

This right relationship is one which the experience would conserve . . . our continual yieldedness to his will is our part in maintaining that right relationship which is the necessary strength of those who serve him.

'And peace.' This assuredly follows, for when we are in a right relationship with God we are at peace with ourselves. Ended is that civil war of which Paul of Tarsus was not the first nor the last to write. . . .

If the moderns despise the apostolic remedy, at least they have to acknowledge the apostolic struggle. 'I hold' said Dylan Thomas, 'a beast, an angel and a madman in me, and my inquiry is to their working and my problem is to their subjugation.' Now if holiness means an integration of life with Christ at the centre so that these warring confusions are ended and inward peace is proclaimed, is that not a privilege?

But more still—'joy in the Holy Ghost'. . . .

The Call to Holiness, pp 42-44

15 September

. . . Christian joy is not an emotion which has to be worked up from the human end but is a blessing which descends unsought upon the man who is in right relationship with God.

So Jesus could pass this gift on to his disciples with the assurance that none could take it from them. When Bunyan heard 'three or four poor women sitting at a door in the sun, talking about the things of God', it was the 'joy which did make them speak' more than their poverty which caught his eye. The half-smile which hovers uncertainly upon the lips of Franz Hals' misnamed *Laughing Cavalier* is faint compared with the 'solid joys and lasting treasure' known to Zion's children. Side by side with a meditation and an account of a meeting, Brengle wrote: 'Next to virtue, the fun in this world is what we least can spare.' And so says every man who has caught the spirit of his Lord. . . .

For as no man is to be denied the opportunity of salvation, none shall be refused the joy of holy living. This privilege, like the wideness of God's mercy, includes all. The gate which God has opened let no man shut. It is the wayfaring man who can walk the way of holiness. And that means me—and you.

The Call to Holiness, pp 44, 45

16 September

In our common usage perfection implies a state not requiring, indeed, not admitting of, further improvement. There are no comparative and superlative comparisons of

204

the adjective 'perfect'. Perfection is the final goal of all endeavour, the summit peak beyond which no climber can go.

Nothing is more natural or understandable than to carry over into the spiritual life the current meaning of this word, and to say that if Christian perfection is a state of grace in which a man is so good that he cannot be any better, then this is not for mortals this side of the grave. We would blush to make such a claim. All our English habit of understatement would rise in protest against it. And were this the meaning of this word when applied to Christian experience, then such comments would be fully justified. . . .

But closer inquiry makes it clear that I am not required to do *what* he does, but *as* he does. That is to say, God does all in love for he is love. Love is not just one of his attributes but the very essence of his nature. 'God is love.' He creates, sustains, redeems and judges in love. And I, on my finite scale, am required to do all I do in the same spirit. Of myself I cannot do this. Love is not my native air. But I can receive of his Spirit who is the Holy Spirit. Of him I already know something for by his power I was first convicted of sin and then led into grace. . . .

The Call to Holiness, pp 46, 47

17 September

. . . The Church of Christ is perfect when she is fulfilling her intended end as the body of Christ, acting as his eyes to search out human need, his feet to run to meet that need, his hands to succour need, his lips to speak comfortable words to those in need. Thus behaving, his Church is a glorious Church, without spot or wrinkle, perfect in the Father's sight because she is fulfilling his purpose for her.

That part of the Church of Christ known as The Salvation Army is perfect when fulfilling her appointed end—seeking in the highways and byways for the maimed and halt and lame so that they may share in the feast of good things prepared by him who keeps open house for sinners. This is not easy work for the Army and, busy with her task, her dress may be soiled, her face flushed, her accent not always impeccable, her grammar shaky under stress of emotion, her appearance not always so collected as others of the Lord's servants, but she is perfect in his household in that she is accomplishing that good thing which is his will for her.

Once this basic truth is grasped, all foolish desire to copy the manners or the methods of any other of God's faithful ministers will disappear. . . . As we are his servants we can abide his judgment. The Lord knoweth them that are his.

The Call to Holiness, pp 48, 49

18 September

. . . That person in that part of the Church of Christ known as The Salvation Army and called a salvation soldier is perfect in the measure in which he fulfils God's revealed will for him. No more than Paul does he count himself perfect in any sense of final accomplishment, but perfect in consecration and intention he can be. Were he ever to account himself perfect in the sense of having nothing more to learn, the strong possibility would be that he had looked away from that perfection which is Christ and fallen back on the age-old refuge of the unprofitable servant, I am as good as my neighbour. What is required of him is perfection of intention, and even the beginner can yield himself so fully to God that in this sense he has a perfect heart towards the Lord. . . .

. . . When we say that a man's heart is the Lord's, we mean that his will is the Lord's. The central and determinative factor within him is in God's hands for him to direct and control as seems him good. No man can be more fully the Lord's than he whose will is the Lord's. That life is perfect in the scriptural sense when the will has been fully yielded to God.

Once again let it be said, not perfect in any degree of finality. That is not possible this side of the grave. . . .

The Call to Holiness, pp 49, 50

19 September

The truth is that our response to God must include the whole personality, the regulative centre of which is the will. I love God when I put his will first in my life.

In any exposition of love in the New Testament sense, it has become commonplace to distinguish between the meaning of the various first-century words which are all rendered in the English language by our one . . . word. Certain current meanings have to be strained away. Affection between man and woman is not intended here. Family unity—the 'blood is thicker than water' idea—has also to be ruled out. The David and Jonathan friendship— 'thy love to me was wonderful, passing the love of woman'—is not what is meant either. Human preference, in the sense of liking this rather than that—'I love a holiday on the south coast'—also falls very short of the New Testament ideal. What the earliest Christian thinkers did was to adopt a Greek word which was something of a waif and stray and turn it to divine use. The word they chose for love to God and man was little known and less used, but they brought it to their mercy seat to be baptised with the power and warmth of the Holy Spirit. Words as well as men can be converted, and this one was sanctified to Christian use so that love as Jesus used the word means caring whatever the cost. . . .

The Call to Holiness, pp 59, 60

20 September

Loveless knowledge is the antichrist of every age. Time and energy have been spent on the task of identifying antichrist with a particular person. The truth is that he belongs to no one country or century. Were this spirit limited to a specific time and place, and identifiable with one person only, he would not be so greatly to be feared for his place and power would be correspondingly limited. This is not to say that antichrist is timeless, for that would in one respect be raising him to equality with God. Antichrist is the opposite in time to the eternally compassionate Christ; the opposite of that love which cares for men whatever the cost.

Antichrist does not care. His reasons for not caring may have the highest intellectual warrant. It may be argued that pure research cannot be halted; that nature demands that men shall solve her mysteries. Ours not to reason why, only to keep on inquiring; others to decide to what use our findings are to be put. Such an evasion of personal responsibility is in itself loveless, and where knowledge is not ruled by love, there is antichrist. Where knowledge is applied without love, there again is antichrist. The highest names may sponsor such research. The most demanding national necessities be adduced in support of the application of such research. But if it be not done in the spirit of care, there is antichrist.

The Call to Holiness, pp 61, 62

21 September

This truth applies to more than the cosmic effect of nuclear physics. If it did not, we ordinary folk might suppose ourselves immune from this spirit of evil. Self-righteously we might welcome the opportunity of sitting in judgment upon our intellectual superiors and supposing ourselves untouched by their temptations. But we are not. Loveless knowledge has its evil way when, from the vantage point of experience or power, a parent dominates his home, a foreman his gang, a teacher his class, a secretary his society, a master his men. Wherever what we know is used regardless of what the other man is, there is antichrist. He can be as evident in the backdoor gossip of a down-town street as in decisions of state. Antichrist is the spirit of not caring. If one of his sayings be recalled as 'Blow you Jack, I'm in the dinghy', then service and ex-servicemen may recognise him when they meet him. His speech betrays him for it reveals his loveless heart. He is sometimes present where least expected in religious circles. By contrast he is gloriously absent whenever a thirsty man asks, and is given, a cup of cold water.

To put down such a mighty one from his unlawful seat requires a mightier yet. There is one such—the incarnate love manifested in the historic Jesus and eternally present in the world by his Spirit. . . . The only conqueror of antichrist is the love of God which 'is shed abroad in our hearts by the Holy Ghost'. . . . It is the first-fruit of the Spirit who would have me care for all whatever the cost.

This gift, though divine, is not exclusive. All who will share its pains may know its joys.

The Call to Holiness, pp 62, 63

22 September

There is an outward as well as an inward witness, for the visible fruit of the Spirit bespeaks his presence within. This testimony is all the more convincing when the ugliness of the works of the flesh are set in intentional contrast, with the fruit of the Spirit. . . .

'When I would do good,' wrote Paul, 'evil is present within me'; . . . Ever since man has begun to reflect on the complexity of his nature he has been aware of this inward division. 'Talk about two natures,' wrote Charles Gordon to his sister Augusta, 'I have a hundred and they all want to rule.' . . .

A Jew by race, Paul would early learn from his rabbinic masters that man was possessed of two impulses—one good, one evil. There was a school who taught that these conflicting powers were present in a baby even before he was born. Another said that the evil nature awoke at nine years of age; another at twelve. All agreed that this impulse was ever waiting, until the last recorded syllable of life, to slip the leash and drag a man to his doom. To love the law was regarded in theory as a stout enough rein to hold evil in check.

But one man at least knew differently. Hebrew of the Hebrews, Pharisee of the Pharisees though he was, Paul knew that the war between the law in his members and the law of his mind brought him into captivity to the law of sin.

The Call to Holiness, pp 52-54

23 September

'Spirit' and 'ghost' are words which have come down in the world. In our common speech these are but disembodied shades. The ghost of Banquo in the banqueting hall of the palace at Forres might unman a Macbeth, but in a century such as ours where time and sense are all, children cheer Marley's ghost in *A Christmas Carol* as only a piece of play acting. They are more amused than terrified. . . .

In the Old Testament the word 'spirit' meant strong breath or blast and was associated with power, not infrequently violent power. So in the New Testament where the Spirit 'driveth' Jesus into the wilderness. So on the day of Pentecost when the coming of the Spirit was likened to 'a sound . . . as of a rushing mighty wind'. . . .

Here was the Spirit of the living God entering men's lives in power. . . .

In the preliminary moments before an orchestral concert begins the instruments will sometimes indulge such fancy as seems them good. The woodwind will run up and down scalic passages with incredible dexterity; the bass violins grunt in the depths; the brass tootle and trumpet. There is anything but music until the conductor enters and at a stroke brings harmony out of disorderly noise. A unifying power is at work. . . .

The musical analogy is not far-fetched when it is remembered that Wycliffe translated John 20:22 as 'He blew on hem and seide, take ye the holi goost'. It is the word of a flute player. The holy breath evokes divine harmonies. Was that why Paul was so disappointed when the Corinthians sounded only like a noisy gong instead of producing the music of the Spirit?

The Call to Holiness, pp 54-56

24 September

The early popularity of the Church in Jerusalem had declined. . . . James the Apostle, son of Zebedee and brother of John, was put to death. As there was no public outcry against this judicial murder, the king—under the impression that this new movement would collapse if deprived of its leaders—arrested Peter. His intention was to execute the apostle out of hand, but, making a show of piety, he deferred any action until after the Passover. Thus, although James was martyred, Peter's life was spared.

We may ask why one should be taken and the other left. Could not God have intervened to rescue James as he did Peter? Yes; so long as we recognise that both events may well have been equally valid expressions of his will. . . . The more important question is not 'why did James die?', but 'how did he face death?' Not 'why was Peter imprisoned?', but 'how did he behave in prison?' Whining or bravely? Cowardly or courageously? As both men acted as true disciples of Christ, the martyrdom of James glorified God as much as the escape of Peter. Both events were in the divine will.

Whatever awaits us—action or suffering, living or the ordeal of dying—can be faced victoriously in the strength of the Holy Spirit. There is no need to resent whatever hardship may come to us through obeying God. It is not pain that matters, but the way it is borne. . . . To know there is a Father who will receive the soul when the body can hold out no longer is to rob death of its sting, and to transform the last enemy into a door which opens into the place prepared by Jesus.

International Company Orders 1939

25 September

Our primary textbook is the Bible, the written record of God's progressive self-revelation to man, culminating in the life, the death and the rising again of the historic Jesus of Nazareth, whom the New Testament calls 'the Word made flesh'. . . .

[Major Harding Young] was, in the presence of his wife and two children . . . arrested in his own quarters in Bandung on 14 April 1942. His one request was to be allowed to take his Bible with him—but this was refused. So during the seven months of solitary confinement which preceded his internment his prayer was for a Bible. This was answered when he was given a 'loose-leaved' Bible—loose-leaved in the sense that it lacked any covers. Nevertheless it was patched up. The dark blue of a convict's uniform formed a backing, a piece of prison pyjama cloth served as edging, and blue paper used to blackout the prison windows did duty as inside lining. One of the two principal means of grace was restored to the major and his fellow internees. No jailor could deny them their personal approach to the throne of grace, and now they possessed the other thing needful. We who are people of *the* Book cannot live without it, nor without such additional books as may help to make its meaning clear and plain. Without them we are as helpless as the legendary plumber who arrives on the job site having left his tool bag at home.

In Good Company, pp 112, 113

26 September

To read the Bible should be a daily habit with us all. I do not say read a chapter a day. There is no virtue in a chapter as such. A chapter may be too long. Sometimes half a dozen verses are more than enough to think over. But the daily reading should never be omitted. A promise of God can strengthen us for work. A word of Jesus can throw light on a difficult personal decision. A sentence from the gospels can provide the best of talking-points for the open-air meeting. And the more we read the Bible the more will we want to read.

There is an Eastern story of some young men who were poking fun at an old man for always reading the Koran. 'You must know it by heart,' they said. 'Do you not get sick of reading the same thing?'

'For me,' replied the old man, 'it is not always the same Koran. When I was a boy I understood it as a boy. When I was a man in my prime I understood it as a man. Now I am old I understand it as an old man. I read it again and again because for me it always contains something new.'

Far more true is it to say that you and I will always find in the Bible 'something new.'

Jesus and our Need, p 53

27 September

Like every other Jewish boy, the Master was brought up on the Scriptures of his race. When you and I went to school we had half a dozen text books and perhaps twice as many reading books. But a Jewish lad had one only—our Old Testament. . . . Every boy had one book only and, as soon as he could read, was given a number of memory portions. The first was the *Shema:* 'Hear, O Israel, the Lord our God is one Lord.' Another was the *Hallel*—Psalms 113-118. A third was the story of creation, and a fourth a collection of sayings from the Book of Leviticus. All this may sound rather dull. No Jack the Giant Killer here, no Richard and Blondel. But Jewish history had a giant killer—David, and the song of Deborah meant as much to a youthful Peter or Jacob as the *Chanson de Roland* to a Pierre or Jean.

But what concerns us here is that these stories, and many more, were committed to memory. That was more a blessing than a hardship, for instead of knowing, as with so many of us, only odd sentences and hackneyed phrases, the mind of a Jewish lad was soaked in noble thoughts about God expressed in noble language.

[But] knowledge about God is not the same as a personal experience of God. . . .

Jesus and our Need, pp 50-52

28 September

Now knowledge about God is not the same as a personal experience of God. Some Jews were none the better for all that they had learnt of the Scriptures in their youth. Their knowledge but rose up against them in condemnation. But Jesus found that the words of Isaiah, of Hosea and of the Psalms came alive for him in his moments of need.

This was so in his arguments with his opponents. Time and time again in the gospels we come across 'Have ye not read . . .?' 'What readest thou . . .?' 'Did ye never read . . .?' 'What is written . . .?' Jesus knew the Scriptures better than the professional teachers of his day. And, what is more, he knew not only their language but their spirit and intention.

See him, for instance, meeting the challenge of those who rebuked him for mixing with sinners. . . . Or read how he met temptation in the wilderness. . . . Or look how Jesus faced death with Scripture on his lips. His last words 'Into thy hands . . .' were taken from Psalm 31:5. This sentence was the first prayer that a Jewish mother taught her child to say before going to sleep at night. . . . And with this goodnight prayer Jesus bowed his head and died. In life and death the Scriptures were part of his armoury. . . .

Jesus and our Need, pp 52, 53

29 September

The Bible can be regarded as one long series of illustrations of the suffering which evil brings upon love. The Old Testament prophets bewailed the fact that a people so greatly loved could behave so badly. There is no wind so keen as that of man's ingratitude. Yet God cannot cease loving and remain true to himself. . . .

A father once complained to a rabbi that his son had forgotten God and turned to wild ways. 'What, rabbi, shall I do?'

'Love him more than ever' was the reply.

That is the only answer we can make to the world's faithlessness. Evil can be met and conquered only by a stronger good. And even when love is slain, as on the Cross, its seeming defeat is its supreme triumph. . . .

In face of faithlessness or betrayal, all we can do is to remain true to our own creed. God's nature is not altered by man's sin. If he treated his world as his world treats him, he would not be the God we know through Jesus. But he abides faithful; he cannot deny himself.

His followers must do the same, for if love has to suffer long, it is also 'the one thing that still stands when all else has fallen' (1 Corinthians 13:8, *J. B. Phillips*).

Jesus and our Need, pp 22, 23

30 September

Many folk consider immoral conduct to be the most serious transgression of the law, and I agree that it is a sorry affair. Seen at close quarters it has little glamour, for usually it is furtive and always it is coarsening. But though virtue goes out of those who indulge in it, Jesus could say to one who had thus fallen: 'Go, and sin no more.' It was for the proud at heart he reserved his sternest words. For pride is no involuntary weakness of the flesh; it is a settled attitude of the soul which shuts a man out of the Kingdom.

Easy as it is to mark pride in another, it is just as difficult to notice it in ourselves. Yet one lad will be proud of his cornet playing; another of the nice home where he lives; another of the school tie he can sport. One girl will fancy her looks, while the second will think that her boy friend is definitely a cut above the rest. All simple, foolish things—yet do we not detest them in others? Must they not then be detestable in ourselves?

The remedy is not to keep on saying: 'I will be humble', for there the 'I' keeps cropping up even in our good desires. The way out is for us to think most of Jesus and to do our work for his sake. Then our interest and attention are turned away from ourselves and upward to the only One in whom we can rightly glory. For when we stand in with Jesus, we just cannot think of ourselves at all. And that is the humility which is commended in the Kingdom.

The Kingdom of God, pp 29, 30

1 October

Pride in a man's heart separates him from God and from his neighbour. Pride makes a man think himself independent of God, as it causes him to fancy that he is superior to his fellows. Some vices—cruelty, lust, sloth, arise from our animal nature but, as has been pointed out, pride comes straight from Hell and can spoil all our other virtues.

That was what was wrong about the Pharisee. It was

quite true that he was neither immoral nor unjust, nor did he behave like a publican. He lived a most respectable life and, in his religious practices, went much further than was expected of him. But his pride in his virtues spoiled his good deeds and so all his giving and fasting and good living were poisoned at their source. . . .

C. S. Lewis has remarked that Satan is quite happy to see us brave and good-natured and honest—so long as we remain proud. For when we commence to take pride in our virtues, thinking so well of ourselves that we attribute our good conduct to our own wit and wisdom, it will not be long before our pride will have a fall. In the opening chapters of Scripture, Satan is represented as a serpent whispering to Eve that disobedience to one particular command would make her and her husband as gods! And they fell for the suggestion.

Ever since pride has been the worst—and the commonest—of the deadly sins. . . .

The Kingdom of God, pp 28, 29

2 October

. . . The apostle [Paul] lists nine graces of the Spirit who is the Lord and Giver of life. He it is who can make the desert of the sinful heart blossom like the rose yet, to do so, he requires our active consent. A series of penicillin injections works independently of a man's willing. They can have the desired effect whether he himself wishes it or not. In a sense he is a guinea-pig. But not so with the work of the Holy Spirit. Our relationship with him is as with a person whose advice we can accept or reject, whose company we may welcome or refuse. If such is our mood we can grieve the Spirit. But if such is our desire he will dwell with us and be in us.

The first sign of his presence is the grace of love—which word must at once be rescued from the emotional slough of despond into which it has fallen. Too often in the spiritual life we read into this term the vagaries of our own human nature. We think of love as a feeling which, like

216

the wind, bloweth where it listeth, its source, object and strength being both unpredictable and uncontrollable. The word (it has been said) can cover everything from Heaven to Hollywood.

But basically to love God is to put his will first in our lives. To love our neighbour is to put his needs before our own. There may or may not be an emotional content in one or both of these relationships, but primarily these are twin expressions of an attitude of the will.

The Call to Holiness, pp 58, 59

3 October

The Christian principle of love is more lasting and purposeful than fondness or preference. Fondness, as such, cannot be commanded at will. We care for certain people—for what reason? We don't care for others—for what reason? A boy and girl 'fall in love'—that is, they find themselves gripped by an emotion over which they may have little control. Often they have no wish to control it; they prefer to be swept off their feet by it. . .

All this has been set out to make it clear that the love we are asked to display as members of the Kingdom is not the enemy of human affection, though rising superior to it. What we are called upon to manifest is a steadfast goodwill which conquers dislike, which is not quenched by hate, which is not overcome of evil but which overcomes evil with good. . . . And if it be argued that this is more than can be expected of any earthly being, the answer is that this activity is not self-induced but born of the love of God shed abroad in the human heart.

Love in the New Testament sense is more than occasional acts of kindness, gracious and praiseworthy though such are. Ordinary folk whom we call 'sinners' are capable of frequent acts of kindness. In every European city bombed during the war, companions in misfortune were kind to each other. Neighbour helped neighbour. One shelter dweller sought to cheer another. As Jesus said, the publicans love those who love them. But the love which he exemplified is born of a new relationship to God,

217

and this is active with or without external stimulus. In short, Christian love is a consecration to God which controls the whole of a man's actions for all time.

The Kingdom of God, pp 13, 14

4 October

Emotion may accompany our love to God. This has been particularly true with some of the saints of past ages who have poured out their hearts in passionate adoration. They have not hesitated to use the most fervent terms for none other could do justice to their devotion to their Lord. So St John of the Cross wrote of his search for him who was his soul's delight:

> That light did lead me on
> More surely than the shining of the noontide
> Where well I knew that One
> Did for my coming bide. . . .
>
> Upon my waiting breast
> Wholly for him and save himself for none,
> There did I give sweet rest
> To my beloved One. . . .

Few among us have the gift of such expression and maybe would not even desire it. So be it; such language is not obligatory. At the same time love to God is never only an intellectual exercise, the chilly assent of the mind. Who can repeat such a hackneyed line as 'My Jesus, I love thee, I know thou art mine' without feeling his heart strangely warmed?

The Call to Holiness, p 59

5 October

Christian joy is the fruit of Christian experience, and this is true at all stages of that experience. . . .
Among the Friars Minor of Assisi joy was rated as highly as chastity. . . . [The Salvation Army] song book can quote Doddridge on his 'glowing heart' telling 'its

218

raptures all abroad', John Newton on his 'solid joys' and Isaac Watts with his 'cheerful songs'. . . .

Tertullian spoke of 'the hilarity of the saints', and this was as true of Saint Francis with his witty repartee which won from Saladin an invitation to remain permanently at the Moslem Court as of 'Saint' William Booth, who could include in a serious letter to his eldest son a funny story he had heard about a Yorkshire preacher.

No less true of 'Saint' Samuel Brengle who, changing quarters, was confronted by an irate removal man who had lost his hammer. 'Where in 'ell's the 'ammer?' he snapped.

'There's no need to go there to get it; the hammer's right here' was the twinkling reply, and the irritation changed to a grin.

No less true of 'Saint' Clara Case who, while making an entry in her personal notebook concerning a most difficult problem which faced her in her Indian command, could add a 19th-century Chinese description of a bicycle. 'No pushee, no pullee, no shovee; ridee onee backee, holdee by ee ears, kickee in ee sides, makee go.' Said one who served her: 'Her eyes moved readily to merriment; there were laughter lines at their corners.'

The Call to Holiness, pp 64-66

6 October

. . . Many folk shy away from the Christian faith because they imagine it will deprive them of the few joys still left to them in a shadowed world.

There are some who suppose that a man is not truly religious unless he is always slightly uncomfortable. Christianity is thought to be life minus, practised by a few odd people who find a perverse satisfaction in going without good things.

This kind of criticism does not shake me, however, especially when I remember how loosely the term 'kill-joy' is used. Anyone who opposes any form of commercialised iniquity is promptly labelled a 'kill-joy'. A man who wants to keep public life clean is dubbed a Puritan. Yet when someone steals a car and, panicking, knocks down a child, he is reported as 'joy riding'. If that is what the world calls joy, then I am rather happy about my preference for the Christian variety. . . .

There is nothing strange about a man who has unexpectedly come into a fortune feeling on top of the world. But there is something almost unbelievable in the joy of a man who is up against it—and that is Christian joy. . . .

Because the unconverted man knows nothing of this he cannot believe that such gladness exists and so derides what he cannot understand. But those who have this gift know it is theirs—for keeps, and are quietly content.

Jesus and our Need, pp 46, 47-49

7 October

Let no one be frightened by the word 'Puritan'. Pay scant attention to what the prejudiced Macauley had to say about them. The Puritans were no kill-joys. If they had no taste for worldly gaieties it was because they had no need of such artificial aids to happiness. They had an inner gladness which expressed itself in their poetry and song. Never forget it was a Puritan poet who wrote of:

'Sport that wrinkled Care derides
And Laughter holding both its sides.'

One of the leading Puritans of the 17th century was John Bunyan. His was a hard life but not a joyless one. Thrown into Bedford Gaol after the Restoration, he cheered himself by playing a flute of his own making, and a violin still exists which bears his name. When he wrote his immortal allegory, he had a pair of virginals in a room at the Interpreter's house, and there was music at meals. Christiana played the viol and her daughter Mercy the lute. One current objection to Bunyan's pilgrim was that 'he laughs too loud'. The 'dismal stories' came from the sophisticated worldlings around him.

We should not find it hard to obey the word to 'rejoice and again . . . rejoice', for we know that the source of joy lies in that mastery of life and circumstance which Jesus alone bestows.

Jesus and our Need, pp 48, 49

8 October

If we inquire how these servants of God maintained their gaiety amidst vexatious responsibilities, we discover the second truth that Christian joy is the fruit of Christian obedience. When God's will is accepted, not sullenly or reluctantly as if it were something from which there was no escape and had to be borne, but as the loving guidance of him who does all things well, then joy abounds and even much more abounds.

'Be it according to thy word,' said Mary to the angel Gabriel. Thereafter she could say, 'My soul doth magnify the Lord, and my spirit hath rejoiced in God my Saviour.'

Acceptance of the holy will of the holy God brings its own joy. This is joy which is born of God and which concerns his Kingdom and his will. It is not joy in what I am or what I can do. Nor is it joy in triumph over another, much less that cruel pleasure in another's misfortunes. The joy which is of the Spirit bears its fairest bloom when I forget myself, my virtues (if any) and my failings (to dwell upon which may be only another form of egotism), and lose myself in the praise of him who was, who is, and who ever shall be, and who has granted me, who am less than the least of all saints, the amazing privilege of preaching the unsearchable riches of Christ. This is surely why the very epistle which speaks most of sharing the fellowship of Christ's sufferings can repeatedly call upon its readers to rejoice in the Lord, and again to rejoice.

The Call to Holiness, pp 66, 67

9 October

What Paul preached to others he himself practised. His words of good cheer were not written from some ivory tower. The heavy clouds of the Neronian persecution were already darkening the sky. The cry was about to rise from the blood of those who were to be made scapegoat for a Caesar's folly. The apostle's life had been no easy one. Nagging ill health, no home of his own, arguments within the Church, failures among the brethren, hunger, the hazards of travel, riots, floggings and now prison had been his portion, yet he wrote that 'if it should be that my life blood is poured out . . . then I can still be very happy'. Like his Lord, he could speak of joy in the face of death, a joy which no man could take from him.

No man can take this joy from us either—yet our own sinning can rob us of it. This is where the experience of holiness not only bears the fruit of joy but is its sole guardian.

This truth is rarely grasped by those outside the fellowship of faith and not always understood by those within that charmed circle. For example, some duty becomes irksome or some corps task provokes unexpected disagreement. The will sags. The soul's temperature drops abruptly. The life goes out of our step and, partly in weariness and partly in disgust, we fall back on some practice from which we normally abstain in order to restore (so we think) our native cheerfulness. . . .

But . . . the relief is but temporary and next morning life awakes with its problem still unsolved. . . .

The Call to Holiness, pp 67, 68

10 October

A business deal goes awry—and there seems to be an inviting magic in alcohol which will banish worry and induce a sense of well-being. . . . Or a man may think to forget the troubles that plague him in a bout of uncontrol. . . . Sex is regarded by some as the equivalent of joy; it is its chief destroyer. . . .

Amid these sad confusions the experience of holiness remains the sole fount and source of abiding joy. Not by adding hours of pleasure to hours of pleasure can be extracted so many moments of joy. There is no distillation of earthly elements which will produce this heavenly pleasure. Joy belongs to God. Joy is born of God. Joy is the gift of God to those who delight in his will.

Jesus is the extreme example of this. Man of sorrows he was and acquainted with grief. That had to be. The sin and unwisdom of men are enough to sadden all who love them.

But man of joy he was as well. 'He endured a cross and thought nothing of its shame because of the joy he had in doing his Father's will' (Hebrews 12:2, *J. B. Phillips*).

That joy his every follower may share.

The Call to Holiness, pp 68, 69

11 October

Peace is the third of the graces listed as being born of the Spirit. We have to consider each of these graces separately, but that is only because of our inability to grasp at one and the same time the multifold nature of the harvest of the Spirit. In practice the Spirit's fruit is one and indivisible. He who enjoys one will enjoy them all. The life of the Spirit is a harmonious whole. . . . One rich fullness includes these nine graces as the rainbow blends all the colours of the spectrum. The parent grace is love and, should that tender bud be frostbitten, little else will grow. But if love flourishes there will be gentleness; if temperance, then joy; if faith, then meekness; if goodness, then peace. If the tree is alive every bough will be laden. . . .

There is a peace which is born of an easy conscience. In the early pages of *Grace Abounding* John Bunyan speaks of a sermon which shook him as no other had done before. 'And so went home . . . with a great burden upon my spirit. . . . But hold, it lasted not, for before I had well dined the trouble began to go off my mind, and my heart returned to its old course. . . . When I had satisfied nature with my food, I shook the sermon out of my mind, and to my old custom of sports and gaming I returned with great delight.' . . .

The Call to Holiness, pp 70, 71

12 October

There is a peace which is born of unconcern. What matter who sinks if I swim. In his picture of Dives and

Lazarus, Gustav Dore painted the rich man's servants driving the beggar away with whips. But factually and imaginatively the painter was wrong. Lazarus was left to die. He starved at the gate of plenty, and plenty was content to let him starve. Had he been driven away Dives might have pleaded the lame excuse that the beggar was out of mind because out of sight.

There is a peace which is born of escapism. The world is evil; let us flee it. Politics are a dirty game; let's keep out. Civic work makes too many demands upon a man's leisure; leave me to watch the 'telly'. To take up a local position in the corps would involve me in corps difficulties; I pray thee have me excused. In short, anything for a quiet life. Peace at any price.

. . . The salutation 'I give you peace' was as common among first-century Jews as 'Goodbye' is with us. Goodbye is an abbreviated form of 'May God be with you' and has been a genuinely religious greeting, though now it mostly means little more than 'I'm off'. The Jewish greeting had also sunk to the level of a conventional phrase. The peace which the world gave was only a form of words without corresponding reality.

The Call to Holiness, pp 71, 72

13 October

This work of love and mercy provoked the Sadducean party in the Sanhedrin to open hostility. They were more bitterly opposed to the Early Church than were the Pharisees—some of whom may even have become disciples. . . . The Sadducees did not believe in any resurrection, and they took action because Peter had declared that the cripple had been healed through faith in the name of the *risen* Lord. They were also annoyed because of the crowds which followed the apostles, and feared lest their converts should so multiply as to provoke conflict with Rome, thereby endangering the means by which they themselves secured their own position.

Note the courage of Peter's reply before the 70 members and president of the Sanhedrin. . . . The council was nonplussed. 'Unlearned and ignorant men' who 'had been with Jesus' could not be brow-beaten. Peter and John announced that they could not give up speaking the things which they had seen and heard. This attitude of Peter was the more remarkable, because this was the man who—not many weeks previously—had been afraid to admit that he had the least connection with Jesus! . . .

What had brought about this change? . . . Has there been any like change in our own lives? . . .

International Company Orders 1939

14 October

Even the *Oxford English Dictionary* may mislead us here for peace is described as 'freedom from war or civil commotion, from quarrels or dissension, from mental or spiritual disturbance, the absence of noise, movement, activity'. The virtue is defined negatively as if its existence did not depend upon its own intrinsic worth but upon the absence of any opposing external factor. Whereas the Christian word regarding peace is that it can be enjoyed in the midst of tribulation. That was what Jesus said. 'These things have I spoken unto you, that in me ye might have peace. In the world ye shall have tribulation.' But the world's tribulation and Christ's peace could exist together because his peace was not—and is not—as the world gives.

. . . When Jesus said, 'Peace I leave with you, my peace I give unto you', he was speaking of a peace which was born of his union with the Father. When he declared that 'I and my Father are one', he meant not only in nature—as when we declare him to be 'truly and properly God and truly and properly man' but one in purpose as well. Is it irreverent to say that here were two minds with but a single thought, two hearts that beat as one? Consequently the Saviour knew a peace which the slings and arrows of outrageous fortune could not disturb. At one with the Father, he was at peace in a world of jangling men.

The Call to Holiness, pp 72, 73

15 October

This peace was part of his legacy to his disciples, among whom we may number ourselves. The peace which is of the Spirit is not necessarily peace with events but peace with God. Every reformer and soulwinner who has ever lived has warred mightily with events. This goes from the Early Church to our own day. This same Epistle to the Galatians describes how Paul withstood Peter to his face—that is, withstood him publicly, speaking to him 'so that everyone could hear'. That must have set tongues wagging in Antioch! . . .

Recall John Calvin finding a vulgar, scurrilous placard in his pulpit in Geneva, of guns being let off outside the cathedral doors as he preached, of being minuted by the Council: 'M. Calvin . . . preached today with great anger. . . . It is ordered that he be called upon to explain why he preached like this.' 'I promised myself an easy, tranquil life,' he wrote to his friend Francis Daniel; 'but what I least expected was at hand.'

Recall William Booth speaking on his 60th birthday. 'My life has been one of almost uninterrupted trial, conflict and difficulty. I was thinking the other day how few hours there have been in which there has not been some cloud in the sky.' . . . Peace depends not on our relationship to circumstances but to the Father.

The Call to Holiness, pp 72-74

16 October

The fruit cannot be enjoyed unless the root has been planted.

. . . The enjoyment of this grace depends primarily not on what we are but on what God is. The soul's peace is based upon the dependability of God and then upon our confidence in the divine character.

That God was dependable was one of the first—and last—lessons to be learnt by his chosen people. They were surrounded by nations who followed after gods whose behaviour was capricious and unpredictable. A god might favour a man today and ruin him tomorrow. . . .

Not so the God of whom Moses and the prophets spoke. At the beginning of the Old Testament story a man sees in the rainbow shining in the rain-washed skies a pledge of the dependability of God. This calamity will not happen again. He and his family begin life anew without terror clutching their hearts every time a cloud darkens the sky.

A tribesman leaves his ancestral tents and treks across the desert to a land he knows not of, depending upon the word of God to guide him and to settle him in an unknown home. Abraham could trust 'the soul's invincible surmise'. . . .

And at the close of the Old Testament a prophet announces God as saying, 'I am the Lord, I change not; therefore ye sons of Jacob are not consumed.' God is dependable, declares the Scriptures.

The Call to Holiness, pp 74, 75

17 October

Who could . . . question the dependability of him who had fulfilled his promise to redeem that which he had created? The apostle Paul regarded this as a self-evident proposition. 'He that did not hesitate to spare his own Son but gave him up for us all—can we not trust such a God to give us, with him, everything else that we can need?'

If God be utterly dependable, then our hearts can be at peace through fellowship with him. We can all relax. Not relax into sin or sloth. But we can sit more easily to life. We can cease trying to lay an apprehensive grip upon the steering wheel of the universe. A wiser hand than ours is at the helm. Nothing that can happen can harm the soul who trusts and obeys. A false faith will try to make out that what you dread may never happen. The true faith says that the worst that can happen cannot make God lose hold of the believing soul. There are only two facts which men and women have to face. One is the fact of life, the other of death—and both are in the control of love. Whether we live or die, we are the Lord's. Therefore 'let not your heart be troubled, neither let it be afraid'.

The Call to Holiness, pp 75, 76

18 October

Longsuffering and gentleness . . . seem passive qualities, but so to dismiss them would be to underrate their worth. One very important truth these two words are declaring is that the Spirit's presence and power are to be seen not only in the extraordinary and unusual—the tongues of fire and the rushing mighty wind—but in that daily growth in Christlikeness which is the hallmark of true holiness.

. . . Most versions, ancient and modern, agree in naming the first three graces of the Spirit as love, joy and peace, but thereafter they part company. Longsuffering is rendered as forbearance (*20th Century, SA edition*), good temper (*Moffat*) and patience (*RSV, Phillips* and *Goodspeed*). Gentleness is given as kindness (*RSV, Phillips, Goodspeed* and *Knox*). Some scholars say that an accurate English equivalent for the word which Coverdale translated as 'longsuffering' does not exist. But the simple believer has to live and so, taking courage where scholarship might hesitate, let longsuffering be defined as patience with a purpose and gentleness be described as patience with a purpose in action.

This at once redeems both words from an undeserved air of passivity. Christian patience is not the spiritless attitude which accepts whatever may be because to try to effect any change would be too much trouble. Here is no spineless acceptance of whatever is—good, bad or indifferent. Patience with a purpose will work to a mark—over centuries if needs be—and never shaken.

The Call to Holiness, pp 77, 78

19 October

The first announcement at Sinai of the divine nature proclaimed 'the Lord God, merciful and gracious, longsuffering'. Moses dared to quote this divine declaration against its own Author when pleading the cause of a generation who, at the gate of the land of promise, murmured about the impossibility of going further.

Surely, said he, the Lord would not summarily cast off his people. Was he not longsuffering? He had need to be with a race whom their own prophets described as stiffnecked and rebellious. It was of the Lord's long-suffering they were not consumed.

The New Testament underlines the same truth in more than one place. The parable of the wicked husbandmen is a parable of the patience of God. Sudden destruction did not come upon them like a whirlwind. Other servants were sent more than the first, and then last of all the son and heir. No hasty action here.

The opening of the second chapter of the Epistle to the Romans makes the same point. After the apostle's searching indictment of the Gentile world he turned on his own countrymen lest they suppose that the judgments of a righteous God did not apply to them. They did apply—and all the more because they were the chosen people. . . . To whom much had been given much would be required. The measure of revelation is always the measure of responsibility. 'Despisest thou the riches of his goodness and forbearance and long-suffering?' In Paul's view his people were trading on the patience of God. They thought they could do a wrong and get away with it.

The Call to Holiness, pp 78, 79

20 October

Zangwill used to say that the patience of God, not his peace, passed his understanding. The very patience of God is presumed upon as though he were unconcerned about evil or powerless to stay its course. How could he go on allowing men to trade upon his forbearance?

The answer is found in his longing, not for man's punishment but for his redemption. After all, man is his child, made in his image. A parent will put up with much—sometimes too much—from his child. Love sinks to the level of indulgence. The refusal to dominate becomes an unwillingness even to direct. God is not man that he should be guilty of man's errors of judgment, but in his patience of purpose he is not less resolved than man.

'If the world had treated me like it has treated God', said Luther, 'I would long ago have kicked the wretched thing to pieces.' The wicked husbandmen killed the heir yet, in purposeful patience, God turned that worst of all sins into the means of mankind's redemption. Here is patience with a purpose, a patience that can bide its time. It is God's intention to bring many of his sons into glory and he is not going to be put off by any silly fractiousness on their part. Of course, if they will not, they will not. Even the divine heart can be broken by unyielding refusal. 'O Jerusalem . . . how often would I have gathered thy children together . . . and ye would not!'

From this picture we have of the longsuffering of God three practical truths follow. . . .

The Call to Holiness, pp 79, 80

21 October

First of all, we must be patient with our work for God. Here the young idealist has a hard lesson to learn. 'We thought', said Cromwell of the Civil War, 'That one battle would have ended it.' 'The war will be over by Christmas', was a common saying in the late autumn of 1914, but one battle, one good meeting, one campaign, is never enough. The children of Israel had to march seven times around Jericho before the walls fell. Likewise generations of believers have been seventy times seven years marching around certain citadels of iniquity and these have not yet fallen. . . .

Carlyle somewhere says that the strong man is not he who, in a sudden frenzy, can lift an immense weight, but he who can carry the heaviest weight the longest distance. Patience with a purpose is of this nature. The inevitable disappointments which are the lot of all who serve God are faced and overcome. The servant of God goes on working for God by good report, by evil report and—hardest of all—without being reported on at all! Is not this a gift of the Spirit, and of him alone?

The Call to Holiness, pp 80, 81

22 October

Here is Thomas Clarkson, colleague and fighter with Wilberforce against the iniquities of the slave trade in England in the 18th century. To complete a particular case he needed the evidence of a sailor whom he had once seen but whose name he did not know. Systematically he went from port to port in this country and from ship to ship in each port till, on the 317th ship he visited, he found his man. Here was patience with a purpose.

Or here is Matilda Hatcher, pioneer salvationist in Japan (her story is told in *The Rising Sun*), summoned in the late evening to visit an outpost where defection had been reported. By the time her train reached its destination the hour was so late that no other conveyance was available and Matilda had to walk the remaining three miles over a flinty unmade road in her straw shoes. Soon she was limping more then walking and in the end almost crawling more than hobbling. On reaching the officer's quarters such a tale of backsliding was unfolded that she collapsed on the floor and wept.

Later she was taken to sleep in a friendly home and part of the way was by the path she had come. In the light of the paper lantern she could see the blood marks of her own feet. . . .

Here again was patience with a purpose—the hallmark of the mature servant of God. It is the inefficient and unskilled who grow impatient—the schoolboy with his homework, the learner at the piano, the apprentice at the bench. Pray God [for] this grace of maturity.

The Call to Holiness, pp 81, 82

23 October

We must also be gentle—which is patience in action—with one another. This will not be hard for him in whose heart the love of God is shed abroad, for 'love is very patient'.

We must be patient because God uses many servants of

231

many temperaments for he has many kinds of work to do. 'There are different ways of serving God,' observed Paul, 'but it is the same Lord who is served.' That truth should enable us to work for God alongside those with whom we may not always agree. We must never think that ours is the only way of serving the Kingdom. Our comrade local officer may be right in his way. Nothing ever entitles us to say: 'If it isn't done this way, I'm finishing.' Everyone who is working for Jesus is working for us as well.

We must also be gentle with those who are not yet fully possessed by this patience with a purpose. There are many Pliables on the way to the Celestial City who never get further than the first slough of despond into which they fall. All they want to do is to struggle 'out of the mire on that side of the slough next to home'—and off they go.

The Call to Holiness, p 82

24 October

While it is true that some offenders merit the judgment that it were better had they never been born because of those whom they have caused to stumble, yet with those who have stumbled, be gentle. We are instructed to rebuke 'with longsuffering'. Wounds require gentle treatment. Surgeons have gentle fingers. Steel is there all right, but no unnecessary roughness. 'Gentle Jesus' is not 'spiritless Jesus'. Gentleness is strength controlled by love.

Last of all, a man should be gentle with himself. This is no plea for self-indulgence, but there is an exaggerated form of self-condemnation which is in essence a refusal to admit the power of grace. If God has hope for a man should any man lose hope for himself? If God has patience with you, why lose patience with yourself? 'The Lord is . . . longsuffering to us-ward, not willing that any should perish.' If there has been failure, then turn to him in penitence, and 'let patience have her perfect work, that ye may be . . . wanting nothing'.

The Call to Holiness, pp 82, 83

25 October

It is a well-known rule that the simpler a word, the harder it is to define. How define goodness? Three of our most-used modern translations give 'generosity' as the best rendering. Others feel that the *Authorised Version* cannot be bettered and repeat 'goodness', leaving the reader to say what the word means.

. . . Goodness gets down to the job. Goodness is love with her sleeves rolled up. Goodness is not afraid of dirty work. The *good* Samaritan bandaged the wounds of the hapless traveller, set him on his own beast, took him to the nearest inn and paid his reckoning in advance. The *good* shepherd sought the sheep that was lost, for he could not lie down to rest even though the ninety and nine were safely in the fold. If required, he would lay down his life for that sheep. The *good* and faithful servant laboured mightily with his lord's five talents until he had made five talents more.

Goodness has willing hands, a ready mind, an eager heart, winged feet. Goodness cannot be idle in face of need. Goodness is the Martha of the graces. She has been compared unfavourably with the contemplative virtues, but Mary might have had less time for meditation had not Martha been busy with the cooking. Activity is not the sum total of religion, and the salvationist has to beware lest his service becomes a substitute for a personal experience of grace. But the ability to get things done in the cause of Christ is not to be despised for in this way the Spirit can work.

The Call to Holiness, pp 84, 85

26 October

Goodness which is born of the Spirit carries itself with an attractive air—and here is where the suggestion of generosity may be of help. Nothing evokes admiration more than a generous deed or a generous speech or a generous gift. Generous is as generous does. Even the ranks of Tuscany are compelled to cheer the generous heart. And it would be a strange omission if this appealing gallantry were absent from the teaching or the practice of the experience of holiness which, on all counts, is the summation of the virtues.

Nor is it absent. Goodness was never intended to look dowdy. The word translated 'good' in our *Authorised Version* carries the suggestion of pleasant or agreeable. In this sense the Creator 'saw every thing that he had made, and, behold, it was very good'. Beauty adorned the work of his hands. . . .

Nothing can be more attractive than the good life well lived. It is goodness of this pleasant kind which is goodness of the proper kind. We can all be so good, so uncomfortably good, so awkwardly good, that we put people off instead of winning them to our fellowship. . . . A general disagreeableness is no sign of piety. Sourness is not the fruit of sanctity. We are intended to adorn the doctrine we profess.

The Call to Holiness, pp 85, 86

27 October

. . . Let us . . . be Christian in our attitude to the world about us. And that world can be defined as society organised apart from God.

This means that with some aspects of the life of the world the believer will have nothing whatever to do. On every count he will dissociate himself from its commercialism, remembering the Master's teaching that a man's life consisteth not in the abundance of the things which he possesseth. Nor will he share in its self-seeking, again remembering that Jesus said that he who would save his life shall lose it. Nor, as grace shall be given him, will he share its sinfulness. . . .

In the relationships of believers one with another, let it be said that the closer our walk with God, the closer our walk with each other, but also the less shall we find in common with those who do not share that closer walk. . . . Yet though there is bound to be an unmistakable difference between the man who belongs to Christ and the man who does not, that gulf should be bridged from our side by our desire for his salvation and for that of the world to which he belongs. After all, God does not hate the world. How can he hate that which is his own creation? . . .

. . . With unwearying patience we who are believers must labour, as did our Lord before us, for the salvation of the world for which he died.

Essentials of Christian Experience, pp 34, 35

28 October

This is our basic need—to commit ourselves so unreservedly to Christ that we may receive of the Spirit of Christ. That is to say, we cannot effectively proclaim Christ as Saviour to others unless we personally know him as such ourselves.

One thing is clear, a nominal Christianity is of little use today. The formalities of religion avail nothing either to the believer or to the cause. A nominal Christianity is a contradiction in terms. The man who is Christian in name only is more of a hindrance than a help. No man can truly be Christ's only in name. 'If any man have not the Spirit of Christ, he is none of his.' A Christianity which is merely nominal is powerless to stand against the forces of secularism. Lacking any inner life of its own, it will capitulate to an enemy which, though irreligious in name, possesses all the dynamic of a religion.

So my : . . . concern is that all of us who bear the name of Christ shall live by the power of Christ because he, who lived and died and rose again, lives by faith in our hearts.

Essentials of Christian Experience, p 35

29 October

It is faith in a Person that saves. Though, as with our friends, we may be hard put to say in so many words exactly why we believe in a particular person. Knowledge has something to do with it, for we do not give a blank cheque to a total stranger. Yet though we may not know all there is to be known about A or B, we have learned enough to trust him. We have seen him under pressure and know he does not panic. We have compared his deeds with his words long enough to regard him as a man of integrity. We feel in our bones that what we do know of him so guarantees what we do not yet know that we can fully and freely confide in him.

Now the faith that saves is based first of all on what we know of God. Not that we know everything there is to know about him. . . . We know in part. But the part we do know is sufficient, as the Scriptures say, to make us wise unto salvation. God has allowed us to see in Jesus enough of his eternal love and power to make it possible for us to have faith in him.

. . . If the love and patience and wisdom and helpfulness which Jesus showed to men in need is a sample of the divine love and patience and wisdom and helpfulness, that should be sufficient warranty for any man. . . . We are asked to believe in the saving power of the God and Father of our Lord Jesus Christ.

Essentials of Christian Experience, pp 42, 43

30 October

. . . The faith which saves not only includes the recognition that God can be trusted but requires from those who would trust him the response of obedience. Saving faith has been defined as that trust in God which leads to obedience to God. . . .

Here, for example, is Emil Brunner saying: 'Faith is obedience; nothing else.' And here is Bultmann saying: 'Faith is not mere cognisance of Christian truth . . . but genuine obedience to it.' 'The notion that commitment plays an essential part in religious faith (declared the Dean of Jesus College in the annual Cambridge Open Lectures for 1964) is one of the factors which has greatly influenced contemporary theology.'

Here is Catherine Booth . . .: 'Saving faith is . . .

commital, the giving of . . . the whole being up to God . . . just as a young woman when she marries commits herself to her husband . . . becomes one in spirit with him and has no separate interest henceforth for ever.'

. . . If faith is the trusting of one's sinful life to God for salvation, it is also the trustful dedication of one's redeemed life in obedient service to him. And it is perhaps at this point that the word of truth searches many hearts most deeply.

It is not for me to try to suggest what God in Christ is saying to you. It is for me to ask you to listen and obey. Faith always says yes to Jesus.

Essentials of Christian Experience, pp 43-45

31 October

In any voluntary association of people the regular attender or worker stands in danger of being overlooked because he is regular. The captain never loses any sleep over Brother Faithful. He will be at the open-air rain or shine. But Brother Fancy, who is here today and gone tomorrow, gets the captain's attention because he is such an uncertain quantity. Poor Faithful thinks that the captain is always on Fancy's doorstep; but doesn't the captain wish he had no need to be!

It is Sister Flighty who gains most attention from the young people's sergeant-major. Sister Faithful is always at the company meeting on time, but for her opposite number the sergeant-major may be standing anxiously at the door ten minutes after the responsive exercises are over. 'Your company is all here,' he greets her. 'The Bibles are ready as well. I've taken care that yours have no leaves missing. Forgotten your *Company Orders*? Look, borrow mine for the afternoon.'

Does Sister Faithful wonder whether her work is over-looked? No one dances attendance on her. But he who has granted her the spirit of trustworthiness recognises how she labours 'with steady pace.'

The Call to Holiness, pp 91, 92

1 November

'With steady pace' was not intended by Richard Jukes as a reflection upon the pilgrim whose journey he hymned. A steady pace is a maintained pace. The race which is set before us is a long-distance course, not a hundred yards' sprint; an affair of years, not of even seconds. Much of the way from here to the Celestial City is, as Evelyn Underhill remarked, through a built-up area. Bursts of speed and flashy cornering are a menace where cross the crowded ways of life. This journey has to be done with due regard for all other traffic and 'with steady pace' is a commendable virtue. Remember Livingstone's 'characteristic forward tread . . . neither fast nor slow, no hurry and no dawdle, but which meant getting there'.

It has been pointed out that this is a little-noticed but most effective point in *Pilgrim's Progress.* Faithful leaves the City of Destruction after Christian but passes him on the way because he never lingers to talk with this one or that. No fellow traveller or chance acquaintance beguiles Faithful from the narrow path. But Christian, who is Everyman, can be counted on to make the most of every possible difficulty. If there is a slough of despond, he will be in it. If Apollyon is about Christian will be bound to cross him. If there are lions in the way he will be sure to face them in their angriest mood. But when he and Faithful meet and Christian asks his new companion how he managed to pass the lions, Faithful answers simply, 'I think they were asleep, for it was about high noon.'

O faithful Faithful! And O discerning Bunyan! This is a master's touch. Though the sun was high overhead and not a shadow for shelter, Faithful plodded on. The lions were overcome by sleep, not he. He passed them deep in their after-dinner nap.

The Call to Holiness, pp 92, 93

2 November

Difficulties disappear for the man who is faithful. It is when we are off duty, or, worse still, neglecting duty, that a net is spread for our feet. But the man who is intent on what God would have him do is delivered from danger unawares. He breasts the rise in the road without noticing the gradient. He covers the distance without marking the milestones. Plain honest faithfulness will make the rough places smooth and the crooked ways straight. Not brilliance, or learning, or personality; just faithfulness.

Faithfulness is a tower of strength in the hour of moral or spiritual danger. In one of his early books A. S. M. Hutchinson told of a girl in a seaside town into whose home comes a young city editor suffering from overstrain and needing relief from the high pressure demands of his London office. In his new surroundings he finds the Bible is read and prayer is offered, habits which he himself had never followed, and slowly a peace from another world begins to invade his heart. He is attracted to the girl as well. With Effie as his companion all his needs would be met, so he proposes that they should go away together. She is flattered—for she cannot parallel his brilliance; but puzzled—for while there has been a declaration of affection there has been no suggestion of marriage. He presses his suit. Let them go away together today, tomorrow. 'And live in sin?' asks Effie, still bewildered.

The Sunday-school phrase angers the man beyond measure. That his offer, from his height, should be so construed is humiliating beyond measure. Why ever did he think that such a girl could give him anything. He will call it off. But the truth was that his offer broke on an unsophisticated loyalty to the teaching of home and Bible class.

The Call to Holiness, pp 93, 94

3 November

Faithfulness to what we know can save us in our hour of peril. No blinding light from Heaven is needed to make us aware of the abyss at our feet. We have but to be faithful to the truth already in us. If there is a suggestion to default on Sunday duty in high summer, we know where our first loyalty lies. If it is said that a glass at a friend's wedding party is neither here nor there, we know without anyone telling us what our answer should be. If a conversation gets too near the bone, then we know full well we are not obliged to take part in it. In a dozen daily matters we need no fresh revelations of truth; just grace to be faithful to the light already given.

The simple virtue of faithfulness can sustain us in the hour of discouragement as well—and that may be a present hour for those who take the work of God seriously. His church is not everywhere like an army with banners. In some places she is being driven back; in others bravely clinging with depleted forces to former strong points. Especially is this true in our large cities where even the well-filled places of worship are but islands set in a horrid sea of paganism. Some believers have lost heart and are swift to say so. They are equally swift to blame some other person or some administrative blunder or some internal strain for their discouragement. But what has really gone awry lies deep in their own spirit. The sober hidden grace of faith has drained away.

The Call to Holiness, pp 94, 95

4 November

Christianity is a minority movement. No convention required any person to make a show of allegiance to the faith. Material prosperity is not linked with religious practice. Indeed, Christian scruples may be a bar to social success. In this setting our faith has to be practised for its own merits and commended on its own right. Are we willing to serve God for naught?

We rise to this faithfulness as we receive the Spirit of him 'who was faithful to him that appointed him'. The phrase occurs in the New Testament where a writer, steeped in the thought forms of his Jewish countrymen, was working out a parallel between Jesus and Moses (Hebrews 3:1-6).

In Jewish history Moses held a unique place. . . . No man had been granted closer fellowship than Moses. To him had been given the Law. One rabbi taught that, in the economy of God, the faithfulness of Moses ranked him higher than the ministering angels. His trustworthiness stood on record for all ages to read. But he was outsoared by Jesus in that the Son must be higher than the greatest of God's servants. . . .

'The heart of every private man' can drink in valour from this divine Captain's eyes. Our faithfulness derives from him who is 'the faithful Witness'. This grace is not our own lest any man should boast. Like the other fruit of the Spirit, it is born of the sanctifying presence of God in the hearts of those in whom he is fulfilling his perfect work.

The Call to Holiness, pp 95, 96

5 November

Meekness has come down in the world of words. Moffatt takes care never to use it in his translation. He substitutes 'gentle', 'pious', 'humble', 'afflicted', 'the poor'; never the oft-misunderstood 'meek'. Who cares that 'it's safer being meek than fierce'? To many such a line only evokes a picture of a nervous and hesitant lad in a barrack room who has decided that the best way to keep out of trouble is to remain unnoticed. It's safer! So as a protective device and to keep out of harm's way he reduces himself to a colourless nonentity.

With savage irony Mark Anthony employed the word over the dead body of Caesar:

> Pardon me, thou bleeding piece of earth,
> That I am meek and gentle with these butchers.

Nor is the grace of meekness over-welcome within the church of Christ itself. Someone has said that the apostle listed it near the end of these virtues because it was one of the hardest to practise. Meekness is wrongly understood as spiritlessness, insipidity, lifelessness; a meek person can be kicked around with impunity.

With the Bible in hand we should know that this is neither the meaning of the word nor its visible sign. . . .

The Call to Holiness, pp 97, 98

6 November

Moses is described as being 'very meek, above all . . . men'. Very meek, not very weak. No spineless character could have brought Israel out of Egypt, nor led a band of ex-slaves through their years of desert wanderings until they emerged a disciplined people.

Malory quotes Sir Ector saying to Sir Launcelot, 'Thou wert the meekest man . . . that ever ate in hall . . . and thou wert the sternest knight to thy mortal foe that ever put spear in the rest.' At Arthur's court great meekness was not incompatible with great courage.

Let an incident from John Woolman's life illuminate this grace further. One June morning in the 18th century he arrived in London and, knowing that the yearly meeting of the Society of Friends was in session, hurried there from the boat. Hunch-backed, less than five feet tall, arms longer than legs, much of his face hidden in a snowy beard which fell over his chest, his clothes undyed, he must have looked something like a troll to staid Friends in London. His reception was as chilly as his appearance was unusual and, after he had tendered his papers, a Friend rose to say that the visitor might now feel his mission was discharged and be free to return home.

Woolman was stricken. He had crossed the Atlantic under divine concern and at no small self-sacrifice. After a silence he meekly rose to say that he did not feel led of the Spirit to leave but, as he could work with his hands he would be glad to be employed by someone so as not to be a burden to any. Before the session ended rebuff had changed to welcome.

The Call to Holiness, pp 98, 99

7 November

Scholars have pointed out that the Greek word thus translated [ie 'meekness'] used to be applied to an animal which had been tamed. A horse which had been broken in and now answered to bit and bridle was 'meek'. The animal had not been robbed of its strength but now used its strength at the bidding of another. Instead of the untamed wildness of the open moor, there was now directed energy for worth-while tasks.

Temperance does not mean that form of self-control by which a man says 'I'm cutting my smoking down to five a day', or 'You'll never see me drunk, I know when to stop'. This control is not of external restraint nor of self-willing, but arises from the presence of the Holy Spirit at the regulative centre of a man's life. In this sense temperance is more properly understood as God-control.

This inner divine control bids us accept ourselves for what we are rather than waste time complaining about what we are not. God has made us as we are because he likes us that way. There is a place in his fields for the bluebell in the forest as there is for the lily in the hothouse. And as exotic blooms have a hard time in some of our comfortless summers, it is just as well that there are daisies and daffodils to cheer the eye.

The Call to Holiness, p 100

8 November

The life controlled by the Spirit will not rebel at the place of service which God appoints. The meek of heart will not complain about being frustrated, which is sometimes a high-flown phrase for not getting our own way or not being in the limelight. Not every man in an aircraft factory can fly at supersonic speeds. There are fitters, riggers, engineers, carpenters, labourers—and the tea boy, each of whom must do his work as competently as the pilot is expected to do his. He who works together with God may be technically unskilled but none is ever redundant. There is more work to do than hands to do it. The Kingdom of God cometh not by automation. In this economy men still count most of all.

Said Bernard of Clairvaux to a young novice whom he found idling in the monastery kitchen: 'If you neglect to wash the pots and pans you will neglect to worship God.' As in family life, so in the Kingdom, there is always a lot of washing-up to be done, and not always before a stainless-steel sink either. Many sinks are too low for the back. In some places the water is hard; in others it is not yet piped on. The elegant host and hostess at table may not take kindly to the after-dinner chores. But they must be done, and character comes out at the sink. For general usefulness, a willing pair of hands may be a greater blessing than a witty tongue. Meekness has an unbreakable strength which can sustain drudgery by treating it as divine.

The Call to Holiness, p 101

9 November

. . . Let it be remembered that all these graces are of the Spirit. They are not our human virtues brushed up and given a high polish. This is not me working at myself until I think I can pass for the very handiwork of God. The fruit of the Spirit is the result of his creative power in my life. And if I am to be like Christ in whom these graces were displayed to perfection, than I must first yield myself to the Spirit who was his without measure.

Such a surrender will bring the harvest in due season. Let none stumble here through lack of faith. Let none suppose the soil of his heart too unpromising. If weeds will grow there, why not wheat? Even the presence of tares shows that the soil will support life.

Look at a seed. It is small, hard, dry, seemingly lifeless. Yet all the possibilities of fragrance, form, taste and colour are there.

All the wonder and glory of the life of holiness awaits the full surrender of the forgiven heart to the presence and power of the Holy Spirit. Let the seed be planted. The harvest will follow.

The Call to Holiness, p 102

10 November

The experience of Christian holiness may finally be defined as one in which the whole man is redirected

244

towards the highest spiritual end—that is, likeness to Christ, and in this he is granted the continual help of the Holy Spirit.

The whole man—for in considering this doctrine we must not make the mistake of supposing that holiness means the eradication of any of our normal human appetites. The redirection and control of all to the divine glory—yes; but the elimination of none.

Whatsoever we do can be done to his glory for no human appetite is of itself evil. To suppose otherwise is a reflection upon the Creator whose handiwork we are. Man is the creation of God, not the devil. His origin is divine, not satanic. Scripture describes him—and Scripture quotes this scriptural description approvingly—as 'little lower than the angels'. Or, as the *American RSV* reads: 'little less than God' (Psalm 8:5).

Man was born to greatness but has fallen away from his high estate. Light was in him, but in many that light has turned to darkness. This makes his ruin more saddening. Lilies that fester not only smell worse than weeds; they look worse as well. We never expect weeds to be anything but weedy. That is their nature. But in lilies we look for beauty and fragrance. And from man, part of the creation which God pronounced to be good, there is high promise but sad performance.

But there is every difference between a good thing gone wrong and something which was bad from the start. . . .

The Call to Holiness, pp 103, 104

11 November

The easy notion that we can blame our 'fallen' nature for what we do is in essence an evasion of responsibility. To excuse an action by saying 'Sorry, but I'm made that way' is to twist the doctrine of original sin to excuse sinning. To lay the burden of my behaviour upon my make-up—as if that was something apart from my real self—is to play with truth.

Sin lies in the will, not in the instincts. There is no sin in the farmyard for there is no choice there. The animal does as his nature dictates. But I am not an animal in that sense, and those who blame their nature most would be loudest in their protests were they treated like animals. The man who demands the right to please himself must accept the fruits of his choosing.

The truth is that no part of me—eye, temper, hand—is in itself evil, though each may be put to an evil end as my will may determine or allow. . . .

Take temper. Sanctifying grace does not mean the abolition of temper but its control and redirection. God does not take a man's temper from him. Why should he? A man without temper is as useless as a knife without temper. . . .

Look at your right hand. Is not so familiar a thing fearfully and wonderfully made, so strong that it can grip a sledge-hammer, so sensitive that it can caress a *pianissimo* from a violin string. It is not in itself evil. . . . But it can wound in the house of a friend. Lady Macbeth's hand could close upon the dagger which would dispatch Duncan sleeping under her roof.

The fault is not with the . . . temper or the hand. Responsibility lies much deeper—and that is at one and the same time a relief and a warning. . . .

The Call to Holiness, pp 104-106

12 November

A relief—in so far that we can gladly welcome a holiness which is not a denial of our humanity. That bypath has been explored, and those gifted with Christian wisdom have been able to halt in time. In a passionate eagerness to make sure that nothing should come between them and the blessing of holiness so earnestly desired, John Wesley and his helpers debated in their second conference in August 1745 whether 'an entirely sanctified man would ever get married'. To their everlasting credit they quickly saw how great was their peril in trying to treat God's good as evil.

Let it be clear . . . that holiness is not the enemy of any human affection. Holiness is not the cuckoo which would drive out of the nest all other cherished satisfactions. Holiness but blesses what is already blessed and hallows what is already holy—the heart's affections.

But if we accept this truth to the enrichment of our joys, let the warning be also accepted that holiness stands like a passionate angel guarding the gateway of our human Garden of Eden, denying an entrance to the licence which would be the ruin of our happiness. Because no human appetite is of itself evil, that does not mean that any may flourish uncontrolled. Hunger is satisfied by eating, not gluttony. Love is satisfied by affection, not lust. Love has its own delicate restraints of which licence is the destroyer. Once a lad and a girl have made that discovery their mutual joy is safe.

To sum up—what needs to be sanctified is the will. As the will is the source of all sinning, so it can be the spring of all right living.

The Call to Holiness, pp 106, 108

13 November

'The more I look on life' said General Bramwell Booth in his journal . . . 'the more clearly I see that it has been the principle of worldliness . . . which has been the foe, the deadly foe, within the city.'

Note—'the principle of worldliness'. Too often worldliness is equated with certain acts in much the same way as sin is loosely identified with particular misdeeds which ought more properly to be called sins. Sins are separate actions, each of which is a defiance of a holy God. Sin—the source of individual sinning—is the egotism which erects the fallen self on the throne of the heart and worships it instead of God. So the world, or the principle of worldliness, is not any single pursuit or amusement, though these all form part of the world. But to be content with so one-sided an equation is to rob the word of its sting. Not so did the first believers think of it. The world had crucified the Lord of glory, and to them the world was held in such mingled dread and abhorrence that one of the foremost of their number declared himself to be 'crucified unto the world'. He could not have used a stronger term.

How shall we define this thing which to Paul was anathema?

The Officer, September, October 1950

14 November

The world to which he [Paul] was crucified was certainly not the world of nature—the wind on the heath, the glory of the sunset, the delight of fruit and flower. . . . Nor can the principle of worldliness be identified with the friendly joys of life—neighbours meeting, the corps social, the works outing. . . . Neither can worldliness be equated with those uncommercial recreations by which a man keeps himself physically fit. . . .

The fact is that some very earnest people have bedevilled this problem by isolating certain acts and places instead, as General Bramwell saw, of fastening on the principle.

The world can be defined as human society organised apart from God. In such a society there is no common or uniting purpose to which every member must subscribe. . . . A worldling can . . . be described as one who takes action only when his own interests are threatened.

Not without reason, then did believers in the past rate the world as their principal foe. 'The world, the flesh and the devil' in the familiar order. The devil we know and the flesh—alas!—we also know. But the world and the principle of worldliness can appear in so many forms and assume so many disguises as to deceive the very elect. . . .

The Officer, September, October 1950

15 November

Wrote Mrs Commissioner Brengle to her husband at a time when he was occupied with much campaigning: 'I think that if this hoisting up of our great men in front of the Cross could be stopped, it would be one step forward to regaining some of our lost power. Continue to insist on this in your case, and I believe that God will greatly reward you. Let them put all the blarney they like in the advertisements, but keep it out of the meetings. I am sure it grieves God. You know I love to hear you lauded, and I can spend many happy hours at it, but when I go to the meeting I want no one mentioned but the One who can save the people from their sin.'

The stronger than the strong man armed who alone can deal with the principle of worldliness is mentioned in that last sentence. The more we make room for Jesus, the less will there be for the world. In our gatherings let his name be praised and none other. Let us preach not ourselves but Christ Jesus the Lord.

For this reason shun the applause of men. Ban fulsome introductions and final eulogies. The one commendation we need is that of the truth openly declared 'to every man's conscience before God'. He who has that inward witness will neither need nor seek any other.

The Officer, September, October 1950

16 November

. . . To bring work and religion, religion and work, together in a holy calling is not a bright idea of the 20th century. This conception of the wholeness of life has its roots in the Old Testament. And . . . this call to present to God our bodies refers, primarily, to this body by means of which I have my being and earn my living. Which is another way of saying that divine service is not limited to a particular hour on a Sunday morning or Sunday evening but covers all that takes place both in my 40-hour week as well as in my hours of leisure. The purpose of the Christian faith is needlessly curtailed if its application is limited to special times and special areas of life. The redemptive purpose of God is as concerned with the way in which a man uses his time and spends his money as the way in which he says his prayers.

'I thank thee, O Father, Lord of heaven and earth . . .,' said Jesus, as he spoke of the way in which the proud rejected him but the humble welcomed him. . . . Our Lord was rejecting, once and for all, the thought that there were areas of life where the writ of his Father did not run. We all know that there is a plain difference between a place of worship and an industrial plant, though the balance of life requires our attendance at both. But to suppose that what goes on in the one—but not the other—is of interest to God, is to put paid to true religion and to deprive man of his only hope of a salvation which can redeem the whole of his life.

Essentials of Christian Experience, pp 26, 27

17 November

. . . The shoe repairer who helps to keep people's feet dry, the shop-keeper who serves wholesome food over his counter, the garage mechanic whose repair job is utterly dependable—and all others like them—can present their bodies, that is to say, what they do, to God as their acceptable service.

In this connection I recall a civil service friend of mine who was, and is, a salvationist, describing how a senior government official came up to him one day and said: 'I'm having a house built and the builder is making a good job of it. I look around most nights and see how things are going and the work is first class; nothing skimped or shoddy. The builder's one of your crowd.' There was a man the work of whose body was 'acceptable unto God' and, because acceptable to God, acceptable also to man.

In the second place, we are to present to God not only what the body does but what the body is. . . . In this sense the body means the whole personality. 'Your very selves' translates the *New English Bible.* This self or personality, presented to God, can be the temple or home of his Spirit, thus becoming yet another human instrument which God can use to accomplish his will on earth.

Keeping this truth in mind, it becomes plainer still that the outworking of the Holy Spirit of God cannot be limited to one particular day of the week, much less to particular hours on a particular day. The man whose body has thus been presented to God will find that his life makes its own continuous witness seven days a week.

Essentials of Christian Experience, p 28

18 November

. . . It may be asked why should any layman take his religion so much in earnest. Cannot so thorough-going a committal be left to clergy or ministers while he, who has to work for his living, gets on with the difficult enough task of keeping a roof over the head of himself and his family?

But to whom was—and is—the New Testament addressed? Not just to those who are professionally involved in the Christian cause, but to all the people of God. And it is we—the total people of God, ministers and layfolk alike—who, recognising the immensity of the mercies of God (which please remember were crowned with the gift of Jesus as Saviour) will therefore recognise that this response to him, with the consequent dedication to the needs of men, is our reasonable service. . . .

The divine appeal is not a sledge-hammer planned to stun our bemused intellect into a numbed assent. God is not seeking the cringing response of some servile creature who does as he is told lest a worse thing befall him. He awaits the free response of the free man who, acknowledging the compulsive power of the divine mercies, answers with a clear head and a willing heart. . . .

And far from this total response cramping any man's style, it ennobles him who makes it and glorifies the God whose service is always perfect freedom.

Essentials of Christian Experience, pp 29, 30

19 November

. . . It has to be said that there are some believers who are the worst enemies of their own cause. The faith which we hold will not be destroyed by the assaults of its foes. Indeed, as I read the press or listen over the radio to the attacks made upon the Christian faith, I am almost comforted. Is this shying at an Aunt Sally all we have to fear? For this figure of straw, set up by some of our assailants for the express purpose of knocking it down, is often a travesty of the faith, bearing little resemblance to its true nature and power.

In any case, we who are believers should remember that it is nothing new for the Christian faith to be reviled and its adherents harried out of their lives. This has been part of the history of the Church from the beginning. Knowing our Acts of the Apostles we have not forgotten the stoning of Stephen, nor the death of James by the sword, nor the attempted lynching of the apostle Paul within the precincts of the Jerusalem Temple, nor the banishment of the aged John to Patmos. And if it is the war of words which we fear, the most savage attack today is mild compared, for example, with the pretty line in invective practised by the second-century pagan philosopher, Celsus, one of whose mildest remarks was to compare believers to frogs croaking in a swamp.

But these are not the folk we have to fear, whether their abuse be verbal or physical. As Theodore Beza said to the King of Navarre after the Massacre of Vassy: 'Sire, it is in truth the lot of the Church . . . to suffer blows and not to return them. Yet I also take leave to remind you that she is an anvil which has worn out many hammers.' My concern has not to do so much with the attacks made upon our faith from without as with its betrayals from within. . . .

Essentials of Christian Experience, pp 31, 32

20 November

The promise is that the gates of Hell shall not prevail against the Church of God, and on that promise we can rely. But it is when Christians are less than Christian that the citadel is opened from within to an enemy who, left to his own stratagems and devices, could never capture it from without. . . .

Let us be Christian in our relationships with one another—for surely charity begins at home. . . .

There are those who see no value in an Earls Court campaign, and there are others who regard Rome as a child of Hell. There are those who refuse the grace of God permission to flow through any ecclesiastical channel save their own, and there are others who look askance upon any Christian fellowship which may rise above denominational barriers. . . .

Let us rather thank God that he fulfils himself in many ways. He can speak through a ritual hallowed by centuries of usage and he can speak through the street corner open-air meeting. He can speak through the cathedral anthem and he can speak through the gospel chorus. He can speak through John Sebastian Bach and he can speak through the Joystrings. He can speak through the priest upon whom episcopal hands have been laid and he can speak through the testimony of the layman whose heart is the Lord's.

Essentials of Christian Experience, pp 32, 33

21 November

Frustration is one of the oldest of human complaints because it springs from our mortal nature. Like our shadow, it haunts us because we are body as well as mind and soul. Complete and satisfying fulfilment, when the broken arc gives way to the perfect round, belongs to another world than this. It is only as time is swallowed up in eternity that frustration shall be no more. Meanwhile the half-light, the dubiety, the misunderstanding. We must accept a health that is vulnerable to illness, a knowledge that has its limitations, an experience which is not always one of clear shining. But ever and anon 'in the cleft of rock' we are bidden take note of those abiding certainties—the eternal might and mercy of God.

We can also apply this truth to what happens within us, that is, in our personal experience.

There are days when God seems withdrawn—and that for no apparent reason. We are not aware of any sin committed which should cause him to avert his face. 'More commonly', Commissioner Francis Pearce used to say, 'I have to hold fast my confidence without a particle of conscious feeling to strengthen my faith.'. . .

It is the Lord who gives and the same Lord who takes away. . . . I have to learn to bless his name in both settings. I am not to bless lightly or irresponsibly for that would be almost as dreadful a blasphemy as to curse him. But I bless because, however dense and chilling the mists, experience will prove that he was close at hand even when I could not see him.

Essentials of Christian Experience, pp 50, 51

22 November

When the pilgrims in Bunyan's story reached Vanity Fair they were quickly recognised for what they were by what they wore, by what they said, and by their indifference to what the shops in the city had to sell. That is to say, theirs was a distinctive pattern of living which was the outward and noticeable expression of their faith. The truth which inwardly they cherished was manifest in their conduct. So we can help to make the message clear and plain by doing what he says. John Baillie had a famous aside that being a Christian made a difference to the way a man tied up his shoes. That was his way of saying that the spirit of Jesus in a man's life is like a drop of dye in a vat of water. Test it by the bucketful or the spoonful, the colour will be of the same intensity throughout. . . . From scheme and creed the light may go out but

> The blessed gospel none can doubt
> Revealed in holy lives.

. . . The more openly we call him Lord, the greater is our obligation to obey him, and the heavier will be our condemnation if we do not the things he says. . . . The question before us is: Am I doing the things he says? The word which comes to us is: Whatsoever he saith unto you, do it.

Essentials of Christian Experience, pp 9, 10

23 November

Seeing we began with Silvia, may we go back to her before the end.

Holy, fair and wise is she;
The heaven such grace did lend her.

That is to say, her adorer felt that her desirable qualities were so sublime—'holy, fair and wise', and note how holy comes first—that they could not be of Silvia's own making. They were bestowed by Heaven itself.

It would be foolish to speak as if the whole weight of Christian theology could either be fastened upon, or deduced from, a lover's poem. I would only make the point that this desirable quality of life described as holy is seen to be Heaven's gift. My only dispute would be with the word 'lend'—as if the gift, once bestowed, could be at any time thereafter withdrawn.

The grace of God, Heaven's gift, enabling us to enjoy a life of spiritual well-being, is not just lent for a season. This blessing can be ours for always. We can know that day-by-day fellowship with Jesus Christ, our Lord and Saviour, which will enable us to follow his example. The resultant life of spiritual health is the life of holiness.

Plainly this way of life is both desirable and possible. And in support of this last proposition, let the testimony of one of the greatest of all believers be quoted: 'I can do all things through Christ which strengtheneth me.'. . . My hope and prayer is that you will not merely hear the text but enter into the experience.

Address—27 June, 1965

24 November

Whether we like it or not—judgment of one kind or another is never absent.

Nature punishes all forms of slackness. The unsound girder sags when tested by heavy loads crossing the bridge. The faultily-mixed concrete cracks and that portion of the newly-made road has to be reset. Nor does organised society tolerate wrongdoing. Its standards of crime and

255

punishment may be defective. But the fact remains that wrongdoing is not condoned. And we who believe that man belongs to God cannot escape the logic of our own creed. God has a right to judge what is his own.

No doubt there has been a widespread weakening in standards of judgment over past years. 'There's so much good in the worst of us . . .' is a general attitude. We do not see our friends—much less ourselves—as black and white. Our characters seem to be made up of many colours. No-one can have anything but reverence for the natural goodness of the average man—the heroism of the miner who goes down the pit for his entombed mates, the courage of the lifeboatman who puts out in the teeth of a storm to rescue a shipwrecked crew. . . . We may freely honour and admire such behaviour, while regretting the way in which otherwise decent folk sit loose to the godly habits of private prayer and public worship.

Fortunately, we are not their judge. The One who is the searcher of all hearts can be trusted to say on which side such men and women really are. . . . Motives more than conduct may determine a man's destiny in God's sight. But determined it will be. There is a last or final judgment.

International Company Orders 1941

25 November

The standard of judgment may seem to be quite pleasant and agreeable. Jesus is concerned about one thing only. Have you been a helper to those in need? Those who have, have done it unto him and are welcomed by him. That sounds easy enough. We like the way it seems to simplify the issues of life. Just this—have you been a pal? Decency and friendliness count for more than rank or creed or status. Yet—on closer scrutiny—this standard is terrifyingly severe.

We shall be asked if we have helped 'the least of these my brethren'. The word 'least' means that our charity should have included every man—from the bottom of the ladder up. But has it ever been easy to love—as Jesus

256

himself loved, for that is the standard of judgment—the person who has done us an injury, the man whose ways and opinions we dislike, the fellow who is our closest and keenest rival? . . . The fact is that if we hurt—by intention or negligence—a social outcast or a determined foe, we are hurting Jesus! Then most of us must often have wounded him! . . .

'Though I speak with the tongues of men and of angels . . . though I have all faith . . . though I bestow all my goods to feed the poor . . . though I give my body to be burned, and have not charity, it profiteth me nothing.' In this revealing light it is easy to see that natural goodness is not enough. None can rise to this searching standard apart from the grace of God made available for us in Christ Jesus.

International Company Orders 1941

26 November

Last of all, the Judge is Jesus. The One who blesses or condemns is that friendliest, kindest of men who played with children, forgave the repentant sinner and shared with his disciples his own love of life. Two truths follow.

The Judge is therefore no harsh, arbitrary being, untouched with the feeling of our infirmities. He who understands all will not—as the proverb puts it—forgive all. That would be to condone evil and put a premium on wrongdoing—a practice not followed even in our courts of law. But even his judgment will be an expression of his love.

Seeing that these solemn words about the inevitable punishment which awaits the wrongdoer were spoken by one who was Incarnate Love, they gain much in gravity. We may rightly allow for language which is figurative, but, commented Catherine Booth:

Surely no one will argue that the judgement itself will be less thorough, less searching . . . than the figures used to set it forth. . . . Can anybody imagine that Jesus will say,

257

'Inasmuch as ye did this or that' to those who never did anything of the kind? Such a proceeding would be very unlike anything he ever did or said when on earth. He was called 'the truth'. . . . Will he be any other when he comes in judgment? . . .

• *International Company Orders 1941*

27 November

Now why is it important that we should take notice of what Jesus said and did? Why should we pay attention to his reaction to injustice, to pain, to friendship, to criticism, to grief and to hate?

The value of a man's opinions on any particular matter depends on his competence to speak. Does he know what he is talking about? Or is he airing views when he hasn't a clue? The respect and obedience which Jesus demands rest upon the truth that he was God Incarnate. He was the revelation in terms of human personality of all that God was, is, and ever shall be.

The next question then is: How do we know this to be true?

. . . There is . . . threefold evidence concerning the claim of Jesus to speak as God.

First of all, there is his own testimony. He declared that he spoke with divine authority. He claimed that he was doing God's saving work among men. When Philip begged to be given a glimpse of the Father, Jesus answered, 'Have I been such a long time with you without your really knowing me?' (John 14:9, *J. B. Phillips*).

When a man claims to be God there are only three possible comments. He is mad; or he is a fraud; or he is speaking the truth. Some of the Jews thought Jesus was mad (Mark 3:21). Their religious leaders deemed him to be a fraud (John 9:29). A man like Pilate could not make up his mind. But those who have experienced what Jesus can do for them know that his claim was sober truth.

Jesus and our Need, pp 7-9

28 November

. . . There is a great company beyond numbering who, from the first half of the first century to the middle of twentieth, have declared that Jesus stands to them as God, and that he has done for them only what God could do. From him they have received forgiveness. By his power the chains of evil habit have been broken. In his strength they do the Father's will day by day.

. . . There is one's own personal testimony which agrees thereto. The Britisher's line is that of understatement. Normally we are over-modest about our accomplishments. But if my account of what Jesus has done for me agrees with what others have said, may not that confirmation encourage me to speak out boldly? After all, even modesty becomes a sin if it leads to a suppression of the truth. And my testimony is never an account of what I myself have done, but of what Another has done for me.

When I am dreaming I may imagine that I am awake, but when I am awake I do not fancy that I dream. Awake and alive unto God, I realise that I have come to him through Jesus who, in the days of his flesh, spoke in God's name, declared God's truth, revealed God's nature, displayed God's power. Were I dreaming I might have imagined this, but I am awake and know it to be fact.

To sum up, what Jesus said and did is of supreme importance because he is to men as God. We do well then to hear him.

Jesus and our Need, pp 9, 10

29 November

. . . It is in Jesus that we see what God is like. . . . In the words and deeds of the historic Jesus of Nazareth we see the eternal God at work in the midst of men. . . .

In the New Testament there is not one but four selections of incidents from his life. . . . When we read the gospels we are doing two things. First of all, we are looking at scenes from the life of One who went about doing good. And further, in those scenes we are watching

God at work, sharing the sorrows of men and, as far as men would allow him, meeting both their physical and spiritual needs.

Of course, there were men in the first century who refused God's help just as there are those who do the same in the twentieth. To refuse God's help on the ground that he does not exist and then to blame him for the jam in which we find ourselves is hardly logical. But perhaps we cannot be expected to be logical when we are in trouble. Yet those who turn to him will find that even in the valley of the shadow they need fear no evil for he is with them. What he offers is something better than an explanation of the changes and chances of life—for this might still prove unsatisfying. He offers his own companionship—as Lincoln found during the American Civil War, for a soiled depression in the margin of his Bible still preserved in the national archives, indicates the verse to which he turned again and again: 'I sought the Lord, and he heard me, and delivered me from all my fears.'

Essentials of Christian Experience, p 4

30 November

Jesus just cannot be set aside. He cannot be 'liquidated'. His Church—which is where he is present with any two or three of his people—lives on even in those parts of the world where the hearts of men are seemingly most set against him. . . . Jesus cannot be bowed off the stage of life. He is there whether men like it or not, and—often ignored, frequently hated, sometimes attacked—there he still remains and will remain until God's purpose in and through him is fully and finally accomplished. . . .

This year is AD, and neither the devil nor man can make it BC. God has entered the world in Christ, and now we cannot have a world without Christ—and this is true whether men admit it or not. Jesus had entered into the life of mankind 'like a dye, the stain of which no washing can remove; like a drop of God's blood which remains ineffaceably there'. . . .

The work of Jesus in an obscure province in the south-eastern corner of the Roman Empire hardly looked like the dawn of a new age. The Jews, who were nearest to it, did not think so. Could a carpenter's son out of Nazareth be the Messiah? As for the Romans, they hardly bothered their heads about it. . . . Yet they were all wrong—as are all those today who, in the notorious phrase of H. G. Wells, rate Jesus as 'a back number'. He will outlast them all.

The Kingdom of God, pp 43, 44

1 December

It is a sorry jest with journalists in the northern hemisphere that they are called upon to prepare their Christmas features amid the heat of midsummer. Mopping their steaming brows and calling for cooling drinks, they labour to produce on paper something of that bleak midwinter when frosty winds made moan. . . . But this capacity to project one's mind into a distant situation is a double-edged weapon—especially in so far as Christmas is concerned, for there is a danger that, instead of taking the familiar story at its New Testament value, we invest it with our own private hopes or fears.

For example, to some earnest souls Christmas is the feast of an almost discredited Christ. Not discredited by them, of course, but they are dismayed by the room given by men both to pleasure and to business, while for Christ there is 'not a place that he can enter'. . . . To other devout spirits Christmas seems to be the festival of the forgotten Christ. Not that they forget him themselves; they do not. They are continually bringing to his footstool the royal gifts of gold, frankincense and myrrh. But when they rise from their knees and look around, they see how small a company they are, while streaming past outside goes the commerce of an uninterested world to whom the season is but two more bank holidays, an occasion for another little drink, or yet another two sets of professional matches with which to permutate. The Author of the day seems forgotten.

Now in both these views there is truth, a measure of truth, yet not the whole truth. . . .

The Officer, November, December 1949

2 December

This neglect is heightened by the contrast between the Christmas message of peace and goodwill and the state of things as they are. To this generation has it been given to know not merely an old-fashioned, openly declared war, but the hazards of a cold war. With sinking hearts good people wonder how and when Jesus is going to come into his own. With his teaching rejected by many and his power ignored, the festival of his birth seems to some to be little more than an historic survival, preserved by the kindness of a benevolent secularism anxious to do its duty by an ancient monument.

If we try to see this unique event through the eyes of those who wrote the New Testament, we shall discover that they regarded it as the festival of the victorious Christ. Approaching the one central fact from different angles, and making use of every figure of speech they could command, they declared with one voice that, with the coming of Jesus, a new age had dawned. God had broken into time. He had intervened decisively in history. His Kingdom had been established. The prince of this world was cast out. The new world had begun and not all the powers of evil 'in Hell, or earth, or sky' could put the clock back.

Epistle and gospel agree on this. 'We know that the Son of God is come' is one such announcement, and it is made with the assurance that nothing could undo this act of God. 'The darkness is past and the true light now shineth' is a similar declaration. 'Amid the darkness the light shone, but the darkness did not master it' echoes the fourth gospel. . . .

That, with variations in phrase expressing substantial agreement, is what the New Testament has to say about the birth of Jesus. . . .

The Officer, November, December 1949

3 December

The incarnation is the turning point of history. Life is broken into two parts, and 'AD' is radically different from 'BC'. No longer do the forces of righteousness stand leaderless on the field of history, for the name of God Incarnate is Immanuel, meaning 'God with us'. God in Christ is present with his people, and thereafter will be present by that same Spirit who was in Jesus. If he be with them, who can be against them?

Not without reason did the Early Church, uncertain of the actual date of the birth of Jesus, fix it on a one-time pagan festival known as 'the day of the unconquerable sun'. After high summer the daylight had been growing weaker, till the nadir of his power was touched on 21-22 December, the winter solstice. Then the days began to lengthen, slightly but perceptibly by 25 December. To primitive man this came as an assurance that the heat and light of the sun were not going to fail after all, and the day was celebrated as the feast of the unconquerable sun.

With an insight which the heathen in his darkness never knew, we can call 25 December 'the day of the un-conquerable Son'. Nor is his a solitary victory. He is no lone Champion, disdaining lesser men in his supreme ascendency. His friends are called to share in his exultation. To adapt slightly two lines in Thomas Kelly's hymn:

> We share our Leader's victories
> And triumph with our King.

As Paul wrote: 'In spite of all, we are winning an over-whelming victory through him who gave us his love.'

The Officer, November, December 1949

4 December

There may be a truth of the imagination which is no less valid than the truth of fact but where relevant imagination does less justice to fact, its shortcomings must be made good.

For example, we sing:

> O Sabbath rest by Galilee,
> O calm of hills above—

as if Galilee were some quiet backwood county where peace and holy quiet reign undisturbed.

In point of fact, geographical Galilee was one of the more densely populated parts of the Roman Empire. More than 200,000 people clustered in the towns and villages about the lakeside. Capernaum was on a main trade route from east to west. Tiberias was a modern city . . . complete with royal palace and public racecourse. Magdala, set in the midst of indigo fields, was noted for its dyes. . . .

Across the way from these purely Jewish communities with Jewish synagogues and Jewish ways were Greek cities where the Greek tongue and Greek traditions prevailed. These were a legacy from the conquests of Alexander the Great, so that in and around Galilee was a ceaseless clash of culture and commerce. . . . So far from being a 'Sabbath rest', Galilee was aboil with what we would now call conflicting ideologies.

So with Phillips Brooks and his:

> O little town of Bethlehem
> How still we see thee lie.

A choice carol—but was Bethlehem truly wrapped in 'deep and dreamless sleep'?

The War Cry, 24 December 1949

5 December

Was Bethlehem truly wrapped in 'deep and dreamless sleep'? Or was not the overcrowded inn on the eve of the census shrill with the laughter of women and coarsened by the rough talk of men?

For it was no high and noble cause which had brought Joseph and Mary—and everyone else present—to Bethlehem that night. An imperial ukase had instructed every Jew to register on a given date at his tribal home. The reason for this was that Augustus wished to secure up-to-date information for his taxation returns, the vital statistics of which he rated so highly that he kept them with his own hand. . . .

So into a world very much like our own was Jesus born. The real Christmas story is no paper and tinsel affair. It began with a bureaucratic order, was shortly afterward marked by a deed of frightfulness which was the work of a local tyrant to whom life was cheap, and finally ended on a cross where sentence of death was carried out 'without the benefit of the clergy'. Far from being a pretty-pretty tale belonging to some never-never land, the Christmas story touches life at its grimmest and rawest. . . .

Christmas declares that God has not forgotten the world, much less does he despair of it. And the final truth is that he who would serve the purposes of God must, in like manner, neither renounce the world nor denounce it, but lovingly labour for its redemption.

This is the task to which the realism of Christmas calls those for whom the season is more than a welcome rest from work or an opportunity to indulge in over-eating and drinking.

The War Cry, 24 December 1949

6 December

Without doubt there are those who for some time have been calculating the number of days to Christmas.

Possibly harassed supermarket managers have been studying their graphs which, based on comparative figures, indicate when they may expect the peak of the shopping rush. Maybe a dad or mum is even now working out how much time he, or she, has left to complete the list of family presents. And some small boy, his mind hardly on the current class lesson, is trying to remember how many days there are in the month and, on his fingers, to tot up how long it will be before he can don the space-suit he has ordered from you-know-who.

Perhaps those warning notices have already begun to

appear in your local paper. Thirty more shopping days to Christmas. Twenty more . . . Fifteen . . . Ten . . . Five. . . .

It seems that even with this happiest of holiday seasons there is an inescapable time factor. No evangelist could exhort us more earnestly than do our main street stores to remember that what we would buy we must buy quickly. There is a last or final shopping day after which the present which has not been purchased must remain unpurchased. The Christmas card which has not been sent must remain unsent. The deadline once passed, what has not been done by way of Christmas preparations must remain forever undone. There is an element of judgment even with our shopping. All our desire to remember some long-forgotten friend is in vain if we don't think of him until Christmas day is half done. We've had it by then— and so has he!

We take too casual a view of this season of the year if we suppose that its happiness rests upon the uncertain hope that a good time will be had by all, for manifestly that is not true. . . .

The War Cry, 19 December 1964

7 December

The virtue of Christmas as a high festival lies in the fact that it speaks of what God has done in visiting and redeeming his people, and our happiness lies in acknowledging him whom God has sent to be our Lord and Saviour. For our attitude to Jesus will reveal whether or not we have begun to understand why there is a Christmas at all.

Among the Scriptures appointed by the Church to be read during the Advent season is one where the apostle Paul maintains that there were certain opinions or judgments which did not bother him at all.

One of these was what other men might think of him— and it was just as well he was somewhat indifferent on this point, for he was called a good many hard things in his time. Neither was he troubled about maintaining a high opinion of himself. He was too much of a realist to be eaten up by a sense of his own importance. But, he went on, 'He that judgeth me is the Lord'. That is to say, he was concerned about how he stood in his relationship to Jesus. So must we all be. . . .

'For my part, if I am called to account by you or by any human court of judgment, it does not matter to me in the least. Why, I do not even pass judgment on myself. . . . My Judge is the Lord. . . . For he will bring to light what darkness hides, and disclose men's inward motives' (1 Corinthians 4:3-5, *NEB*).

The War Cry, 19 December 1964

8 December

He whose coming we remember at this time of the year is not just a Baby about whom we sing sentimental lullabies for a few days in December and then forget for the rest of the year. It is by him we are judged, and that is one of the soberer truths of which this season reminds us. Like the number of shopping days to Christmas, which bid us make up our mind what we want to buy while we still have time, we have to make up our mind about Jesus while yet—in the old evangelical phrase—we are in time and out of eternity. There is a deadline with faith as well as with the shopping list.

In one of his poems, Studdert Kennedy imagines a Cockney soldier, whose life had been far from blameless, dreaming that he was in the other world and facing the Judge who knows all. Said he:

> And day by day and year by year
> My life came back to me.
> I'd see just what I were, and all
> I'd 'ad the chance to be.

'I'd see just what I were.' That is just what Jesus does to us. In his presence we see ourselves as we truly are.

That is what happened when he came as the Babe of Bethlehem.

At the news of One born to be King, Herod's first concern was for the safety of his own throne. . . .

267

Shepherds and wise men came to worship and, when they found him who was born to be King they laid before him their gifts. These men rose or fell by their attitude to Jesus.

Ah, Lord, before thou dost become our Judge, persuade us to accept thee as Saviour!

The War Cry, 19 December 1964

9 December

To what then shall we liken the act of him who for us men and for our salvation came down from Heaven? Would it be improper to give imagination reverent rein and say that in celestial councils it had become increasingly clear that there was something amiss with the state of God's creation. Instead of tuneful praise, discords were ascending to the divine throne, discords more wilful than any modern atonalities. It seemed as if every man had become his own conductor, beating time as seemed good in his own eyes to any improvisation as sounded good in his own ears.

Cherubim and seraphim looked at each other in speechless dismay. The noise which assailed them was certainly not according to the Father's will. Angel and archangel realised that so harsh a cacophony could not continue, without let or hindrance, and so the watchers and the holy ones were not entirely taken aback when the Son announced that he had accepted the Father's will that he should descend to earth to restore harmony.

'May I hope,' said Michael, speaking with profound reverence, for all knew that the Son was not of the nature of angels, 'that you will arm yourself with such thunders and lightnings as were used at Sinai. They had great effect then, and the more superstitious of the earth's inhabitants still think that thunder is the voice of the gods. Some such aids are bound to impress them, and there is precedent for their use.'

. . . But God's triumphs are gained only in God's way.

The Officer, November 1952

10 December

The Son was silent. . . . Uriel stepped forward. 'I trust that you will take several legions of angels with you. Twelve at least. . . .'

The Son did not seem to take this freedom of speech amiss though still he did not speak.

'Then maybe you will do something dramatic, such as alighting on a pinnacle of the temple. Some of the Jews expect their Messiah thus to appear.' Either Phaltiel or Jeremiel said this.

'Thank you all, but I think not', said the Son, voicing his thoughts at last. 'I intend to appear as a poor man, the son of one betrothed to a carpenter.'

It was the turn of the angelic host to be silent. Then one of the company, unable to restrain himself, broke out with, 'But is that not a risk, sir?'

The remark was not answered directly, for the Son went on as if thinking aloud.

'You see, the children of men have such queer ideas about power and glory. Look at those Romans now. Such a level-headed people might have learnt from the glory that was Greece and the grandeur that was Babylon. Here is Nineveh no more and the splendour of Solomon but dust, and yet they go on thinking that the greatest among them is he who can command the instant obedience of the largest number. How will they know, unless I show them, that he who would be great, must become as one that serves?'

. . . God's triumphs are gained only in God's way.

The Officer, November 1952

11 December

'But suppose men do not recognise you, sir?' asked Raphael, bold in comment because he was one who was continually in and out before the throne. 'The Jews have made a habit of stoning the prophets and killing such messengers as the Father sends to them. . . . I ask your pardon if I repeat the word "risk". We would not have anything untoward happen to you.'

The Son smiled—if so weak a word may be used to describe the exceeding brightness of the glory which irradiated his countenance. 'I agree. There is a risk. But I go not to do my own will but the will of him that sent me.'

Pure imagination? In one sense, yes—as all metaphor is imaginative. But if imagination be reason in her most exalted mood, no.

Every fact is true. Jesus was born son of the betrothed to a carpenter. He was a poor man who had not where to lay his head. He was largely unrecognised, for he came unto his own and his own received him not. The princes of the age were faced without any legions of angels. Scorning the methods of force and fear, he was able to save from their sins such as believed on his name.

The Bethlehem story is no cunningly devised fable. It is a true account of a victory won by God's weapons as God wished. He who came down from Heaven to save men was armed only with a Cross. That is the one sword which God's people can draw if they wish to share in the victory of God's Son. Other weapons, other victories.

The Officer, November 1952

12 December

For a season men were willing to rejoice in that light, but then darkness overcame the light and the best of his followers stumbled and fell. Three of them had seen the light of the glory of God at the transfiguration, and some were so sure of immediate victory that they tried to book places in advance for the coming triumph. But it was eclipse instead, unexpected by the disciples but accepted by Jesus who knew that to save his life he must first lose it. This is a law which governs the universe, and to it God and his purposes are subject. If we attempt the impossible and try to paint in words what happened, the picture we get is that of a strong One stooping lower and lower until he almost disappears from sight in order to get his back beneath a burden which no one else could shift. If he was

270

to move it, he first must stoop. And as the load bows him to his knees it almost breaks his back. But he steadies himself and moves off with the burden of the sin of the world upon his shoulders. God had to bend to lift, to stoop to raise, to descend to reascend. Fully to reveal himself, he had to take the veil of a crucified workman. That itself scandalised—as Paul noted—middle-class propriety. Yet this disguise assumed in love was the supreme disclosure of his power. Almighty power and almighty love are never in opposite camps. That is a false and misleading contrast for which our own imperfect thinking is responsible. God's power is ever one with his love and thereby becomes not less, but more, adequate for every situation. His submission to man's sinful treatment became the divinest means of grace. Seeming defeat turned out to be eternal victory.

The Officer, November 1947

13 December

. . . How does God, source of all power, reveal his almighty power?

The lesson begins in its simplest stages in the Old Testament where it is the seemingly weak who give the decisive twist to history. The autocratic Pharaoh has to summon to his aid an unknown Hebrew prisoner. Goliath falls to the sling and stone of an unsophisticated country lad. The unarmed prophet shows himself master of the Syrian host. 'Not in the fire, nor yet in the earthquake,' but in the still, small voice is revealed the energy of God.

Old Testament history is a theme with variations on the triumph of supposed weakness. The things that are not bring to nought the things that are. A small and unpopular people is chosen of God. They are slaves, . . . despised by their masters. After many setbacks they at last come into their own and seem set for becoming a great power. But their military strength lasts no more than a couple of generations, and then the kingdom splits in two. Vassal states revolt. Defeat, not victory, is Israel's portion. The larger part of this divided people disappears from history, and in less than a century it is the turn of the remnant that is left. But in an age of national disaster the great prophets arise, and out of the remnant a remnant survives. After exile comes another deceiving season of brief prosperity, till again the vineyard is broken down and the inheritance given to another. But, as before, out of death comes life. The dying agonies of the Jewish nation are the birth pangs of the Christian Church.

The Officer, November 1947

14 December

There seem to be two Christmases, each distinct from the other though, trying to make the best of both worlds, we attempt to combine them.

The popular Christmas of snow-covered roofs and village waits carolling under a frosty sky we owe largely to Dickens and his Pickwick pictures of life at Dingley Dell. To him more than to anyone else is due our simple but mistaken belief that old-fashioned Christmases were always white. Meteorological records for the past 100 years show that snow fell in Britain six times only on Christmas Eve and on 12 other occasions on Christmas Day. Approximately one English Christmas in five has, during the last century, registered an average temperature on or below freezing point.

The trimmings of this sentimental Christmas are mostly of recent date. Christmas cards are of Victorian origin. The Christmas tree was introduced into England by the Prince Consort from his homeland. Many of our favourite carols owe their revival to the discovery in 1850 of a commonplace book (now in the Balliol Library, Oxford) which a 16th-century London grocer had filled with riddles and puzzles and words and airs which he did not wish to forget.

But there is another Christmas. . . .

The Officer, November 1947

15 December

. . . There is another Christmas which celebrates in humbling and austere fashion the unattended birth of a Baby in a stable. According to the mystery of the gospel he so born was God incarnate. The Christian affirmation is that this Child of Mary, who served his time as a carpenter, whose three years' ministry ended in a death on which a curse had been set, was God-in-man. And more— that this brief revelation lasting no more than a moment against the background of eternity, a flash of divine lightning momentarily riving the darkness of night, was God's most significant demonstration of power. Indeed, it was the supreme illustration of the weakness of God which is stronger than men. This stupendous claim must either be very truth or utter nonsense.

The possession of power and its use has been a vexed question since time began. 'My soul doth magnify power' is a cry as old as mankind. 'Our strong arms must be our conscience, swords our law', exclaimed Richard III. Is such a line morally justifiable? And, if it is, does he who so acts gain that on which his heart is set? It is not: does the means justify the end, but do these means even secure the desired end?

In private and in business life we meet those who 'throw their weight about'. Their strong arm is their conscience. In world politics we see nations who follow the same tactics. In secular society money is valued because it is regarded as a means to power. And in religious societies the problem is not banished, only altered. . . .

It is time to go back to first principles. How does God, source of all power, reveal his almighty power?

The Officer, November 1947

16 December

. . . Gentiles provided Paul with a ready-made constituency on his missionary travels. Dressed as a qualified rabbi, for such he was, he would enter the synagogue on the Sabbath. After the prescribed readings of Scripture, the president of the meeting would invite the visitor to speak, whereupon Paul would begin on his daring, darling theme that the promises of God to Israel had been fulfilled in Jesus. Again and again a 'host of devout Greeks and a large number of leading women' believed his message. This explains the bitter opposition of the Jews who saw their own adherents being taken away from under their very noses by one whom they regarded as a renegade. But the rage of men could not stay God's flowing tide. Those early missionaries had the divine word which human hearts were seeking. The seed fell 'into good ground, and brought forth fruit, some an hundredfold.' . . .

To sum up—the state of human society favoured the spread of the gospel. Unwittingly, certain races had been helping to 'prepare the way of the Lord'. The wood and coals were laid ready; the coming of the Light of life set the fire ablaze.

The epistles describe how the world was waiting. The Greeks sought for wisdom (1 Corinthians 1:22) which would explain the mystery of human existence and solve the dark riddle of sorrow. The Jews required a sign—that of a conquering Messiah who would restore the Kingdom to Israel. Was it by chance that, while the ancient world was on tiptoe, Jesus came? or was not that the moment for which God had been waiting from 'before the foundation of the world'?

IHQ Archives

17 December

. . . It was not 'odd of God to choose the Jews'. Jesus did not appear to a people with whom he had nothing in common. 'He came unto his own', to a race which had been taught to believe in a righteous God and who regarded the individual and looked for righteousness in him. Jesus never needed to argue about the existence of Almighty God, Maker of Heaven and earth. In this matter the prophets had paved the way for him. There was this strain of deep seriousness in the Hebrew character—is there

274

a comic line in the whole Bible?—as if the fact of sin and the need of salvation did not permit of any jesting. The Jew was not greatly liked by his neighbours. His exclusiveness, his abhorrence of idols, his queer food laws, provoked general resentment. Nevertheless, there were Gentiles who were one with the Jews in loathing the licentiousness of the age, and who sought moral strength by frequenting the synagogue and studying the law.

The dispersion increased their number and made a further contribution to the spread of the gospel. . . . The Jews living in Palestine were only a fraction of their race. . . . Seven per cent of the population of the Roman Empire were Jews . . . but of that figure only 700,000 lived in Palestine. . . .

Here then was this powerful race scattered around the Mediterranean. Every town of any size had its synagogue—Rome had 16—for wherever 10 Jews could congregate they set up their own place of worship. In many a Greek city the synagogue attracted thoughtful Gentiles tired of 'uncharted freedom'. Cornelius was one such who served the true God and followed certain principal Jewish observances such as prayer and alms-giving. Lydia was another 'God-fearer'.

IHQ Archives

18 December

To Amos (9:7) the coming of the Philistines from Caphtor and the Syrians from Kir was as much the handi-work of God as the deliverance of Israel from Egypt. Isaiah (10:5) thought of Assyria as God's rod chastising Judah . . . Jeremiah (5:15) saw God bring down the enemy like a wolf on the fold. . . . He could make and remake nations like a potter his vessel. . . .

Was it by chance that the three Macedonian dynasties which arose out of the wreck of Alexander's empire had to bow before the growing strength of the republic of Rome, whose power, in turn, policed the ancient world and so facilitated the spread of first-century Christianity? History is the action of God; it is an expression in time of his eternal will. The truth about the destiny of nations was uttered once and for all by Jeremiah (18:9, 10): 'At what instant I shall speak concerning a nation, and concerning a kingdom, to build and to plant it; if it do evil in my sight, that it obey not my voice, then I will repent of the good, wherewith I said I would benefit them.'

Though carried in the interests of empire, Caesar's standards were blazing a trail which the followers of the Son of God were to use to go forth to a nobler war. . . .

IHQ Archives

19 December

The supreme instance of the strategy of God is to be seen in the hour when 'the Word was made flesh'. The incarnation was not a happy accident. Not by any fortunate coincidence came 'the word of God unto John, the son of Zacharias' in the fifteenth year of Tiberius Caesar'. This revival of prophecy, when hope of prophecy was almost extinct, meant that the long-expected Messiah was about to visit his people. The Kingdom of God was at hand. As Paul wrote to the Galatians (4:4): 'When the fulness of the time was come, God sent forth his Son.'

Why did Jesus appear on the stage of human history at this point of time and none other? Why in a country no bigger than Wales? . . . Why this unique revelation in the first century AD? Why not earlier? Or later? Perhaps we may not be far wrong if we write down Roman unity, the Greek tongue and the Jewish religion as three factors which conspired, under God, to prepare the hour for the Man.

The suggestion is in harmony with the teaching of Scripture, for, from the eighth century BC onward, the prophets had believed God was at work using other nations, in addition to their own, to accomplish his purposes. . . . Greece and Rome—pagan though they were—helped to make straight in the desert a highway for God.

IHQ Archives

276

20 December

Those who know their New Testament will be aware that Matthew prefaces his description of the nativity by a lengthy account of the family tree of Joseph and Mary. Four women are mentioned in it—Rahab, Tamar, Ruth and Bathsheba—which, remembering the social climate of the day, was in itself most unusual. But look at the four so singled out. Ruth was not even of Jewish race and the other three had known life's darkest shadows. But the place which their names occupy makes it clear that even a sinner can be included in the redeeming purposes of God. The wideness of God's mercy has room for both men and women of every character.

William Lecky cannot be accused of any bias in favour of the Christian faith, but in his *Rise and Influence of the Spirit of Rationalism* he had this to say about the influence of Christianity upon social life: 'For the first time woman was elevated to her rightful position, and the sanctity of weakness was recognised as well as the sanctity of sorrow. No longer the slave or toy of man, no longer associated with ideas of degradation and sensuality, woman rose . . . to a new sphere.'

But I would be doing the Christian faith the sorriest of injustices if I ended in the past tense. This is but a most abbreviated account of the difference which Jesus has made. . . . And one of the most important by-products of the Christmas story is the truth that the world's Redeemer stands in the midst of our common life not as a passive observer but waiting to possess your heart as Lord and Saviour.

The War Cry, 25 December 1965

21 December

It is true that a few folk are still searching round to find a few bits that match so that some shadow of this former idol may dominate our community life in the name of racial superiority. But they labour in vain. Whatever the gods whose help they may invoke, they cannot invoke the name of the God and Father of our Lord Jesus Christ.

He made an end to any distinction between slave and free man; as, indeed, he made an end to any distinction between Jew and Gentile which, in the Mediterranean world of the first century, was a barrier not unlike the ideological barrier which separates east and west today. That is to say, this was a difference which went too deep to be bridged by any of our customary practices of give and take.

Christmas tells how all sorts and conditions of men gathered around the manger. Shepherds came—and they were despised by the orthodox of the day. Wise men came—and long tradition has always made one of them an African. Later on Simeon and Anna—two people made wise and gentle with age—used the Scriptures of their race to praise God for the holy Child.

Everywhere and at all times all men are welcome to share in the worship of Jesus. God will not have any of his children turned away from his throne of grace. Our notions of an integrated society are but a shadow of the reality of the divine family in which men come from the east and the west, and the north and the south, to sit down and eat bread in the Kingdom of God.

The War Cry, 25 December 1965

22 December

Suppose that this was not AD 19—(AD standing for the year of our Lord, a year of grace) but was a year dating from some other event—the capture and sack of Rome by Alaric, or the discovery of the New World by Columbus, or the dropping of the atomic bomb on Hiroshima . . . the resultant world would not be the one we know, and there is a sentence in the New Testament which sums up what the difference would be.

'Now that Jesus has come' (says one translation of Galatians 3:28) 'gone is the distinction between slave and free man, Jew and Gentile, male and female.'

Take each of these three assertions in turn.

Suppose the apostle Paul—and his were the words quoted—returned to our western world today, one of the first facts which would amaze him would be that there were no slaves to be seen.. ... Western man realises that he is not his brother's owner. ...

It is a commonplace today that, as Thomas Rainborowe said in 17th-century England, 'the poorest he ... hath a life to live as the greatest he'. Neither colour nor race can bar the tidal wave of this truth. This is one of the end scenes in the eternal drama which began in a stable in Bethlehem. Then and there was lit a slow fuse which has burned through the long centuries until there was such an explosion that the iniquity of slavery disintegrated into so many pieces that, like Humpty Dumpty, it can never be put together again. ...

The War Cry, 25 December 1965

23 December

Small use writing a pretty-pretty piece about the lights in Oxford Street or the decorations in Bourke Street when we face the fact of the incarnation—the Word made flesh.

This is not because I am a curmudgeon or a square. My only reason for avoiding the West End at Christmas time is that to be caught up in a traffic jam is not my favourite way of spending a leisure hour. And nothing would give me greater pleasure than to walk down Bourke Street again, for it has never been my lot to be in Melbourne over Christmas. But Christmas does not centre around any of the multitudinous actions of men but rather the greatest of the acts of God—his coming to earth in Christ in the form of a servant and in fashion as a man.

Scholars have pointed out that the word 'great' in 'Great is the mystery . . .' means of great importance, not difficult to understand. All the same, we had better take it both ways. Undoubtedly of great importance, but undoubtedly difficult to understand as well. As William Temple used to say: 'If any man says that he understands

279

the relation of deity to humanity in Christ, he only makes it clear that he does not understand at all what is meant by the incarnation.' Great is the mystery! . . .

The War Cry, 23 December 1967

24 December

A truth can be mysterious . . . and yet still valid. I must not say that what I do not understand is therefore not true. The limits of human knowledge are not the final limits of reality. And because neither I—nor anyone else—can explain the coming of God in Christ to the world, that is no reason for saying that here is one more fairy tale—the most fanciful of the lot—which decorates that ancient fantasy called the Christian faith.

Maybe we have started at the end in thinking about the divine humanity of the Redeemer. To our imperfect understanding of God we have added our imperfect understanding of our own human nature, and have supposed that the addition of these two imperfections could account for the perfection of Jesus.

But whatever Jesus is, he is not the summation of our ignorance. It is true that I can better understand my own nature in the light of his, but I do not more fully understand his nature in the light of my own. Mine illuminates nothing in its own right. Every virtue I possess is derivative. While Jesus is rightly called the first-born among many brethren, I cannot therefore deduce what he is from what I am, child though I be by grace of that same family of God of which he is the Elder Brother.

. . . Jesus Christ was 'truly and properly man'—as we are men—but here . . . the resemblance ends. What I am is small clue to what he was. We are in a dead end and will have to start again. . . .

The War Cry, 23 December 1967

25 December

An ellipse is described about two foci; a circle around

one. The nearer those focal points to one another, the nearer the ellipse approaches a circle; the farther apart, the greater the difference. When the foci coincide, the ellipse becomes a circle.

The divine humanity of Jesus is most clearly seen in the realm of the will. His life on earth had but one centre—the fulfilling of his Father's will. Both circles coincided, for both had a common centre. Here was a mutual agreement of purpose which held good in all weathers.

In the person of Jesus, God and man were joined in the unity of a common end. When Jesus entered human life, God entered. What Jesus did, God was doing. What Jesus suffered, God suffered. God was in Christ, was the apostolic explanation. In Jesus we see God; in Jesus we also see man—both joined in the dedicated unity of a single being. . . .

Christian teachers have never denied that such doctrines as those of the incarnation, the atonement and the resurrection are mysteries of which our understanding cannot be other than incomplete. Yet to know in part is still to know—which is entirely different from being led up the garden path. . . .

And though this act of God in Christ transcends our understanding, faith returns grateful thanks to him for his unspeakable gift of a Saviour. Acceptance of this truth can turn any man's holiday into an unforgettable holy day.

The War Cry, 23 December 1967

26 December

That God should visit and redeem his people is a dream as old as time. The nations of the ancient world each had their myths of gods who took human form. This popular expectation is illustrated by the account given in the Acts of the Apostles of the reception accorded to Paul and Barnabas at Lystra. . . .

Just as nowadays it is the political parties who promise the nearest equivalent of a new Heaven and a new earth, so it was the Caesars who did so centuries ago. And as promise (both ancient and modern) has succeeded promise—each more resounding and at times more empty than the previous one—so it has become increasingly clear that man's deepest hopes are not to be met by any secular salvation. His technological triumphs cannot deliver him from his basic fears.

On his voyages in space man can take with him only that which he is. . . . Nor can man bring from outer space any magic which can warm a heart chilled by loneliness or deliver a will from the evil thrall of some compulsive habit.

For our salvation we look neither within ourselves nor without to space. Instead we turn to him in whom dwelt 'all the fulness of the Godhead bodily'.

Arnold Toynbee was once asked how he thought the world would look in 2,000 years' time. Very sensibly he replied that he did not know, but of one thing he was sure. Two words now so important to men and women would be equally important then. Those two words are Jesus Christ, for in him God once resided on earth for us men and for our salvation.

The War Cry, 24 December 1966

27 December

. . . No spring is born without a winter. No corn grows unless the seed is first cast into the ground and dies. No child is born save through the living death of the mother. No power is generated without dissolution. The atom must be 'split' if energy is to be liberated. Life is born through death. 'Whosoever will save his life shall lose it; but whosoever shall lose his life . . . the same shall save it.' This rule holds good for individuals, for nations, for religious societies, for God himself—as both the incarnation and the atonement, the two focal points of our faith, show. The Creator did not exempt himself from the law which governs his creation. How could he? He abideth faithful; he cannot deny himself. Through death, which is not mere physical dissolution but that death of the will to which Paul referred when he spoke of dying daily, through this death of self comes life.

This is a costing experience. The dying is real, not a form of words, not a make-believe. From enduring it even Jesus shrank. 'Father, save me from this hour.' Where he hesitated, lesser mortals may be forgiven their reluctance. Superficially, the story of Jesus may enthral us, but a closer reading should stagger us. This life-from-death principle meant not merely that he was humble in spirit, but that he was humiliated in person. He was despised and rejected, with nowhere to lay his head. His words fell on stony ground. He suffered many things at the hands of sinful men. He was mocked and scourged and spat upon. Finally, he hung with nothing but a loin cloth around him.

Is that power? Christian insight claims that it is. . . .

The Officer, November 1947

28 December

. . . The world, thinking of power only in terms of the police state, . . . sees little in the incarnate God but another being suffering in the first century those dehumanising tortures which have become the tragic commonplace of the twentieth. The story may move the unbeliever, but only as failure arouses a passing pity. This misses the truth that this endurance of the worst that man could do transformed the wrong done into the means whereby man, the principal offender, could himself be saved. Salvation came through suffering, life out of death, to be glorified from being crucified.

This is the only power that abides. . . . Final victory is not with the strong, the swift or the cunning. That illusion dies hard. . . . Empires which copy the methods of the brontosaurus end in the same place—the museum. . . . The Caesars are no more, but the Son of man still has power on earth. The finger of God can still cast out devils. . . . The rejected stone remains head of the corner. . . . The Kingdom abides in power, and wherever men receive Jesus and have faith enough to follow him they reign as he reigned—not on thrones but from the tree. Perplexed, they are not in despair; cast down, they are not destroyed; bearing about in the body the dying of the Lord Jesus, they also manifest his life.

Is this too hard a saying? Easier to get back to shopping and presents and toys, and forget this paradox rooted in the universe? Yet we could not so much as buy a Christmas card had not God stooped in Christ to conquer, lost to gain, died to live.

The Officer, November 1947

29 December

. . . Just as there is ample evidence of man's need of a Saviour, so there is ample evidence that Jesus is the Saviour they need. Again I will not quote from Scripture . . . [but] from a paperback with which was associated the Oscar prize-winning film, *The Bridge on the River Kwai.*

The author, himself a prisoner of war, describes camp conditions on two successive Christmases. Christmas 1942 saw men robbing the sick, ill-treating one another, caring not whether their cobbers lived or died. Compassion had vanished. Morale was at its lowest. Despair prevailed. But on Christmas Day, 1943, 2,000 men assembled for worship, sang carols and listened to the word of God. Said one prisoner of war: 'This is a merry Christmas, especially when you compare it with last year.'

How had the change come about? Simply because two or three men had held to their faith. Their acts of self-sacrifice had silently rebuked those of the 'Blow you, Jack, I'm in the boat' school. As the author comments: 'The camp had been dominated by sickness and despair. Yet I had seen a Power at work to renew many of us. Men were still men, and I had seen selfishness. But I had seen love. . . . To see Jesus was to see in him that love which is the highest form of life.' It was Christ who made the difference to that camp. No wonder the author called his book *Miracle on the River Kwai.*

This same miracle can be repeated in the lives of all who commit themselves to Jesus as Saviour and Lord. 'The

Father sent the Son to be Saviour of the world'—and he is the Saviour we need.

Essentials of Christian Experience, p 5

30 December

To call Jesus Lord was to ascribe to him supreme authority. The secular significance of this title is made plain in the court scene where Paul appealed to Caesar. The charge against this unusual prisoner had the Roman procurator baffled. It fell under no legal category known to him. 'I have no certain thing to write unto my Lord' said Festus to Agrippa. The *New English Bible* translates: 'I have nothing definite about him to put in writing for our Sovereign.'

Caesar, sovereign, lord—these were the titles for the supreme authority in the Roman world. And 'Lord' was the title which believers applied to Jesus. 'God hath made that same Jesus, whom ye crucified, both Lord and Christ.' If his is the name high over all, then better never acknowledge him as such than so to address him and then disobey him. This is to fall into the greater condemnation.

Our Lord himself said this too often and too plainly for anyone to mistake his meaning. The contrasts he continually drew were between saying and doing. 'Not every one that saith unto me, Lord, Lord, shall enter into the kingdom of heaven; but he that doeth the will of my Father which is in heaven.' 'Many will say to me in that day, Lord, Lord . . . and then will I profess unto them, I never knew you.' 'Ye call me Master and Lord: and ye say well . . . I have given you an example, that ye should do as I have done to you.' Profession without practice was worse than useless.

Essentials of Christian Experience, pp 6, 7

31 December

Over the years there have been many encounters with the media—by far most of them on a friendly basis, but from the centenary onwards one of the oft-repeated suggestions was that this piece of Victoriana known as The Salvation Army was surely on its way out. Was it not one with the bustle and the hansom cab—a quaint 19th-century survival whose day was virtually done? . . .

The question misjudges both the nature of man and the nature of our society. The fact that a man may not consciously desire a Saviour is no proof that he does not need one. Discount the biblical word that man does not live by bread alone, we are still left with R. H. Tawney's description of him as 'that timid staring creature so compounded as to require not only money, but light and air and water, not to mention such non-economic goods as tranquillity, beauty and affection'. So long as the soul of man thirsts—be it ever so faintly—for a drink divine, so long will there be needed those who know where the fountains of living water are to be found.

As for the nature of our society, as long as there are broken homes and chronic alcoholics, compulsive gamblers and panders who prey upon human weaknesses, children who are socially deprived and adults who are socially inadequate, rebellious adolescents and lonely pensioners, the young who at heart fear life and the old who are afraid of death, so long will there be needed men and women who are willing to pay the price of caring. In face of these incontrovertible facts . . . I am well content to soldier on in this Christian regiment because here there is no continuing city. We seek one whose builder and maker is God.

No Continuing City, pp 150, 151